AT THE GRAMMYS!

AT THE GRAMMYS!

BEHIND THE SCENES
AT MUSIC'S BIGGEST NIGHT

by **Ken Ehrlich**

HAL•LEONARD®

Hal Leonard Books
An Imprint of Hal Leonard Corporation
New York

Published in 2007 by Hal Leonard Books
An Imprint of Hal Leonard Corporation
19 West 21st Street, New York, NY 10010

Printed in the United States of America

Book design and composition by Dovetail Publishing Services

Library of Congress Cataloging-in-Publication Data is available upon request.

ISBN-10: 1-4234-3073-5
ISBN-13: 978-1-42343-073-5

www.halleonard.com

This book is dedicated with much love and gratitude

to my parents, Art and Lucile Ehrlich,

who always inspired me to do better but be happy,

and to Marty Faye,

who long ago said to a young publicist who really wasn't sure

where his life was headed, "Hey kid, want to produce my TV

show? It's $75 bucks a week, but you get to see a lot

of free shows, and we'll have some fun."

Contents

Foreword

By Bono

First, a confession: In the early eighties, as lead singer of post-punk combo U2, I remember recommending to our band that we never play an awards show. Yes, your honour . . . guilty of the scourge of hip. At twenty-one years old, our world was black and white, not colour. We were lost to the big music, but it was coming to a garage near you, not a stadium, and TV just made us look small. Our singles went down the charts when we appeared on *Top of the Pops* in the UK. Bruce Springsteen affirmed this paranoia with the admonition "never put yourself in a place where other people have control over the volume". The Grammys were for grown ups. We called them "The Grannys". Snobs, we did not want to hear anything about music from anyone older than us. The Clash sang, "If you've been trying for years we've already heard your song," and that was good enough for U2.

I recall exactly when 'the scourge' lifted from me. I was in the bath at the old Gramercy Park Hotel in downtown Manhattan and the Grammy Awards were on television in the next room. I could see the TV through the doorway. Of course, having at that point absolutely no chance of being nominated I was blowing bubbles through the acceptance speeches. If I had not been naked and submerged, I would have pulled the plug.

And then the Staple Singers came on. Mavis and her sisters singing like they hoped that God's mercy will be stronger than His vengeance, and Pops, speaking with the voice of a weary angel while playing his guitar with the sting of a pitchfork. It was all there: anger, love, forgiveness, family, community and the deepest sense of history. A tear from my eye ran down my cheek and mended the sneer on my lip. Here was the full power of American music challenging my arrogance.

I watched the rest of the show with new eyes. The Grammys invited jazz, country, rock, soul and classical into the same hall. No regard for demographic studies of what would deliver ratings, no radio call-out research—a mad amalgam of the profound and the absurd and the creeping realization that one man's Mozart is another man's Vegas.

When he was given his Lifetime Achievement Award, the great Ornette Coleman said, "I guess art and culture come from the heart of human beings who are interested in sharing love with other human beings. At least that's what I think and what I'm trying to do." That is a pretty good summation of why we are all in this and why the car crash between art and commerce, exemplified by the Grammys, can actually be a good thing. Those of us who have been blessed by success, but do not wish to be ruled by it, appreciate that someone out there attempts every year to do the impossible—to pick examples of the 'Best Of' among artists who can get into fistfights over chord changes. You know when going in that no one's going to agree on anything, and yet the Grammys tries again and again to find something like consensus. Who could decide if the record of the year should go to John Coltrane or the Beatles? Marvin Gaye or Joni Mitchell? Radiohead or Jay-Z?

Like everyone, I have been enraged by the Grammy votes some years (Eminem was robbed!) and delighted others (Bonnie Raitt! Santana!). I guess I think the Grammys are great when they agree with me and a travesty when they don't. . . .

We all want to win. As proud midwives we want to see the baby we brought into the world get the medal. But when you sit in that arena and hear your band's name put up against Michael Jackson, Bob Dylan, Paul McCartney, even a long-practicing megalomaniac experiences that most foreign of emotions—humility.

U2 have been lucky enough to stand on the Grammy trapdoor on 22 occasions over the last 20 years and every time it causes a sharp intake of breath. Not just the winning or losing, but the mad flowering of the song that brought you to the party. It's remarkable—something that started as a seed when you walked down your garden path in Dublin can carry you from Tokyo to Morocco to Los Angeles on the waves of a radio. It's remarkable that it can drop you in an arena full of your peers, under the brutal attention of a hundred cameras.

To compete for awards against other singers, songwriters and musicians is an honour and an embarrassment. And in the end, ego aside, we all sign up for it out of respect for the music. What really goes through your mind when you step onto the podium to accept a Grammy? Five words, a line from a song: "How did I get here?"

The answer is easy: the music brought you.

Introduction

There are few artistic endeavors that touch the spirit and the soul, or become that magical thing that triggers memories, as much as the music that weaves in and out of our lives. Cliché as it may be, "the soundtrack of our lives" is an extremely apt phrase, since so many of us match the benchmarks of our existence to the songs we associate with those events. Tune the radio to a random station, browse your iPod, or take a walk through your CD collection and you're likely to think about your wedding day, the passing of a loved one, riding around with your high school buddies cruising for chicks (or guys), or any of a thousand life experiences. Be it emotional, or intellectual, our fondest, saddest and most enduring memories are linked to the music that was playing when they happened.

Over the past 50 years of the Grammys, we have experienced vast changes in the musical landscape. Often those changes have either affected or reflected social change, cultural change, even political change. The year 1958, when the first Grammys were given out, was only four short years after the birth of rock 'n' roll that blasted its way into the consciousness of a young generation. We had entered into a folk music renaissance that was to form the basis of an intense social revolution in the '60s, and were only five years away from the Beatles, the group who were to affect every aspect of American life and quite literally change the world. All of that occurred within a ten-year period—and it only gets more interesting from there.

As the Recording Academy prepares to celebrate its 50th anniversary as the producer of record for over two-thirds of the Grammy Awards CBS shows, I was approached by numerous friends to look back on my 27 years of bringing "Music's Biggest Night" to millions of music fans each year since 1980. They were less interested in the facts and figures than in my personal observations, the highlights and the low points, the stories behind the story, my favorite moments and my least favorite moments.

What they didn't know, because I had kept it to myself, was that I had been keeping a private diary of my observations, usually written in the quiet moments of the first few days after each show was completed, when the memories were the freshest, and my thoughts most immediate. These reflections may not have had the benefit of distance from the show for objectivity, but neither did they suffer from second-guessing or rewriting history, something quite common in the entertainment business.

And, might I add, they are all personal, and subject to interpretation, in this case, *my* interpretation, which admittedly, carries the bias of having been there in the heat of battle. I believe them to be reasonably accurate, but please forgive me if I miss a date here or there, or lose a nuance or two.

I suspect that many, if not most, of the events described will be familiar to you, particularly if you've watched Grammy shows, and you'll find it easy to connect the dots between what you saw on television and what happened behind the scenes. If you detect a bias, it will be from a producer who works primarily in the field of "music on television," and televised live musical events in particular.

I think these shows are not only the most difficult, but also the most exciting and energizing type of television there is. With the Grammys, the intense production period for the show is usually about eight weeks, from the nominations to show day, an incredibly condensed period of time to get a show together from a blank page to three and a half hours of live TV. No televised event, save the Super Bowl, has more room for spontaneity, for the potential for surprise, for things to go wrong, or right for that matter, on the night. For those men and women who work with us yearly on the show, the work may become habit, but it's never predictable.

So, while this book is by no means the official story of the National Academy of Recording Arts and Sciences, it will reflect the Academy's direction of the event and the show, its mandate to always elevate the community of music and to represent that community and its membership to music fans as the organization of record. And because that involvement is so critical to the success of the Grammy show (the usual "thank-yous" are reserved for the end of the book), I'll begin with a tremendous expression of gratitude to all of the NARAS executives, staff, and committee members who have worked to make the Grammys the preeminent music awards show in existence, a fact that is indisputable.

There's no question that the Grammy Awards are a product of the teamwork of an incredible group of television professionals, originally put together by my mentor, Pierre Cossette, in 1970 for the first televised

Grammy show. This show could not be what it is without the ceaseless dedication of the remarkable teams that have changed over the years. And while it's always tricky to single out individuals, there's just no question that this book, and the experiences contained within, could never have happened, and would have been nowhere near as much fun, if it weren't for the incongruous connection that Pierre forged when he put Walter Miller and me together in 1980. My relationship with Walter, 16 years my senior, has been one of the most interesting, nurturing, at times combative, more often loving, and overall, rewarding experiences of my life.

And finally, we could put together the most amazing production possible—a phenomenal looking set—beautiful lighting, 5.1 surround sound and high-definitioned like crazy, and if we didn't have the artists to stand on that stage and perform their hearts out, you really wouldn't watch, would you? Over the years, on the Grammy shows and on so many other shows we do, I've had the privilege of working with nearly all of the best (and a few of the worst), the most talented (and lucky) artists in the music world, and if you're one of them, please accept my eternal thanks and gratitude.

I hope you find this book enjoyable on a number of levels: first and foremost, as a reminder of some of your favorite memories of the Grammys, both positive and, quite likely, some less so. The simple fact is that the show, like the artists who have appeared on it over the years, engenders no shortage of extreme debate, and perhaps the success of the show lies in our ability to try and provide something for everyone over the course of each show. We've never taken for granted that Usher fans are Green Day fans, or that a teenager who likes the Black Eyed Peas will even know who Lynyrd Skynyrd is. And yet, all four of those acts appeared on the 2005 show, and millions of fans watched.

Second, if you have more than an abiding interest in award shows, you may find this book fascinating on another level. By the time the show gets on the air, it all looks easy: the massive set changes that take place in six minutes, the pacing and structure of the show designed to keep viewers around for the whole three-and-a-half hours, the directorial challenge of shooting a hip-hop performance with 50 dancers and then, five minutes later, capturing the intimacy of Bruce Springsteen alone on a stage. The following pages may give you some insight into just how hard we work to make it look so easy.

And finally, if you're a music fan, then the backstage tales of many of your favorite artists, on their best behavior—or their worst—some personal opinions on the talent (or lack of talent) may be of interest to you. I'll tell you this—it's a much more accurate and balanced portrayal of most of them than you get with either *Entertainment Tonight* or *People* magazine. None of these stories have ever been seen or written about in either of those places, and I'm amused when I see their second-hand reporting which is often way off base, no matter how many times Billy Bush says "and you saw it on *Access Hollywood* first." First maybe. Accurate? Not really!

But having said that, the truth is that I respect many or most of my musical acquaintances. Note that I didn't say *friends*, a term tossed around quite easily on these shows. When we're in a working environment with these artists, there often exists an easy, positive relationship, need based though it is, and it's almost always a great deal of fun. But, with some notable exceptions, I stick to the credo, the one that I try and relate to kids coming up in the business who ask me how I've survived this long in a business that eats people alive: "they're not your friends." Oh, I'd go to the mat for many of the artists I've worked with over the years, mainly because history has brought us through some rough waters together, and it's been collaborative, enjoyable, and mutually productive. But that doesn't change the bottom line that a producer needs to separate himself personally from the talent he's working with, because at some point along the way, you need the objectivity. It's a difficult job. It takes a little intelligence and lot of patience. It takes the ability to subjugate your ego for the ego of the talent you're working with, and sometimes it takes the ability to look them in the eye, tell them they're wrong (they don't often hear that from people who are working for them) and let the chips fall where they may. Quite often, they respect you for your honesty, although sometimes they think you're an asshole. I'll take either one, although I much prefer the former.

I haven't written a lot about the early days of the Academy, although as someone whose career has been so intertwined with the organization, I've studied those early years and the men and women who are responsible for the platform we enjoy today.

This book is dedicated to them; people like Paul Weston, Dennis Farnon, Lloyd Dunn, Sonny Burke, and Jesse Kaye, record label executives in the mid-1950s who, in answer to the Emmys and the Oscars, decided to form an organization to recognize achievement in the record industry.

People like Val Valentin, who more or less designed the "Grammy" and like Chris Farnon, who for years was the unpaid, and then underpaid, executive director of the Academy, and held it together with spit and glue; people like Henry Mancini, Frank Sinatra, Sammy Cahn, and others who were there in the early days when the Academy needed credibility and famous faces; and people like Pierre Cossette and his friend Andy Williams who created and shaped the show in the '70s through its formative television years and beyond and became its public face.

This book is not an attempt to glorify the Grammys or the institution that stands behind them. I'm not even a member of the Academy, and although I have close ties to it, over the years I've shared some of the same feelings and frustrations you have when the names are announced and artists come up to accept their awards. I've stood backstage for 26 of its 36 televised years, witnessed everything from performer meltdowns to artistic triumphs. I've seen more than my share of overjoyed winners and despondent losers, and watched helplessly as the vicissitudes of live television caused amplifiers not to work and microphones to go splat on the stage, and I've have seen presenters walk out with the wrong envelopes.

I've witnessed a wastebasket delivered offstage as a hyperventilating Bette Midler came close to vomiting; walked Stevie Wonder onstage and into position, clipping his bow tie on 30 seconds before he was to perform before millions; and have come out onstage at the end of one show to tell Luther Vandross that his entire performance was cut off by the network due to the show running long. And no less memorably, I escorted Aretha Franklin to the stage, where she filled in for an ailing Luciano Pavarotti, and I watched her turn "Nessun Dorma" into her personal anthem, singing it for the first time backed by a 65-piece orchestra and a 30-man chorus. Because at the root of it all, it's about the *music.*

Here then, with no apologies, is the story of the modern Grammy years, by no means objective and quite possibly a bit defensive, hopefully informative without being salacious, but most certainly with all my love.

CHAPTER 1

The 1971–1979 Grammy Awards

The National Academy of Recording Arts and Sciences was "born" in May 1957 at the Brown Derby in Hollywood when a group of music industry leaders finalized their plans to create an organization that would be to the music community what the Motion Picture and Television Academies were to their respective arts. Though an awards show was part of the plan from the beginning, it wasn't until 1963 that an annual show, not live but produced with taped performances by some of the winners months later, made it to television. That show, *The Best on Record*, was sometimes taped before a live audience and at other times without an audience at all. Although it was sanctioned by the Academy, other than the presentation of Grammys to some of the winners, who obviously knew they had won by then, it bore no resemblance to the live-event award show that was to finally find its way to the air in 1971. In fact, the official awards ceremonies for a number of those years were held separately, on both coasts, with winners accepting either in New York or Los Angeles.

Because my affiliation with the Grammy Awards as producer began in 1980, the bulk of this book deals with the televised awards shows from that year on. But to provide some perspective, I've condensed a brief, historical recap of the first nine broadcasts, based on conversations I've had with people who were there from the beginning.

In 1971, with only the Oscars, the Emmys, and the Tonys as television award show staples, Pierre Cossette, armed with the rights for a live broadcast, managed to make a deal with ABC for a live, two-hour broadcast of the 13th Annual Grammy Awards. This was a million miles ahead of the closed, industry-only event the Grammys had been for its first 12 years, and even with tremendous difficulties in getting talent to perform, or convince them why it was important, Pierre managed to swing appearances by some of music's biggest names, including Duke

Ellington, Herb Alpert, Burt Bacharach, the Fifth Dimension, Henry Mancini, and Pierre's friend Andy Williams.

Broadcast live from the Hollywood Palladium, the show featured numerous performances, although in the major categories, most of the nominated songs for Record and Album were cover versions, performed with mixed results. No question that Aretha Franklin nailed "Bridge Over Troubled Water" (which she would then go on to record and win a Grammy the following year) and that Dionne Warwick did a great "Let It Be," but the Osmond Brothers' cover of "Everything Is Beautiful" and Anne Murray's version of James Taylor's haunting, introspective "Fire and Rain" were seriously lacking. The only nominees to perform in the major categories were the Carpenters, who performed "We've Only Just Begun," not too prescient, as Simon and Garfunkel picked up the Grammys for Record and Album of the Year for *Bridge*. But with presenters that included John Wayne and Zsa Zsa Gabor, a full house, and great ratings, the live Grammy Awards show was born, and it was on its way to becoming music's most important evening on television for the next 36 years and counting.

The following year the Grammys moved from Los Angeles to New York, where they took place at the Felt Forum, the smaller theater in Madison Square Garden. The big winner was Carole King who won Record, Album, and Song in short order but didn't make the trip to New York to accept her awards. The show definitely seemed to move up a notch production-wise, featuring performances by the cast of *Godspell*, Tammy Wynette, B.B. King, Three Dog Night, and again, the Carpenters. Though once again the ratings were excellent, the 14th Annual Awards would see the beginning of the "Grammy-bashing" tradition, with several lukewarm reviews of a show that certainly appealed to a broad segment of the viewing audience. Several of the entertainment and music trades took the show to task for not recognizing a number of mainstream artists including Elton John, Traffic, the Allman Brothers, and Sly and the Family Stone. Grammy-bashing was launched and would become a yearly pastime for television and music critics, to the point where it would seem as if they would just reprint the same column every year, changing only the names.

In 1973, the Academy, wanting to expand its reach, scheduled the show in Nashville. But ABC, which was generally very happy with its

Grammy arrangement, was not happy to hear about Nashville, which held for them the perceived down-market aura of country music (times would certainly change). ABC threatened to pull out if the show came from there. As Pierre tells it, he accepted their no and went on a no-holds-barred, full-frontal assault campaign to get his friend at CBS, Bob Wood, to take the show. Pierre resorted to camping out in front of Wood's house, eventually winding up in bed with Bob and his wife one Sunday morning; Wood relented "just to get Pierre off my case," and the Grammys were picked up by CBS, where they have been ever since. The Nashville show was obviously country music–heavy, with performances by Charley Pride, Donna Fargo, and Mac Davis in addition to Helen Reddy, Loggins and Messina, Curtis Mayfield, and Don McLean. Country presenters dominated, but the major award categories didn't follow suit, with George Harrison's *Concert for Bangladesh* winning for Album of the Year and Roberta Flack's "The First Time Ever I Saw Your Face" winning both Record and Song (for writer Ewan McColl). The rating for the show, a phenomenal 53 share, made Pierre and CBS look like heroes and certainly didn't make ABC happy—so unhappy, in fact, that they went out and offered Dick Clark a slot to create a competitive awards show, and that's how the American Music Awards (AMAs) came about.

As acceptance of the Grammy Awards grew and expectations for the show more intense, it seemed to raise interest in pop music in general, and the horse race concept for the major awards began to surface and become reasonably integral to the success of and interest in the show. The 1974 show, now back in Hollywood at the Palladium, was a great example of the growing interest in the show, primarily due to the nominations. Five records, nearly all of which remain classics today, fought it out for Record of the Year: "Killing Me Softly with His Song" (Roberta Flack), "You Are the Sunshine of My Life" (Stevie Wonder), "You're So Vain" (Carly Simon), "Behind Closed Doors"(Charlie Rich) and "Bad Bad Leroy Brown"(Jim Croce), had all been huge hits and resonated with a wide span of music fans and viewers. "Killing Me Softly" took Record of the Year for the second consecutive win for Roberta Flack, and Bette Midler was named Best New Artist. Stevie won the Grammy for Album of the Year for *Innervisions* and there were numerous popular wins, but again rock was severely underrepresented, a fact that was pointed out again and again by critics. The show itself, which today looks extremely middle-of-the-road, was certainly representative of the hitmakers of the day with performances by Charlie Rich, Al Green, Gladys Knight and the Pips, and a great version of "Dueling Banjos" (from the film *Deliverance*) by Eric Weissberg and Steve Handell. Some of the presenter pairings were either ingenious or bizarre depending upon your orientation. Jazz drummer Shelly Manne paired with the Jackson Five, Alice Cooper presented with Helen Reddy, and—creating a moment that we still run today when we put together our compilations of Grammy moments—Kris Kristofferson came out with Moms Mabley to present Best Pop Vocal Performance by a Group. At no time has the term "the family of music" been given such poetic license.

That year, even more of the winners were on hand to take their Grammys, and once again the ratings of the show were strong. But a new wrinkle had entered the equation: several of the awards, and some of the performers, had appeared on the AMAs a few weeks before the Grammys, and though it would take some time to simmer, it was the beginning of a battle between the shows for talent. Although at the time it seemed to be "friendly" competition in which both competitors said two shows would only benefit the music business, the "friendly" part of it would begin to fade and be replaced by a pretty intense struggle that would last for almost 30 years until the wounded American Music Awards were moved from just before the Grammys to the end of the previous year.

⤳

Grammy-bashing reached new heights with the 1975 show, which returned to New York for its biannual visit. In fairness, there still weren't any dedicated rock categories, and the nominations for the major awards were very mixed, with safe choices like Olivia Newton-John and John Denver competing against progressive acts like Elton John and Joni Mitchell. But whatever might be going on outside the Academy walls, it didn't seem like the organization cared a whole lot about what the critics were saying; the public liked the show, and once again the ratings proved it. It probably didn't help the cachet of the Academy that Marvin Hamlisch was named Best New Artist (although the category, which included Johnny Bristol and David Essex, might have been in for more severe criticism if they had won). At least Stevie Wonder won again for *Fulfillingess' First Finale*, an album that has stood the test of time. John Lennon showed up at the show and presented the Record of the Year Grammy with Paul Simon to Art Garfunkel, who accepted for Olivia Newton-John's "I Honestly Love You." Stevie performed the anti-Nixon work "You Haven't Done Nothin'," The Spinners tore it up opening the show with "Mighty Love," Harry Chapin did "Cat's in the Cradle," and Aretha did "Ain't Nothing Like the Real Thing"—probably the strongest set of live performances in the Grammys' short four-year live history. David Bowie then presented Aretha with a Grammy for Best R&B Vocal Performance, Female. Bowie, Lennon, Paul Simon, Aretha . . . now you're talking major names and way beyond what fans had seen a month earlier on the American Music Awards. It was a shot across the bow, but not one that wouldn't be answered as the competition between the shows heated up in subsequent years.

At the 1976 show, the 18th Annual Grammys and the first Grammy show I attended, Natalie Cole led things off with a spirited "This Will Be" and was followed by performances from Ray Stevens, Bert and Ernie (from *Sesame Street*), and Janis Ian, all of whom performed before Paul Simon came out and sang "50 Ways to Leave Your Lover," followed by Barry Manilow's "Mandy" to close the show. While there were only seven performances on the show and a couple of those might have been questionable, the Album nominations—Paul Simon, Elton John, Linda Ronstadt, and the Eagles—were certainly reflective of what was going on in music in that bicentennial year. That "Love Will Keep Us Together" won the Grammy for Record of the Year served to mitigate some of the credibility of the Album category, but Captain & Tennille were very popular that year. That the Eagles were shut out created a bad feeling by the group for the Academy and the show, a feeling that was to bite both the Academy and the Eagles in the butt two years later, as we'll see. And although 1975 was certainly a breakthrough year for Bruce Springsteen, he was found nowhere in the nominations, a big miss that would take the Academy years to come back from.

The 1977 show was all about Stevie Wonder, who not only performed "Sir Duke" on the show but also won the Grammy for Album, Best Pop Vocal Performance, Male, and Best R&B Vocal Performance,

Male. *Songs in the Key of Life* was his most ambitious album to date, and Stevie was well on his way to becoming one of Grammy's most honored artists. Other performances that year included Barry Manilow, Sarah Vaughan, the Starland Vocal Band, Wild Cherry (can anyone forget "Play That Funky Music, White Boy"?), and Marilyn McCoo and Billy Davis, Jr. Natalie Cole opened the show for the second year in a row from the same venue (the Palladium), and by the time Barry Manilow sang "I Write the Songs" (which he didn't write) and Barbra Streisand came out to present Record of the Year to George Benson for "This Masquerade," the story of the show had already been written "in the Key of Life." Perhaps the most remembered moment of the show is one that has gone down in Grammy history as one of our lesser moments, when Andy Williams, the victim of a bad satellite connection to Africa where Stevie Wonder was performing, uttered the now famous "Stevie, can you see me?"—an ad lib that created a major brouhaha after the show and ultimately cost Pierre's friend Andy the show. After having moved to Los Angeles the previous year, I was glad to see the show beginning to feature a number of artists with whom I had growing and positive relationships, including Stevie Wonder, George Benson, Barry Manilow, and others. It only made me feel more determined that someday the Grammys and I would get together.

⌐

To celebrate its 20th birthday, the Academy decided to move the show from the smaller Palladium venue in Hollywood to the Shrine Auditorium, a move that opened the show to the general public, with 3000 of the 6000 seats being sold and resulting in a fan-based show, if not a fan-based award structure. It was a move that in years to come would be emulated by the American Music Awards (always in our footsteps) as well as the Academy Awards and other music-based shows. The trades and consumer press critics rewarded the move with generally favorable reviews, and the ratings reflected the increased interest in music. The choice of John Denver (an artist I liked personally but wasn't crazy about musically) as host seemed to mark a step backward for the show in its performance choices, which included Denver doing a medley of the Song of the Year nominations, Debby Boone doing "You

Light Up My Life" (she then went on to win Best New Artist), Shaun Cassidy (!) doing "That's Rock 'n' Roll" (it was not, not by any stretch of the imagination), and a fairly tepid Crystal Gayle performing "Don't It Make My Brown Eyes Blue." The only high spots were a spirited Joe Tex doing "Ain't Gonna Bump No More" and a retro Count Basie Orchestra version of "Sweet Georgia Brown." These performances in a year when the major category nominations included Fleetwood Mac's *Rumours*, the "Love Theme from *A Star is Born*" (Streisand), Steely Dan's *Aja* and the Eagles' *Hotel California*. The Eagles were still holding a grudge against the Academy and the show, and though manager Irving Azoff swears to me that they were just down the block at a Hollywood Mexican restaurant, Lucy's, they never even showed up to receive their award for Record of the Year. James Taylor passed on attending the show as well, but Fleetwood Mac (who won Album of the Year Honors), Streisand, Debby Boone, and Lou Rawls were there to pick up their Grammys. If there was a tip to Grammy watchers for the following year, it was the Pop Duo or Group Vocal award to the Bee Gees, who were already the biggest pop act in the world and about to win just about every award possible for their soundtrack to the upcoming film *Saturday Night Fever*. Coincidentally, having done a *Soundstage* show with them a couple of years earlier, I entered into their lives in a big way for the next two years while I waited for Pierre to call.

It was supposed to be a Bee Gees sweep of the Grammys in 1979, but a compact, defiant and always publicly belligerent Billy Joel spoiled the party by wresting both the Record of the Year and Song of the Year Grammys from the Aussie vocal group with his huge hit "Just the Way You Are." Aside from that, it was definitely Bee Gees fever at the Grammys, once again beamed live from the Shrine Auditorium and full of screaming Bee Gees fans. *Saturday Night Fever* went on to become the biggest-selling soundtrack of all time, only bested 20 years later when *Titanic* outsold it.

The nominations were once again a series of mixed blessings, with albums and records from the Rolling Stones, the Bee Gees, Jackson Browne, and Billy Joel competing with offerings from Gerry Rafferty (remember "Baker Street"?), Chuck Mangione, and Anne Murray. Once again, though the show scored, the press took the Academy to task for some pretty poor judgments in the nominations. And though I say this with mixed feelings, the performances on the show reflected a safe, middle-of-the-road approach with appearances by A Taste of Honey ("Boogie Oogie Oogie"), Alicia Bridges, who opened the show with "I Love the Night Life," and Mangione, who performed "Feel So Good." No Stones, no Bee Gees, no Billy Joel, and again a medley for Song of the Year by John Denver, which included "Just the Way You Are," "Three Times a Lady," "You Don't Bring Me Flowers" and "You Needed Me."

Even accounting for the shift in the musical landscape that was occurring at the time, with disco going full bore and syrupy ballads competing for the few chart positions not held by disco, it was sad that this was the best the music industry leader could field in a year when sales set new records every month.

For me, the Bee Gees' win was a great omen. Even before the Grammy show, they had asked me to produce their first network television special (for NBC), and that would be followed up with the first-ever special to come from the floor of the United Nations, an epic show that would bring together the biggest names in pop music for a benefit for UNICEF. The cast list included Earth, Wind & Fire, Kris Kristofferson, Olivia Newton-John, Andy Gibb, and many others, including the man I would work with the following year on the Grammys, John Denver. I loved doing the shows, the Bee Gees were wonderful to work with, and my executive producers, the high-riding Robert Stigwood and his partner the sly David Frost, turned out to be great partners all the way down the line with both shows.

But the production team that Pierre had hired to do the 1979 Grammy show had obviously not lived up to what the Academy expected.

Fortunately Pierre had not lost my number.

CHAPTER 2

The 1980 Grammy Awards

*Some Grammy Firsts: Bob Dylan, Neil Diamond and
Barbra Streisand, and the Doobie Brothers*

My involvement with the Grammy Awards began with the 22nd
Annual Grammys in 1980. I had been in Los Angeles for three
years, following four years at the Chicago Public Television station,
where I had created and produced the *Soundstage* series, a pop music
series that has been credited as being the forerunner of *Unplugged* and
a number of other "real" music shows. Its bare-bones look and honest
approach had not only been instrumental in breaking a number of
acts, but, appearing as it did at the time of the singer-songwriter era in
popular music, had done a great deal for artists like Harry Chapin, Judy
Collins, Arlo Guthrie, and Randy Newman, as well as a number of R&B
acts, owing to my love of black music. It had also caught the attention
of Pierre, with whom I had met prior to our move to L.A., and who had
invited me and my then pregnant wife, Harriet, to our first Grammy
Awards, in 1976 at the Palladium. It was an experience I'll never forget,
and for someone as much in love with music as with music on television, seeing Paul Simon, Janis Ian, Natalie Cole, and others perform
in one place was amazing. Pierre and I spent some time together, and
I was obviously hoping that one day soon he'd call and bring me into
the show.

In L.A., I had moved up the food chain significantly. In addition
to a stint at *The Midnight Special*, I had done a number of high-profile
specials, including two with the Bee Gees, who were the hottest act in
the business at the time.

One day in late 1979, I received a call from Pierre. Though we had
stayed in touch over the years, three Grammy shows had passed since

we had first met. In fact, in 1979 Pierre had changed producers, dismissing Marty Pasetta and bringing another veteran producer for the 1979 show. That show opened, as described earlier, with a very dated dance number of Alicia Bridges' "I Love The Night Life," a forgettable disco tune that had somehow not only reached the top of the charts but garnered some Grammy nominations as well. I can still remember watching the show and thinking every step of the way what I would have done with the music that year.

I met with Pierre, who told me he was putting together a new team to do the show, and that he was considering me as producer. There were a number of other producers in Hollywood with many more television credits than me, but he believed in me, and if I could work with a director he was considering, Walter Miller, he'd support me with the network and with the Recording Academy. I told him I could work with the Devil himself if it meant producing the Grammy Awards, and he went to work. As he tells it now, it wasn't easy selling either the network or the Academy on me, but with three years of successful credits and his wholehearted endorsement, I was able to get the OK.

His phone call telling me that I was going to produce the Grammy Awards remains one of the highlights of my professional life. Though there were still shows to do before we headed into the Grammys, I poured myself into the show, and long before the nominations had come out, I had played much of the show out in my head.

Past relationships once again paid off. Bob Dylan, who had never appeared on a Grammy show before, remembered the tribute show he had done for me for John Hammond in Chicago and signed on. Charlie Daniels, who had a huge hit record in "The Devil Went Down to Georgia" agreed to perform, the Doobie Brothers, with whom I had already done three shows previously (one *Soundstage*, one cable special, and *The Midnight Special*) also agreed to perform, and Dionne Warwick, who had one of the biggest records of the year, came on board.

Best of all, although I knew he was somewhat wary at first, Walter and I had a shorthand that started with the music and spilled over to a very similar approach to how music should be presented on television. And, to my surprise and delight, Tisha Fein, my old friend from

The Midnight Special, had come over the year before and was the talent booker on the show.

Walking into the Shrine Auditorium for our first production meeting is a moment I'll never forget. In my still youthful zeal for the project, and for what I was doing for a living, I arrived at the venue long before anyone else and walked into an empty auditorium, the house lights spilling light on the building's 5000 seats but only a single work light on the stage. It was both eerie and exciting at the same time. I remember thinking that less than two months from that day, this empty arena would be filled with 6000 people, rocking for two hours on the biggest night of music of the year.

If I had this feeling of exhilaration, I could only imagine what Pierre's mind had been like two years earlier when he had moved the show from the Palladium to the Shrine. Since its first telecast, the Grammys had always been held at smaller venues, most often at Hollywood's Palladium, a 2,000-seat venue that sorely lacked the production elements necessary to do this kind of show. As I was to learn during our 25-year-plus relationship, Pierre has always dreamed of making the show physically bigger and bigger—witness our move in recent years from venues like the Shrine (6,000) and Radio City Music Hall (6,000) to Staples Center (14,000) and Madison Square Garden (15,000). With Walter, Tisha, and me in place, the scope of the show was now equal to the size of the venue, and we all shared a feeling of unlimited potential as we moved into production of our first Grammy show together.

The 22nd Annual Grammy Awards opened on February 21, 1980 with Charlie Daniels performing "The Devil Went Down to Georgia" to a standing ovation, the first time the words "son of a bitch" ever went out live on television. I walked Johnny Cash and his wife June Carter Cash to the podium to present the first award, and cheered as loudly as anyone in the house when Charlie won. It was the first of more than 600 award presentations where I would try and predict the winner ahead of time and often have them perform just before the category. Sometimes it worked, and sometimes it didn't. I guess it's a good thing we're not a hundred percent, or people would think that we knew the winners, which, on the Grammys at least, is never the case.

Dionne Warwick followed her performance of "I'll Never Love This Way Again" with a win, and as we went to commercial, we started to set up for Bob Dylan's first-ever performance on the Grammys.

Earlier in the day, Bob had rehearsed "Gotta Serve Somebody," the gospel-tinged record that was his first hit since "Hurricane," the song he wrote about Rubin "Hurricane" Carter, which he had performed on the John Hammond *Soundstage*. It was also to be the last charted single he would have for almost 20 years. At the rehearsal, he had taken me aside after he finished rehearsing and asked me what I thought he should wear for the show. I was taken aback by his question, thinking to myself, why the hell is *Bob Dylan* asking *me* what to wear? I had no answer other than to tell him that it was a black-tie night but that performers were free to wear what they usually performed in.

Kenny Rogers was the host that year, and I had written an introduction to Bob that I was to use again and again for him, only needing to update it to reflect the next twenty years.

In the '60s, he was the conscience of a generation through songs like "Blowin in the Wind" and "Don't Think Twice, It's Alright." In the '70s, he created classics like "Knockin on Heaven's Door" and "Tangled Up in Blue," and now in the '80s, he's back with a new sound and a new message. Ladies and gentlemen, Bob Dylan.

Standing offstage, I looked as Bob entered with his band, everyone tuxed up to the hilt. He had taken me literally and put on a tux, perhaps for one of the first times in his life. "Gotta Serve Somebody" smoked that night, but the best part of it all was that Bob Dylan won his first solo Grammy ever, a fact not lost on the press the next day when the overwhelmingly positive stories about the show came out.

Piling on performance after performance, the Doobies, with whom I had done both a *Soundstage* show and a *Showtime* special from Alpine Valley in Milwaukee, 90 miles from Chicago, came out next and nailed "What a Fool Believes," pretty much a Michael McDonald performance, but with some great guitar lines from Patrick Simmons. Their album *Minute by Minute* was my first wrong pick for Album of the Year, and Billy Joel's *The Stranger* picked up the Grammy. I loved Billy's album, which had outsold the Doobies, so I was torn when the win was announced.

After that, we did the first of what would become a Grammy signature performance in the gospel categories. Because both rock and R&B had their roots in gospel music, I had always loved its purity, not to mention its rawness when performed by performers who "went to church on stage," and that night the Mighty Clouds of Joy and Andraé Crouch went to church like it was Sunday morning on Tuesday night. Another standing ovation and another Grammy win for both Andraé and the Clouds.

And then came the big one, the one that is generally credited with starting the phrase "a Grammy moment." I set up what I knew would be a showstopper.

As always, the president of the Academy—this year it was Jay Lowy, not one of America's great speechmakers—came out from the wings to deliver the annual message from the president. As he droned on, poor guy, I watched the eyes of the live audience begin to glaze over and only imagined what was happening in millions of American homes. As he brought his speech to its climactic conclusion, rather than any intro at all, we took the both the house and the stage lights down nearly to black, took an uncomfortably long ten seconds of dead air, and then . . . from one side of the stage out came Barbra Streisand, and from the other out walked Neil Diamond, two of the biggest stars in music, singing the song they had recorded separately and had never performed together, "You Don't Bring Me Flowers."

How that duet came about is almost as interesting as the excitement it generated. Both Barbra and Neil had recorded versions of the song independently, and a disk jockey in Chicago, Roy Leonard, aided by producer Peter Marino, had figured out that you could carefully put the two versions together and make one amazing duet. The combination was, of course, magical, but there wasn't a record—let alone a record that could be nominated for a Grammy, and we had rules about performing songs on the show that weren't nominated, let alone not even recorded. I made my case to the Academy Television Committee, the NARAS appointed group that oversees the show from the Academy perspective, lobbied hot and hard, and at the end of the day they agreed that this was too important not to try and get for the show.

My attorney at the time, a lovely man named Jeff Ingber, was Neil's attorney as well, and after explaining what we wanted to do, he enlisted Neil on our behalf to go to Barbra and ask her to do it. Her television performances were both rare and legendary, and when she accepted early and graciously, we were rocking.

My first call to Barbra to talk about staging the number wasn't two minutes old when she asked for my home number. Thus began a series of phone calls, all focused, and all pertinent, with every possible question you might figure, and many more that you couldn't predict. Yes, Barbra likes to be in control.

"Ken, it's Barbra [like I didn't know]. What do you think? Should I touch Neil's cheek when we get to the last chorus and give him a caress? Do you think that's cheesy?"

I would have given her any answer just to get off the phone at that moment—it was 1:15 in the morning, I had just gotten home and had to be back at the Shrine at 7:30—but it struck me that once again she had added the one element to an already great moment that would take it even higher. I told her I thought that would be a lovely idea and said goodnight.

The next night, near the end of the song, Barbra reached out and touched Neil's cheek and America swooned, we made a bit of television history, and I crumbled at the side of the stage hoping that we could ever do something as exquisite again.

The rest of the show never reached that high, but did have some pretty wonderful moments.

James Galway elevated John Denver's "Annie's Song" to high art, Sister Sledge rocked "We Are Family," an ill-matched Kenny Rogers and Donna Summer performed a medley of the five songs nominated for Song of the Year (a production element we were to abandon as quickly as possible), and the show was almost over, save for the presentation of Record of the Year.

As if it were kismet, some of the internal workings of the Academy worked to my advantage. As if on cue with my arrival, and I ascribe no deeper meaning than coincidence to it, the Academy added four rock categories, and it was an eye opener to me to attend the nominations and see on the list names like the Allman Brothers Band, Frank Zappa, Dire Straits, Wings, Bob Dylan, Rickie Lee Jones, and Bonnie Raitt (who knew what a great Grammy queen she would become ten years later?). One of my favorite reviews from that, my first show, came from the now defunct *L.A. Herald-Examiner* which declared the Grammys "an evening in which pop music vanquished disco." I took that as an omen of things to come.

And, though I had actually looked forward to having John Denver to work with as host, in fact Pierre, who took pleasure in booking the host for the show in the early years, asked Kenny Rogers to do it. A great booking, as Kenny was hot as a pistol and was actually nominated for both Album and Record of the Year. What I knew that many others didn't, though, was that Kenny is dyslexic, not normally a good quality in a host who has to wade through pages of teleprompter copy for two hours on camera.

When I met with him I asked him if he was sure he'd be OK, and all he asked was for us to write slowly. I never quite understood whether he was referring to our teleprompter which sat in the middle of the house, or that I should take my time with the copy I was writing, but just to be safe, I did both. Kenny turned out to be a terrific host, with the exception of his insistence that, as with past hosts, he be allowed to perform the five nominated songs for Song of the Year. I really hated this tradition, but suggested to him that if he really wanted to do that, I would ask Donna Summer, who had a stronger voice than Kenny's and could handle "more difficult" material, to join him and do the medley as a duet. He agreed, and they did a more than creditable version of the songs. As much as I disliked this segment, it would be a couple of years before I would be able to have the original artists themselves reduce their songs to medley form so that I could once and for all bury this old-fashioned variety-show form.

In the awards world, Billy Joel took the big one again, winning Album of the Year and Best Pop Vocal Performance, Male, and it was a popular win. But I was thrilled that the Doobies, Charlie, Dylan, Dionne, and Andraé and the Mighty Clouds of Joy all won. Presenters for the first time were much more appropriate to their categories, save

George Burns (who was managed by Tisha's father at the time), with whom I paired a pale Debbie Harry to present Best New Artist.

The ratings were great, the show was a critical success, and the 22nd Annual Grammy Awards went into the history books as the beginning of a new generation of awards shows. And no one was prouder of what we had done than Pierre, who had put together the team that was to stay together (with a couple of minor hiccups) for the next 28 years.

CHAPTER 3

The 1981 Grammy Awards

"I Want to Be a Part of It, New York! New York!"

After the success we had with the first Grammy show at the Shrine Auditorium, it was clear that we weren't going to take a step back for the 1981 show. The thrill that I had received when first walking into the Shrine the previous December was nothing compared to the feeling of first walking onto the Radio City Music Hall stage in New York.

The first order of business however, was finding a host, and since I had worked with Paul Simon, and he was such a New York icon, I wanted him. At first he was reticent, but when we agreed to give him a performance, he relented, and said he'd do it.

Next came the bookings and it was a tall order, considering the nominations. There was a Who's Who of the elder statesmen in the music business, represented first by Frank Sinatra, who was nominated both in the Album and Record of the Year categories. Next came my friend Barry Gibb and Barbra Streisand, both also nominated for Record and Album, and then in the Album category came Pink Floyd and Billy Joel (a Grammy favorite over the past few years) and finally newcomer Christopher Cross, nominated for both Record and Album. In the Record category, Kenny Rogers and Bette Midler were also nominated.

Although we knew that we needed to have the old guard represented, the show needed to reflect some modernity, and at the time Kenny Loggins was riding high, so we booked him to perform "I'm Alright" from the film *Footloose*. Another film had a huge hit record, and when we realized what production value we could get out of starting Irene Cara outside Radio City on Sixth Avenue and having her and a gang of dancers come through the back of the house to the stage, we jumped at opening the show with the theme from *Fame*. Country music was having a huge revival at the time, with all kinds of acts crossing over to pop, among them Barbara Mandrell, the Oak Ridge Boys, and to a certain extent George Jones, so we put together a medley that featured all three and made that one of the keystone numbers of the show.

And since we were in New York, how could we ignore Broadway, which at the time was dominated by Andrew Lloyd Webber's latest venture, Evita, featuring a huge hit version of the song "Don't Cry for Me, Argentina." Patti LuPone, who starred on Broadway, was added to our growing cast. Remember, in those days we did a two-hour show and only had about eight performance slots over the two hours, so the last slot needed to be filled with a jazz performance. Manhattan Transfer was booked to perform with Chuck Mangione, and it turned out to be a terrific performance. With Paul's performance of "Late in the Evening" (a song he still performs in live shows), it looked like we were booked, but we wound up listening to an amazing contemporized version of "The Lord's Prayer" that featured a host of gospel performers and a great choir, so we found room for that.

And finally, we decided to feature the Song of the Year category in a new way, rather than having the host do a medley, which was growing tiresome if not musically dumb, we brought the five songwriters for the category together to perform a mini-version of their nominated songs. That added Lionel Richie ("Sailing"), Dean Pitchford and Michael Gore ("Fame"), Amanda McBroom ("The Rose"), John Kander and Fred Ebb ("New York! New York!") and, fortunately as it turned out, Christopher Cross ("Sailing") to the party in one extended segment.

And just when we thought we were complete, Aretha Franklin decided to make one of her rare visits to New York. This was well before her well-known fear of flying, but even in those days Aretha was not one for traveling. But when we asked her to perform "I Can't Turn You Loose," a great live performance opportunity, she accepted the invitation and made plans to come to New York.

And although the show had some great performance highlights from many of the aforementioned artists, it was overshadowed by one of the strangest and most unexpected award runs in Grammy history. It was the night of Christopher Cross's sweep of the awards, winning all three major categories, Record, Album, and Song, in addition to Best New Artist. It was the first time anyone had ever done that—and the critics sharpened their knives. Forgetting that many of the nominations were for an older generation of artist, everyone questioned how such a middle-of-the-road artist could sweep the awards, even if all we did with him on the air was about two minutes of the nominated record.

What was overlooked was the Rock category, which featured the never-before-nominated Bruce Springsteen (his Grammy days were to come much later) as well as rock legend Paul McCartney. Offers were made and turned down, and the award ultimately went to Billy Joel, a Grammy favorite in those years, although the album *Glass Houses* contained Billy's hit, "It's Still Rock n' Roll to Me." Let's face it—it really wasn't rock 'n' roll to anybody else. Billy can rock when he wants to, but that wasn't it.

There was an impressive list of presenters (for the time), including Diana Ross, Barbra Streisand and Barry Gibb, a quirky Todd Rundgren, and the unlikely pairing of Anne Murray and Rodney Dangerfield, but they all worked and worked well.

The real highlight of the evening, though very sad in retrospect, was Paul Simon's closing talk. The show was held just three months after John Lennon's tragic murder only 15 blocks away, and Paul's remarks at the end of the show not only put a period to the show, but resulted in one of the quietest moments I've ever experienced on a Grammy show, or any show for that matter. Nobody questioned it when Paul left the stage, spoke to no one, and headed for his dressing room, obviously moved at the emotion he had created in himself—not to mention 6000 people in Radio City and millions more at home.

> *Most people my age can remember where they were and who they were with when each Beatle album came out . . . they were so much a part of the fabric of our lives.*
>
> *I just want to say how sorry we all are at John Lennon's death and how much we'll miss his music, his humor, and his common sense. I'm sure we all share a sense of outrage. I personally would like to thank you all for coming here tonight. This has been a pleasure for me. Goodnight.*

CHAPTER 4

The 1982 Grammy Awards

"I Think John Is with Us Tonight"

For the 24th Annual Grammy Awards, we came back to Los Angeles, a little wiser with two hugely successful shows under our belt and ready to stretch again. This year's nominations were still not very cutting edge, but they were starting to be more reflective of what was going on in the music world—with some notable exceptions.

Although though Bruce Springsteen's *The River* and the Police weren't even represented in either the Best Album or Record categories, it was rewarding for us to at least find Lennon's *Double Fantasy* in the Album category, especially in light of his tragic death.

It would be one more year before the show would move to its now standard three-hour format to celebrate our 25th anniversary, so again it became a challenge to fit as much music as we could into two hours. But even though in those days we could run over a bit, we jammed the show full of ten performances and represented a variety of music.

I thought Quincy Jones would fall off his chair when I called him and told him that we wanted to open the show with James Ingram's version of "Just Once," a soaring soulful song that had achieved No. 1 status, but certainly wasn't an uptempo production-type number that shows like the Grammys usually opened with. But I had a feeling that sending out this former demo singer who had nothing to lose could provide one of those amazing underdog moments that you wish for, and my hunch was realized when James took the stage at the top of the show. I was standing backstage with him, watching him shake like Jello before walking out to the 6000-strong crowd at the Shrine, close his eyes, and deliver a song that would create a lifelong career for him. It did more than soar, it reached the heavens, and it got the show off with its first standing ovation; the folks got it, they were present at the birth of a major talent.

Following James we performed what was fast becoming a Grammy tradition, packing three country numbers into one segment; Dottie West sang "You're the Reason God Made Oklahoma," followed by Terri Gibbs's abridged version of "Somebody's Knockin'" and brought home by the Oak Ridge Boys' No. 1 pop single "Elvira," which scored big in the house. But the best was yet to come. I had asked Jerry Lee Lewis and his cousin Mickey Gilley to present the Country Awards preceded by a short performance, and they knocked the crowd out with a version of one of my favorite Jerry Lee Lewis songs, the classic Hank Williams song, "You Win Again." It received the second standing ovation of the night, and nothing could have made Jerry Lee happier than for people to consider their presentation academic after scoring with this brief barn-burner. The fact that neither man had shown up for rehearsal is long forgotten—as Jerry Lee said to me that night, "It wouldn't have helped."

After George Carlin made a mockery out of the Haskins and Sells auditors, explaining the Grammy rules (a must on any show that hands out awards) with his own twisted bent, the cast of *Sophisticated Ladies*, the Ellington show, rocked the house with a full-out dance version of "It Don't Mean a Thing (If It Ain't Got That Swing)," followed by the award for Musical Cast Album, which was won by Lena Horne. We had desperately wanted a performance from the 70-year-old Horne, but illness prevented that pleasure for a few more years, when she did come and sing.

The show was nearly one hour old when Rick Springfield's "rock" performance was followed by the second-year-in-a-row snub of Bruce Springsteen, whose magnificent album *The River* was beaten by Springfield's tepid *Jessie's Girl*. It was an even more embarrassing moment because I had learned just before the show that Bruce had actually come to the Grammys for the first time, only to be shut out. And backstage after the show, his mother showed up and we talked for a few minutes as I told her how much I loved the album, and how Bruce's day at the Grammys would probably come long after he had made his place in history (I was about ten years off).

With the success of our songwriter's segment the previous year, we tried it again, and it was a big score. Even though several of the writers weren't household names, their interpretations of their own songs (pardon the pun) struck a chord with our audience, and it was a beautiful understated segment, primarily due to the acoustic nature of the material itself. Peter Allen and Carole Bayer Sager kicked it off with a touching version of "Arthur's Theme," followed by Bill Withers, Ralph McDonald, and Bill Salter's exquisite intimate version of "Just the Two of Us," and then Lionel Richie came out Diana-less to do a solo version of "Endless Love," followed by Jackie DeShannon and Donna Weiss doing "Bette Davis Eyes."

When "Bette Davis Eyes" won as Song of the Year, both writers, with tears in their eyes, much like the subject of the song, made eloquent speeches about the importance of writing.

As always, after intimacy, it's time to blow the roof off the sucker, and that's what happened after we returned from commercial. It was the segment I was waiting for, and it delivered on all counts. Al Green tore up "The Lord Will Make a Way," losing ten years in the process and preaching to the converted. Then, in a nod to the contemporary gospel category out came Joe Cocker and the Crusaders who delivered a blistering version of the song that was Joe's comeback recording, "I'm Glad I'm Standing Here Today." After he ripped the paint off the Shrine, Al Green returned and finished with a shout that probably reached from the hall at least to Felix Chevrolet down the block, and perhaps to some of the dormitories at USC, blocks away from the Shrine. It was the highest moment in an already dramatic show, but the real moment of the evening was still ahead.

The place erupted as Tina Turner and James Brown not only walked out together, but riffed a few impromptu steps before remembering that they were at the Grammys. It was a moment for the ages, and gave even the youngest Grammy viewers the sense that funk didn't begin in 1983 with Rick James, it started in Mississippi and Georgia at least 20 years earlier with these two legendary performers, who could get screams out of the crowd with less effort than it took for Rick James to set up his keyboard.

The excitement was only heightened when they read the nominees and then gave the Grammy to a still shaken James Ingram, who barely got through his acceptance speech before running offstage and heading to the bathroom. As they left the stage and walked past me, the entire backstage crew gave them a rare and spontaneous ovation.

Al Jarreau was the next performer to go out and demonstrate the roots of black music, even though he performed "Blue Rondo a la Turk," a jazz tune written by two white musicians, Dave Brubeck and Paul Desmond. It was a virtuoso performance, aided by the wailing saxophone of Pepper Adams, another nominee in the jazz category. Moments later Al came back onstage to accept his Grammy.

Though John Lennon's spirit hung over the place throughout the entire show, it wasn't until the Album of the Year award was up that the night took a different turn. We had several conversations with Yoko's representative, Elliott Mintz, and she and Sean had agreed to come to the show if they could be kept backstage unless John's work was recognized. They had already lost three awards, including Yoko's nominated "Walking on Thin Ice," and though I checked with Elliott to make sure they were still around, if Album passed them by, they were leaving. Herb Alpert and Barbara Mandrell, two Grammy mainstays, took the stage and read the nominees. All of the nominees save Steely Dan and John Lennon had already won Grammys that night. It was left to this one category to see if the Grammys would do right to his memory.

They opened the envelope and Yoko and Sean calmly walked onstage to accept the honor that was due John. Her words rang through the room and are still as meaningful today as they were then: "I think John is with us here tonight. John and I were always proud and happy that we were part of the human race who made good music for the earth and for the universe."

As the nominations for Record of the Year were read immediately following the album category, Walter very innocently caught Yoko crying in the audience. The Record of the Year Award went to "Bette Davis Eyes," though after the show Kim Carnes told me that she was secretly hoping that "Just Like (Starting Over)" would win.

The show received generally good reviews, but the rating was down from the previous two years. Maybe it was that there weren't a number of superstar names nominated, which we looked at with mixed feelings. On the one hand, there was a new crop of recording acts starting to populate the landscape, but television has a mandate for familiarity, and with certain exceptions, this year didn't feed into that.

I was pleased however, with most of the wins, particularly *Double Fantasy* and "Bette Davis Eyes." That Rick Springfield bested Bruce Springsteen, however, was something that was not only personally rough for me, but it would make my quest to bring Bruce to the Grammys even more difficult.

As we made our way to the parties that year, I was struck by a couple of thoughts. Though these shows were beginning to feel like old home week for me (the relationships over ten years of doing music shows were now finding more and more return encounters with talent), I realized that I would never get the chance to work with John Lennon, one of the musical figures who had a profound influence on my wanting to do what I do in the first place, and I was saddened very much by that fact. It would take 17 years for an event to occur that would allow me in some small way to express the feelings that I had for John on television, and when it did, it was to be a moment again tied to tragedy.

Shortly after the Grammy show in February 2000, Faith Hill's manager, Gary Borman, invited me to lunch to meet with a woman who was the West Coast head of an organization called the Violence Policy Center, one of the leading gun-control groups in the country. They were interested in doing a fundraiser that might be appropriate for television, and Gary had thought it would be a good idea for her to meet with me. Right from the beginning, I was sympathetic to the cause, and committed to doing something that could possibly influence the hearts and minds of people.

Normally, the lifespan of one of our event specials is about six to nine months from conception to airing. There are exceptions, of course, and if I wanted to be technically accurate, I could probably point to numerous shows that came together in less time, and a few that probably took longer. But it was to be nearly 18 months from that first fateful meeting with Fiona Fitzherbert from the Violence Policy Center, until the evening of October 2 when the opening notes of "Imagine" sung by Yolanda Adams accompanied by Billy Preston were heard at Radio City Music Hall and in approximately seven million homes around the country.

A tribute to John Lennon seemed perfect. Here was one of pop music's true icons, a member of pop's most important group who then went on to create some of music's most enduring anthems on his own, and a man who was cut down on the eve of what might have been his greatest comeback by a deranged man with a gun. What better way to call attention to the issue of gun control than to use as an icon one of the most universal stories of the impact of our careless gun laws?

Fiona and Gary both loved the idea, and when I took it out to pitch it to the networks, several showed intense interest. Both ABC and TNT came up with substantial offers. Although ABC would have provided the biggest audience and thus guarantee the greatest awareness from the show, I was extremely fond of Brad Siegel, the president of TNT, with whom we had worked on several shows in the past few years, and I felt that Brad would be supportive and committed to the gun-control issue. It was a feeling that was to be affirmed many times in the next year and a half.

The first step in the process was, of course, to get the approval and support of the Lennon estate, and in particular, Yoko. I put together a short treatment that I sent to Elliott Mintz, Yoko's (and John's) longtime publicist, and sent it off on a Friday afternoon in April. Monday morning I received a call from Peter Shukat, Yoko's attorney, saying that she had read the treatment over the weekend and wanted to move ahead immediately. He emphasized that she felt this project was very important and would be completely supportive in whatever way we wanted. It was a great call, and so positive that my normal excitement about all of the projects we do was even exceeded.

With TNT and Yoko on board, we began to develop a list of talent, hopeful of putting the show on in October of 2000, but as we moved ahead it became clear to me that the show was not going to be easy to book, and that both Radio City and Madison Square Garden, the two iconic venues in New York where this show had to be done (New York of course was the only place that was ever considered for the show because of John's association with the city during his life, and also as the location of his death).

So even though we took a great run at trying to do the show for the fall of 2000, it was looking more and more bleak that it could get on at that time.

And even though doing the show in 2001 wouldn't have the same commemorative connection that 2000 was, the concept of the show was strong enough on its own. We all agreed that we should put the show off until the spring of 2001.

During the 2001 Grammys, we continued the preproduction process on the show, only to find that once again, while Radio City was open, it was not an easy show to book. Many of the major artists who should have been there for us for the show were scheduled to tour in the spring or in some cases declined our invitation. We had put together a good list of younger artists, performers who had been influenced by John, but I was frankly surprised to find that people like Elton John, Mick Jagger, and some others who I thought would come to the party just didn't want to do it.

Frankly, it was reaching the point that despite the support of Sandy Shapiro at TNT, Elliott Mintz, and Peter Shukat, we were frustrated at every turn, and I was nearly ready to throw in the towel. Beginning with the booking difficulties, it had been an extremely difficult period, and I wondered whether or not we'd ever get a show on.

But as I thought it through, I became more aware of the critical need for gun-control reform in this country. As I watched the Bush administration show blind support for the gun lobby, I reconsidered my feeling about walking away and became even more committed to seeing the project through.

Yoko's attitude was absolutely inspirational. She agreed to do a significant amount of promotion for the show, was amazingly cooperative with the use of John's image in the promotion and production of the show, and took the initiative to reach out to several of the artists who had initially declined to participate. We began to have regular conversations, and I became increasingly fond of her straightforward, reality-based but tremendously supportive feeling for the show. The team that I had hoped for from the beginning was beginning to become a reality.

Creatively I had wanted to avoid the cliché clip packages of a biographical nature that would provide the material between the musical performances. Instead, I had asked Elliott, who had over 150 hours of interviews that had been done with John over his lifetime, to cull through them and find soundbites from John on a number of subjects, ranging from the obvious issue of violence, to John reflecting on the future, on kids, and on life and death. Elliott had done an amazing job of finding these bites, and one afternoon my friend and writer David Wild and I went over to Elliott's to listen to his first pass. As we sat in his media room and listened to an hour's worth of John's voice, we were struck not only by the remarkable emotional range that John displayed, from humor to anger to happiness to sadness, but with his insight and just how appropriate so much of what he said was to the gun-control issue.

We had also put together a terrific group of artists to participate. Stone Temple Pilots were going to do "Revolution," Alanis Morissette would do "Dear Prudence," Dave Matthews had committed although he hadn't decided on a song, and Moby, Cyndi Lauper, Beck, Marc Anthony, Natalie Merchant, and Shelby Lynne had all agreed to do the show. If we didn't have a group of superstars, we had a group of some of music's most credible artists, all of whom had a sincere feeling about John, his life and his work.

Kevin Spacey had agreed to host the show, and that was a big score. I felt it was critical to have someone front the show who was doing more than reading the prompter, to find someone who when he spoke you really believed what he was saying. And though the few times we had worked with Kevin he had always delivered on that desire, even we had no idea just how much he would bring to the show.

As the summer was coming to a close, things were looking good. We were still hoping an Elton, a Clapton, a Bono would come in, but that wasn't to be. Instead, the songs chosen by the artists were becoming even more important to delivering the message of the show. Shelby Lynne, who was witness to her parents' murder-suicide, chose John's "Mother," while Cyndi Lauper agreed to do "Strawberry Fields Forever" which we planned to shoot as a remote in Central Park at the memorial for John just across from the Dakota, where John had lived and was shot. And we were getting non-committal but positive signs from Paul McCartney, who planned to be in New York at the time of the show. (George politely declined due to health reasons, and Ringo had already exceeded the time he could spend in the country for tax purposes.)

I had been talking to Yoko about both Julian and Sean, and she had asked us to extend invitations to both, which we did. I received a series of e-mails from Julian, none of which gave me much hope, but I knew that Yoko was talking to Sean, and though she wouldn't confirm him, I felt that he was planning to participate.

On Labor Day, everything was looking very good. The show, which had gone on sale three days earlier, sold out immediately even though the tickets were priced at benefit prices. It looked as though over $300,000 would be guaranteed to the charities from the house, not to mention a generous amount that Yoko had promised each of the gun-control organizations. There was a buzz about the show, and all of the artists were being amazingly cooperative in trying to keep their costs down so that the maximum funds could go to charity.

And then, September 11.

As I drove home from the Forum after the cancellation of the Latin Grammys that day, my mind turned to the Lennon show that was to take place nine days later. As the events of the day unfolded, I knew we were not going to do a show on the 20th, but the bigger question was whether or not we would be doing this show at all.

On September 12, we had the first of several conference calls to discuss the future of the show, although like the rest of us at that time, putting a television show in perspective in light of what was going on seemed almost ludicrous. But with people and equipment leaving for New York the next day, decisions needed to be made, decisions that had to be made with a decided lack of information about a lot of things.

The severity of the tragedy in this country was just starting to sink in as we talked. In retrospect it was to be even greater than we realized, but among our considerations at the moment were things like what else was coming from the terrorists, when would Radio City even be open for business, what was the proper time to wait to hold any kind of public event, and how would the city feel about us doing a show?

Though we didn't make a final decision that day, by Friday of that week we were prepared to move ahead and do the show on October 2, three weeks to the day after the tragedy, but only if we had the blessing of the city.

A highly placed AOL/Time Warner executive made a call to the mayor's office and was strongly encouraged to put the show on, expressing a desire even at that time to get the city back on its feet.

It was obvious to all of us, however, that while gun control was an important issue, and certainly one that was appropriate for a Lennon tribute, there was an even greater need to address if we were to proceed. We called the two gun-control organizations and after explaining to them what we wanted to do, they agreed that the proceeds from the house would go to helping the victims of the Trade Center bombing. We contacted helping.com, the website that was acting as a clearinghouse for fundraising organizations needing help, and arranged for their website to be broadcast throughout the show. And we began to turn the script around from the gun-control issue to the immediate needs of the city of New York, the city that John Lennon had loved so much, and the city that had considered him its "first citizen" during his years there.

And then we moved toward putting the show together, dealing with a city in turmoil.

I'm so proud of the way our entire staff pulled together to make the show happen. Even with the post 9/11 fears of flying, and facing the difficulties of doing a show in a city going through major trauma, everyone seemed to realize that not to do the show was giving in to the terrorists, and even more important, realized that we owed it to the city of New York to be there for them.

And that's the way it was throughout our entire time in New York.

Even though our staff is usually great about the gypsy world we live in, doing shows on the road half the year, they were even more sensitive to the realities of working under crisis conditions, increased security precautions, and facilities that required double the patience of the normal production situation.

Show day arrived, and it was incredible. A calm descended on everyone involved, the rehearsals went smoothly, and with each passing hour from the beginning of the rehearsals, it was as though everyone knew we were doing this show for a higher purpose.

I normally do a warmup before the show to deflect the artificiality of the television situation. I tell the audience to forget about the cameras, to "get into the show," and to feel free to let loose when the performance deserves it. I knew that this particular warmup had to go way beyond that. I assumed that more than half the audience at Radio City that night was probably together in a crowd for the first time since September 11. I assumed that the security they had to go through to get into the theater itself hadn't exactly relaxed them, and that there was reasonable cause to assume that many people were even feeling guilty about being out to have a good time that night. For one of the few times in my life, I actually wrote it all out and put it on prompter so that I wouldn't forget it. And while I normally have no nervousness about going out in front of a crowd of 6000 people, I was plenty nervous that night.

Talking to those people that night is something I'll never forget. In front of a set that recreated the "white room" where the video for "Imagine" had been shot by John and Yoko 21 years earlier, I spoke from the heart, and people got it. I was nearly finished, and nearly emotionally drained from the experience, when one of those things that you wish you had thought of afterward happened on its own. In the midst of all of these emotions spewing forth, my cell phone rang. The entire audience erupted as I took the phone and spoke to my friend at CBS, Jack Sussman, who was calling to wish me luck that night. As I turned the phone off, the audience spontaneously broke into laughter and applause, and the edge was off. I could tell that these people were ready for relief, and release, and we were going to give them a show that gave them both.

Every performance was a stunner. Yolanda Adams and Billy Preston soared on "Imagine." Kevin's opening was interrupted five times by applause from the audience as the impact of his words of hope and promise touched them far beyond any opening comic monologue could have (even one delivered by the master, Billy Crystal). And one by one, the artists delivered. And it seemed as though each song, most of which had been selected before September 11, took on new meaning for that audience there and the millions at home.

And then there were the clip packages. While most of the ones we had selected earlier were still to the point, I went into John's interviews even deeper and found sound bites that were even more poignant, and at times, prophetic. In the piece that preceded Stone Temple Pilots' "Revolution," John said, "I want to know what happens after you bomb Wall Street." A stunned silence fell over the house and then Scott Weiland launched into a version of the song true to the original, but with a live intensity that brought the audience to its feet. Even the one biographical piece, footage of John's life that was shown on the big screen behind Dave Matthews, seemed more touching as he performed "In My Life."

And when Sean came out and performed, doing "Across the Universe" with Moby and Rufus Wainwright, and then came back later in the show to sing "This Boy" and then "Julia," a good part of the audience was in tears, tears not only for the loss of John, but for the loss we were all in the midst of remembering 21 days after our national tragedy.

Other performances touched the audience as well. Alanis's "Dear Prudence" took us all back to the simpler days of the '60s and John's connection with the Maharishi, while Marc Anthony's "Lucy in the Sky with Diamonds" was preceded by John's explanation of how he was confused by the public's interpretation of the initials LSD. Musical director Dave Stewart rocked with Nelly Furtado on "Instant Karma," and Lou Reed brought a ferocity to "Jealous Guy" that brought down the house. Cyndi's remote from Strawberry Fields was so sparing and intimate in its delivery that the house gave her a standing ovation although ostensibly she wasn't even in the house.

And then came one more surprise; Kevin Spacey, who I had seen sing several weeks previous to the show at a Latin Grammy benefit show, performed "Mind Games" and shocked the house with his presence, his commitment, and his voice. Gone was the weak character from *American Beauty* and the warped slyness of one of the *The Usual Suspects* and in their place was a performer who could have held the stage with any rock star around today.

Yoko came out and spoke briefly but eloquently, and then the entire cast came out and ended the show with a dual message that demonstrated the range of John's thoughts and John's ability to translate those thoughts into words and music: "Give Peace a Chance" followed by "Power to the People."

When it was over, two hours live to the country and the world, in our minds at least, we had created a small but meaningful turning point for the city of New York, and hopefully for the country. We had been the first event after the attacks to come entirely from New York to the world, and we had shown that New Yorkers were ready to move forward in a positive direction, and that there was a tomorrow. It was a night to remember, and those of us involved would certainly remember it forever.

CHAPTER 5

The 1983 Grammy Awards

*Marvin Gaye, Count Basie, Willie Nelson,
and a Night of Musical History*

To celebrate the 25th anniversary of the Grammy Awards, CBS gave us a "one time only" order for a three-hour show, expanding it from its traditional two-hour time slot. Even though Walter and I had only done the show for three years, it was the most welcome thing that could have happened, and we knew that we would never go back to two hours again. We could expand from about eight or nine performances to thirteen or fourteen, increase the number of awards given on the air, and find the time to open up the show to present some special segments, which I had already begun to call "Grammy moments," several of which found their way into that very first three-hour show in 1983.

Being a keyboard player, I had long loved the idea of putting two or more piano players together to create something special. I guess it all started for me when I was a kid and my mother took me to see Ferrante and Teicher, the first of the pop pianists to put two pianos together. They had a bunch of hits in the '50s, the two biggest being the themes from the two films *Exodus* and *The Apartment*. I loved the sound, and when my mother learned that one of them (Teicher, I believe) had a Cleveland relative, she hunted that person down and took me over to meet the two of them. Her secret motive was that it would re-inspire my interest in classical music, but I had already started to focus on popular music, so it didn't work, other than the thrill I felt when I met them.

On *Soundstage*, years later, I put Chick Corea and Herbie Hancock together to perform "Someday My Prince Will Come," and repeated the piano trick several times before the upcoming Grammy show in 1983. I wanted to open the show with as many great pianists of different styles playing together as I could, and with the palette that was the Grammys, within a few days we had booked an amazing group: Count Basie, Little Richard, Jerry Lee Lewis, Ray Charles, and Elton John. This was going to be the dream combo of my life, and my plan was to have them all do a snippet of one of their classics and then finish it all off together doing Ray Charles's signature "What'd I Say."

The simple fact is, I would have probably done the segment with any one of them, but this would be the first time I would have a chance to work with Ray, my first musical idol and influence. I had grown up with Ray as the constant in my musical life, beginning with those great Atlantic 45s and albums, and had tried to copy his style in songs like "What'd I Say," "Hallelujah I Love Her So," and an obscure track called "Greenbacks," a song about a guy who gets taken by a hooker. I actually performed a medley of those songs when I was a junior in college as the talent part of a Homecoming King competition, and it had secured me second place in the event. And if I had a total LP collection on any artist's work, it was Ray's. Whenever I was blue I would listen to the two live albums he had recorded in the '50s and they would always lift me up.

Over the years, we would be lucky enough to work with Ray a number of times, and he would be one of those few artists who I would sheepishly approach in awe and haltingly speak to about what I wanted him to do. It was reasonably uncharacteristic of me, but I just couldn't ever get over the fact that I was in his presence.

Ironically, twenty years after this first meeting, and shortly after Ray's death, I would be in a position to honor his amazing career achievements on two highly visible television events, one a CBS special that we did to help open the Jamie Foxx film *Ray*, that featured some of the greatest tribute performances I've ever done on television, and the second, on the Grammy show itself, where his final CD, *Genius Loves Company*, was not only nominated for a number of Grammys, but ultimately won the big one, Album of the Year. The Grammy show featured an amazing duet of "Georgia on My Mind" with Jamie Foxx and Alicia Keys, as well as a piece of "Do I Ever Cross Your Mind," the Ray Charles/Bonnie Raitt duet, which I used as the centerpiece of our "In Memoriam" segment. The "Genius: A Night for Ray Charles" special also featured "Georgia," done by Usher, as well as some pretty awesome versions of other Ray masterpieces, including an opening number version of "Night Time (Is the Right Time)" by Elton John, Mary J. Blige, and David "Fathead" Newman (Ray's original bandmate), as well as an inspiring "What'd I

Say" performed by Al Green, with help from an aspiring young piano player, Ken Ehrlich. It was a pretty incredible show that went on to win an Image Award from the NAACP and a directing award from the Directors Guild of America for Bruce Gowers, thus becoming one of the most honored shows of the year.

We had already developed the style of surprising the audience with performances on the Grammys any time we could. Television show or not, it was important to us to keep the audience in suspense so that the element of surprise gave an extra rush to the performance. The shock of seeing these five amazing piano players revealed one at a time until it built to the greatest collection of keyboard heroes playing together was very enticing.

The only problem was that while I could hide a band behind a flying screen or curtain, the idea of hiding five pianos spread out across the stage and then revealing them one at a time was a physical impossibility. Or it was until I came up with what I thought was a brilliant idea. We would construct giant circular curtains which would begin at floor level around each player and instrument, and then be "flown" one at a time revealing the artist. Rene Lagler, our scenic designer at the time, drew up the plans, and we even went to the expense of making them. But when we got down to the Shrine and looked at them on camera, they looked like giant socks. Walter kept calling them socks, and after the continuous, and well-deserved abuse that I took for wanting to use them, we abandoned the idea and instead created one overall reveal for the entire group of stars.

And then the second hitch in my plan developed. I was thrilled when Elton John accepted our invitation to be one of our superstar piano players—and then heartbroken when for the second time in four years he cancelled on us.

But Ray Charles, Count Basie, Little Richard, and Jerry Lee Lewis ain't chopped liver, so we moved on toward making this the best opening a Grammy show had seen to date. And it was.

Ray kicked it off with a smokin' "What'd I Say," and though the others were supposed to lay out and give Ray his moment, standing offstage I couldn't help but grin as I watched the others do some brief fills as Ray brought the audience to its feet for the first of four ovations. Then, with the same sparing triplets that were Basie's signature for nearly 50 years at that time, he went into "One O'Clock Jump" and the crowd erupted for a second time. By the time he finished, we had already made a little bit of music history—and Jerry Lee and Richard hadn't even started.

By the early '80s, time and hard living had taken its toll on Jerry Lee, but the company, and probably the competition, spurred him on a slightly slower, but amazing version of "Whole Lotta Shakin'," and then it was Richard's turn. He was still in his "I don't sing no rock 'n' roll no more" stage, but he had agreed to take the classic licks of every Little Richard song and put them "to God's work" in a song called "Joy Joy Joy." The fact that all of his early hits were actually gospel songs with secular lyrics helped, and the crowd went crazy once again.

Then the competition began. Basie played more notes than usual, but stayed above the fray, and Ray, who had never felt the fire of JL and Little Richard even in the days when they were fighting for chart positions, just took his traditional turn as we came back to "What'd I Say." But Jerry Lee and Richard began a battle of the keys that must have rivaled the old unit show days when they toured with ten or so other one-hit acts in the '50s. As I stood and watched it, I can remember thinking about the legendary Jerry Lee Lewis story that has survived the years about the time Alan Freed had booked Jerry Lee and Chuck Berry on the same bill at the Brooklyn Paramount. Chuck always closed his shows, as did Jerry Lee, and it was only Alan's persuasive nature that got Jerry Lee to agree to be next-to-last on the show, with Chuck to follow. After a blistering set which nearly destroyed the piano, and certainly destroyed the audience, Jerry Lee, who had poured gasoline all over the piano prior to his appearance, stood up, lit a match, and set the keyboard on fire. As he walked triumphantly offstage, he was alleged to have hurled a racial slur at Chuck.

Well, no pianos burned on the night of the 25th annual Grammy Awards, but we were off to a mighty high start, and our four pianos were a hard enough act to follow. And it was only because of a second special segment we did that night that it could even be followed.

For years, the Grammys had been accused of not paying proper homage to black music, though the show often had artists like Stevie Wonder, Gladys Knight, and others perform. Considering the role that

R&B, in its richest form, had played in modern American music, we certainly could do more.

I had laid out a tribute to R&B that started with one of my favorite doo wop songs of all time, "The Ten Commandments of Love," and had reunited the legendary performer/producer Harvey Fuqua with the rest of the Moonglows to do it. From there it went to Gladys and the Pips doing the stone R&B version of "The Way We Were," then on to the Spinners and their mightiest song, "Mighty Love" then it was to come home with Marvin Gaye's first-ever Grammy performance, "Sexual Healing." The rehearsals were met with standing ovations from cast and crew. Except Marvin didn't show up.

On show day, for the dress rehearsal, he was finally there, but never really gave us anything to indicate the power of what we were going to see a few hours later. The audience was even further thrown off when host John Denver, not really known for his R&B roots, offered a well-meaning, but not particularly convincing setup for the segment.

But it soared from the first note; Harvey and the Moonglows made it seem like 1954, and we were all in the balcony of the Apollo Theater.

Then Gladys took the stage and as I had learned from a number of experiences with her, she was there to make a statement. The Spinners were all over the stage as well as in the audience as they did "Mighty Love."

And then, we came back to the podium for one of the more unlikely intros in Grammy history, John Denver welcoming Marvin Gaye to the stage.

I was standing next to Marvin and I knew that there was a little something extra in his system that night. He had arrived late, stayed pretty much alone until his performance, and then seemed not to see anything but that one spot at the center of the stage as he walked out to a thunderous ovation. Now, any Marvin fan will tell you that while "Sexual Healing" was by the far the best of the new Marvin, it wasn't "What's Going On" or "Mercy Mercy Me." But the new Marvin had a lot of the old Marvin that night, and probably extended the life of the R&B male vocalist in pop music by five more years with that performance. It was transcendent, and though there was still over an hour of Grammy show yet to come, I'm not sure that anyone remembered anything else after Marvin finished. The audience leapt to its feet, and Marvin sauntered backstage to find the on-camera backstage position where we always made the previous performer suffer while we announced the results of the just-performed category. Thank God Marvin Gaye won, came out and made it through his speech. It was to be one of his last performances, and a year later he was dead, shot to death by his father in his home.

There was a third performance on that show that people remember to this day, and it, too, had both a historical and a historic musical context to it.

Lena Horne had been booked to perform the year before but wasn't able to be at the show due to illness. She promised to come the next year, and she was there singing what had become her modern anthem "Believe In Yourself" from the concert album that Quincy Jones had produced. No one seemed to notice (or care) that Lena was performing the year after her album was nominated (or won). Once again, as it had with Jerry Lee, Count Basie, and Little Richard, the years melted away and you would have thought you were watching a young and vibrant Lena as she belted the song for all it was worth.

There were other memorable performances that night, and although Willie Nelson's live remote from Austin, Texas (the show that year was on the same day as one of his traditional hometown party shows) was terrific, it almost set a precedent that could have killed the Grammys. Over the years, a number of artists with scheduling conflicts have offered remotes to us, and we've always turned them down. To do it for one could likely mean that it could grow to more than one and eventually turn the show into a live origination and a bunch of remotes, and lose the importance of the event itself. Other than one other time and a Lifetime Achievement Award to the Rolling Stones that we did from London, there have been no other remotes in my 26 years doing the Grammys.

It was probably a good thing that we set up the remote, however, as a bit later in the show, Willie's song, "Always on My Mind," won the Grammy for Song of the Year. It was the first time in many years that a country song had been given that honor ("Little Green Apples" had won in 1968), and Willie would sweep the Country awards that year as well. It was his biggest hit ever, and deserves the standard status it has achieved over the years.

As to other "moments," Leontyne Price's "Vissi D'Arte" was one of the highest classical moments of any Grammy show, and was certainly in contrast to another moment that took place fifteen minutes later when a host of country performers that ranged from the legendary Bill Monroe to Ricky Skaggs and Crystal Gayle saluted country on the show. And Joe Cocker topped his previous Grammy gospel appearance (and spurred a comeback) when he and Jennifer Warnes performed "Up Where We Belong" and earned another standing ovation.

The studio group, Toto, earned both Record and Album honors for "Rosanna" and *Toto IV*, and though I remember liking the production of the album, I've forgotten what it sounds like now. Their win drew the ire of many of the reviews for the awards themselves, particularly in those two categories in which they were up against Paul McCartney, Billy Joel, and two extremely interesting breakthrough albums, one *The Nightfly* by Steely Dan's Donald Fagen, and the second, Joe Jackson's *Steppin Out*, which had become one of the year's most popular tracks. The fact that the others wound up being shut out of the awards gave the press and critics fodder for the now-familiar lack-of-relevance outcries that were becoming almost rote for the day-after reviews.

And, once again, pretty much because it was part of our arrangement with John Denver that he would perform, we put together a medley, but this time, rather than nominees for any category we couldn't book with the originals, we thought about putting together a medley of Grammy-winning songs. Looking back at the performance, it might have been less than brilliant to have John perform "A Day in the Life," and even less appropriate to bring out Joan Baez for them to duet on "Blowin In The Wind," but at least we ended it with everyone onstage doing "Let the Sun Shine In," which of course by 1983 had become dated. One of our less successful efforts, but every once in a while I look at a still picture we took of all the Grammy winners onstage and think about the uplifting nature of music and the true harmony it can provide. There onstage was everyone from Marvin Gaye to Linda Ronstadt, Bill Monroe, and Leontyne Price.

The ratings were strong that year, up nearly three rating points from the previous year, assuring that the three-hour format was here to stay. And though I can recall saying to Walter how tough it was going to be to top the show the following year (that seems to be our Grammy mantra), we didn't count on what was going to become one of the biggest stories in the history of modern music the next year: a little album from Michael Jackson that would go on to become the best-selling album of all time, *Thriller*.

CHAPTER 6

The 1984 Grammy Awards

*One "Thriller" of a Night—Thanks to Herbie Hancock's
"Rockit" Ride and Annie Lennox as "Elvis"*

With each Grammy show that Pierre, Walter, Tisha, and I did together, we began to get into a rhythm—the show has never fallen into a pattern, but we were getting to know each other's style and learning how to feel each other out to get the best we all had to offer to work together. And even though our first three-hour show the year before was a high point, we knew that the show that was fast approaching in 1984 had the potential of topping even that previous effort. We were already well used to the three-hour format, even though we had only done it once before.

Even though there was the obvious Michael Jackson factor to be considered—he received a record *12* nominations—we were determined not to turn the Grammys into the Michael Jackson show, but rather to use his appearance to create an even higher pedestal for the fourteen other spots we had to create for the show. That certainly wouldn't be a problem except for one thing—even after his record nominations, Michael hadn't said yes to performing, and without him, it could be wildly embarrassing.

Even though Pierre had built the show into a very important event even before we got there, there were acts who didn't want to do the show, and for very obvious reasons—the failure of the Academy to be responsive either to what was really going on in music, or to nominate some of the right things, and then give awards to the wrong artists. Some of that criticism still exists today, but Mike Greene's total revamping of the Academy in the years to come would change a lot of that. Today the awards and certainly the show have become not just credible, but also the most important music event of the year.

In any event, we needed Michael and the early signs weren't positive that he'd perform. His manager at the time lived down the street from me, and he scheduled a very quiet, discreet meeting at his home for us to talk about what we wanted to do. We sat, Michael barely talking, and when he did, directing his words to the manager, and I knew that we were up against it. No matter where we went, it wasn't going to be satisfactory. I left very discouraged.

We had allies. The people at Epic Records, Michael's label, wanted him to perform. His father wanted him to perform. Janet, with whom I was then working at *Fame*, talked to him about performing. But no matter what kind of pressure was applied, there was no budging Michael. He wasn't going to do it. And then we discovered that as with other artists, he had felt mistreated in the past by the Grammy voting process, and this was his way of getting back. Even Quincy Jones, a great friend of the Grammys, was unable to sway him, and we went into the Grammy show Michael-less.

To make matters worse, Michael had suffered the singed hair incident at the very same Shrine Auditorium where the show was taking place (when he was making that famous Pepsi commercial) only six weeks before, and here we were in the same venue without him performing for us.

Again, adversity often creates a platform for trying harder, perhaps with a bit of vendetta thrown in. We were determined to do a show without Michael that made everyone forget about him. Boy, were we wrong about the forgetting part. He swept the show, winning a record eight awards, most of which were given on the show, and all of which were accepted by Michael, who sat regally in the front row bemusedly watching the proceedings with a detached sense of wonder. And to this day I wonder whether the show that he saw up on the stage that night made him feel as though he had missed the boat by not performing. On the other hand, he was to perform a few years later and give one of his greatest-ever television performances, so perhaps he was right in spurning the 1984 show since the Academy had done the same to him in previous years.

╰╮

Donna Summer, she of the disco hits and more, opened the show with a full-out dance production number of "She Works Hard for the Money," made all the more amazing to those of us backstage since her limo had stalled blocks away from the Shrine Auditorium, and she ran into the house, winded, about two minutes before the hard wall rose on the number. But it was a big score, Walter nailed it directorially, and it set the stage for the yin of credibility to the yang of disco when presenters Bob Dylan and Stevie Wonder walked out to present the first award of the evening, in which Michael had not one but two nominated performances. Jaws dropped in the Shrine Auditorium and in living rooms around the world as Bob uttered the name Sting as the winner for what was arguably the Best Song of the Year for "Every Breath You Take."

And then, as if to add insult to injury—or at least to give the Police their just due before the *Thriller* assault began—Sting, Andy Summers, and Stewart Copeland were announced as the winners of the next award for Best Rock Duo or Group. I was thrilled, as my son Matt had played *Synchronicity* until the grooves were worn out. (Grooves, for those of you under 25, were those round things that filled the 12 inches of something called vinyl records in the Middle Ages.)

Joan Rivers joined Culture Club's Boy George to give "the rules," and it was hard to figure out who was more lost, Joan or George. But it took the edge off what was shaping up to be a disappointing night at best for those millions of kids who were there to see Michael Jackson sweep the Grammys.

In the meantime, we were now well over an hour into the telecast, and other than the occasional audience shot, and the nomination packages, there had been no sign of Michael, who had already won a handful of awards in the pre-telecast segment of the ceremony.

But the show wasn't suffering, and before Michael would take the stage for the first time, we had scheduled a special tribute to Chuck Berry that was to feature two of rock's hottest guitarists of the time, Stevie Ray Vaughan and George Thorogood. Chuck was another of the Grammy's overlooked legends, and we wanted to correct it, even if it meant working with Chuck, who ain't easy.

Walter and I had gone up to San Francisco earlier in the year to meet with Chuck after one of his shows, and he seemed to love the idea that we were going to do something special on the show that involved him playing with these two other guys. And nothing changed until he hit the stage for the rehearsal two days before the show, and then it really changed. Dick Alen, Chuck's longtime William Morris agent, took me aside and told me that Chuck would love to perform, but not with them. Thus began a negotiation that took place while we were rehearsing the act before him and really didn't end until after the performance on the show itself. I'm always trying to find the weave, the middle ground that will make everybody happy, but will always work for the show. And this one was proving tough. We finally agreed that Chuck would come out first, do "Maybellene," and then would *leave* the stage while Stevie Ray and George did "Roll Over Beethoven"—and then he'd come back for 45 seconds to do "Let It Rock" with them. Forty-five seconds and not a second longer. That's Chuck for you.

Chuck cut the song off precisely at the 45-second mark, and my hope of making musical history with the three of them jamming was just that, a hope, and not a reality. But we did the right thing by Chuck, and late as it was, Chuck had his Lifetime Achievement Award from the Grammys.

After the obligatory commercial, Michael fans everywhere were able to salute their hero as he and Quincy Jones were named Producers of the Year for *Thriller* and they took the stage together, with Michael uttering 22 words and Quincy having to be "played off," that thing we all hate when we fear that we won't get to Record of the Year because all of Quincy's numerous children needed to be thanked.

Michael's micro-acceptance speech was soon forgotten thanks to one of Grammy's all-time surprises and great performances.

The Eurythmics had been nominated for Best New Artist along with Culture Club and a couple of other faceless acts. I loved the entire album, but was crazy about "Sweet Dreams," such a different sound and that magnetic voice of Annie Lennox. They were one of the first bookings on the show, and during rehearsal everybody had loved them. But Dave and Annie had a surprise up their sleeves and told no one what they had planned. Annie had said something to me about "keeping an eye on her" during the rehearsal, but I laid it off to the usual small talk. Purely by accident, I happened to run up by their dressing room midway in the show (I always give the performers one last shmooze before they go onstage, but it was rare that I'd be anywhere near the dressing room). I saw Dave but I could swear Annie wasn't there, until I looked more closely at the person whose back was to me, and I realized that there was Annie doing her best Elvis, sideburns and all.

They came to the stage, and I got on my headset to Walter in the truck and told him he was in for a little shock. When the house saw them, they went crazy, and that was nothing compared to what happened after the house witnessed what was for most of them their first live performance by the Eurythmics.

I held my breath, and then closed my eyes as the unlikely pairing of Cyndi Lauper and Rodney Dangerfield (thanks again, Tisha!) read the nominations for Best New Artist and then called out Culture Club as the winner. The voters had done it again—passed over the brilliant Eurythmics for a two-hit wonder!

But Cyndi and Rodney weren't the presenting highlight of the evening. Following a performance by the cast of *La Cage Aux Folles*, Mickey Rooney and Ann Miller came out to present the award for Best Cast Show Album. To this day I can't tell you whether Mickey was a little hammered or he's just that way, but within moments of his arriving onstage and having trouble with the microphone, he had dropped to the floor, pulled the microphone down with him and was hamming it up as if his life depended on it. In the truck, Walter was going crazy, asking me to go out onstage and pull him off, anything we could do to end this embarrassing moment. But Mickey wasn't having any, and by the time he and his more-than-humiliated partner, Ann, had finished, we felt we had just seen one of the most ridiculous Grammy moments ever. It wasn't one that we repeated when we would do our highlights pieces over the years, but, trust me, it was memorable.

With the earlier wins that the Police had, when the Beach Boys came out to present the Grammy for Album of the Year, it was still anyone's game, and nobody even ruled out Grammy favorite Billy Joel, nominated along with Michael, the Police, David Bowie, and the predictable *Flashdance* soundtrack.

Michael picked up his second on-camera award, and talked a bit more, which didn't stop Quincy from once again being whisked off to music. But Michael's number of wins was building up, and with it, we knew, the handicappers who had hyped the show to viewers as the Grammy show that could make history in terms of the highest number of awards ever won by one artist on one show.

But we weren't through in our quest to make people forget about Michael for a while, and it was Herbie Hancock who made it happen. I had met with Herbie earlier that year about a television project that was still a few years off, and he had told me about this amazing video he was making for his *Rockit* album with video directors (and artists) Kevin Godley and Lol Creme. He sent me an advance of a bizarre group of robots shaking and moving their electronic eyes to the dance beat of an electronic track that was so far removed from Herbie's Miles Davis days that I thought I had the wrong video on when I first played it. It was very, very cool, and when it was nominated (and won in the Best R&B Instrumental Performance), I knew we had to do something on the show. We located the original robots, worked on a system of making them work live (it had taken four days to tape the video), and it was far and away the performance of the show. The crowd loved it.

The show also marked the Grammy debut of Wynton Marsalis, who became the first performer ever to perform two different numbers in two different categories (classical and jazz), winning Grammys in both. Jazz and classical are two of the genres that separate the Grammys from all other shows, and when we can help make them score, it's amazing. And Wynton's double performance was certainly one of those.

Following Wynton's performance, Richard Stoltzman, a well-respected classical clarinetist came out to present the classical awards, and though he read the winners with the usual excitement that always accompanies the classical awards, it wasn't until he finished that he gave the Grammys one of our most remembered presentations. He opened the envelope to find it empty, and vamped as only a classical clarinetist can until one of the accountants rushed out onstage to give him the right envelope. Oh well, live television is interesting.

If Wynton delivered a great performance (which he did), he wasn't the only trumpet player on the stage that night who wound up the crowd. I had heard this gospel recording of "Amazing Grace" by a guy named Phil Driscoll, and it was absolutely breathtaking. We hunted him down, got a tape of him doing the number live, and knew that it would be one of those surprise "Grammy moments" that we lived for . . . someone no one had really ever heard of walking onto that big stage in front of the royalty of the music industry and literally blowing them away. And Phil Driscoll (who we had never heard of before and quite honestly haven't got a clue as to where he is now) walked out and did just that. The ovation was deafening, and he gave the Grammys the performance of a lifetime.

We were set up for the big award of the night for Record of the Year. And even though Michael was the odds-on favorite, the earlier double win by the Police, coupled with the huge popularity of Lionel Richie's "All Night Long," meant that a Michael Jackson win was by no means a fait accompli.

Michael did win, bringing his total to eight, and once again he spoke more briefly than Quincy. In an unprecedented move, Columbia Records president Walter Yetnikoff walked onstage with the two of them, creating a buzz within the industry and perhaps marking the beginning of Walter's fall from grace.

The show, probably because of the heat that Michael had brought to the entire music industry as well as our show, became the highest-rated Grammy show ever, scoring a 30.8 rating and 45 share. The show held for the entire three hours—this only in our second year of doing a three-hour show.

CHAPTER 7

The 1985 Grammy Awards

A Night for Tina Turner

The 1985 Grammy Awards show has been remembered by most people as the "Tina Turner Awards," both for her triumphant comeback and for one of the most dramatic entrances and performances in the show's history. But for me, there were two other remarkable appearances that year that live in my memory.

The first took place less than an hour into the show when host John Denver introduced Cyndi Lauper. Cyndi had been nominated for several Grammys that year, and though it was expected that she would perform "Girls Just Want to Have Fun," which itself was nominated for Record and Song of the Year, Cyndi and I talked about the drama that would be generated if she did another song from the *She's So Unusual* album, "Time After Time." It was an introspective, dark ballad, which we staged with such simple production, a carpeted multi-level environment that allowed the audience at home and at the Shrine Auditorium to focus on nothing other than this transcendent artist and the lyrics to an intensely personal, highly emotional song. And while most people thought of Cyndi as this quirky, almost comedic character as defined by "Girls," in fact, Cyndi was, and is, a singular performance artist whose own persona is defined by her commitment to her art, in this case, music.

She brought in the well-known theatrical stager and choreographer Pat Birch to help her choreograph some catlike moves on the multi-level platform, and just before she went onstage, I watched her enter an almost trancelike mode, psyching herself for this very important four minutes and thirty seconds. Then she walked onstage and hypnotized America and the world, and from that moment on, nobody ever thought of Cyndi Lauper as a novelty act again. Once again, Walter captured this ironic mix of Cyndi's strength and vulnerability with close-ups that were magical.

Even though she projected a kind of tough New York street mentality to those around her, I could sense a heightened vulnerability and almost "outsider" sensitivity, confirmed as she walked to the stage earlier in the show and sobbed her way through her acceptance speech for the Best New Artist award.

What was most gratifying to me was that Cyndi was sincerely grateful to us for the way in which she had been treated by all of us on the show, and I warmly added her to the growing list of artists I knew I wanted to work with much more in the future, hits or no hits. It was a decision for me based not only on the huge talent contained within that small body, but because I sensed in her the same thing I had been able to sense with artists like Paul Simon, Herbie Hancock, Sting, Bono, and others—a strong sense of self combined with an understanding that the musical experience we all share didn't start with their own rise to popularity, and wouldn't end there. It was based on a historical perspective that went back generations, and would continue to evolve beyond what they would add to it. And further, that for the time being, they were the keepers of the flame and needed to do their best to keep the line intact. It would prove to be a quality I would treasure each time it came into play in working with special artists.

The other performance that killed that year was Prince, whose career was already in high gear, but who was coming to the Grammys for the first time. And while *Purple Rain* had been an obvious choice to be nominated for Album of the Year, I was personally disappointed when "When Doves Cry" was slighted for both Record and Song of the Year nominations.

Walter and I hadn't seen a live Prince performance, always a must for us before booking an act. His live shows were legendary, and so we traveled to St. Louis a couple of months before the show to witness for ourselves the amazing artist and his over-the-top live show. Like other great shows I had seen in the past, this was one of those shows where the audience was on their feet from beginning to end. It had everything—a great look, a great vibe, some amazing musicianship, and towering above it all, this slight intense artist whose sexuality was infused with elements of James Brown, Elvis, and the Beatles all rolled into one.

The vision of it remains today as one of the most memorable concerts I've ever seen.

Getting to talk to Prince about the Grammys was another story. His management was very protective of him, and his day-to-day manager, Steve Fargnoli, was even tougher. Despite their insistence that we could work through them on all elements of production, I insisted that we have a sit-down with Prince to talk about ideas for his performance of "Baby I'm a Star," which we had mutually agreed would be performed on the show.

We had scheduled a meeting with him at a downtown hotel about two weeks before the show, and showed up around 10 P.M. for the 10:30 meeting. We were taken to a suite where we sat and waited for nearly an hour before His Princeness would see us. We were then ushered into a darkened room, set up with purple drapes, candles, and not much else other than two exotic-looking women, one on either side of Prince. My style for first meetings has always been to elicit ideas from "the other side" rather than to jump in and say something stupid. So, sensing that this was not going to be one of those traditional mutual glad-handing sessions, I said a few words and waited for something to come from Prince. He just sat there saying nothing but with a slight smile that indicated very little at all. He was waiting for us, and we were waiting for him. After an uncomfortable silence, I went into a few of the production ideas we had, and though he acquiesced through head movements, not a word came from him. After I had run out of things to say, I waited for some sign, but once again, nothing. He looked at Fargnoli and the woman from the record company, and we all knew that the meeting was over. We stood up, he didn't, and we exited, not knowing whether or not anything we had said meant anything at all.

As we walked toward the elevator the record company representative shocked me by saying "that was a great meeting, you know." I didn't know, and wouldn't know until three days later when we got a call saying that Prince had liked everything, but had one or two surprises that he didn't want to talk about until we got to rehearsal for the show.

As rehearsal day approached Walter and I grew more and more curious about Prince's "surprise," and when after his rehearsals nothing out of the ordinary appeared, we thought maybe he had forgotten about it altogether. But he had not.

He rocked that night, lit up the house both vocally and with a blistering guitar solo (I have always believed that along with being an amazing showman his guitar playing ranks right up there with Eric Clapton and Jimi Hendrix). Still no surprise, but then at the end, he and his entire troupe headed down the stairs that were used by winners to come up onstage and he ran out of the house, leaving a bare stage for the 5000 people to applaud. And to this day, I've never seen a house give greater applause to an empty stage. Which didn't help Walter, who was stuck with nothing to shoot until a hastily summoned John Denver was rushed out to move the show along.

Following the next commercial, Dionne Warwick and Joni Mitchell took the stage to announce the Album of the Year Grammy, and Prince, nominated for *Purple Rain* lost to Lionel Richie's *Can't Slow Down*.

And don't think that Prince, later The Artist, and now again Prince, didn't remind me of that moment often as we worked together over the years. Yes, he does talk, but only when he has something to say. And I love him dearly. As it has turned out, though I would have him on other shows in the interim, it took me 19 years to get him back on the Grammys to do his career-changing opening duet with Beyoncé on the 2004 show.

Performance-wise, before we return to the remarkable Tina, there were some other highlights on the 1985 show worth remembering.

With the significant success we had gotten from our "four pianos" the year before, and not being a person afraid to cannibalize myself, I came up with what I thought would be a great follow-up grouping for this show. The electronic keyboard revolution was in full force, and so I decided we should do our own tribute to those keyboards by filling the stage with a sea of them and put together their greatest interpreters for one bang-up number. Both Thomas Dolby and Howard Jones (remember "She Blinded Me with Science"?) were riding the British techno revolution with hits here and abroad, and we booked them as a part of the piece. And my friend Herbie Hancock was definitely on the leading edge of this technology, having used synthesizers on record almost from the beginning. The missing piece of course came in with the presence of Stevie Wonder, who had also been an early proponent of electronic music.

Stevie and Herbie took the lead in putting together the medley which consisted of pieces from all four artists blended together and then multi-tracked and played live on a sea of keyboards which were on various levels on the stage. Because it was a mixture of Brits and Yanks, they even wove in "God Save the Queen" mixed with "The Star Spangled Banner," and called Walter and me about four days before the show to come to a rehearsal at Stevie's studio to hear it for ourselves.

As I think back on that show, having already related our late night with Prince, this show could have been the Late Show, because as you may or may not know, Stevie's time clock is a little different from ours. He works all night and sometimes sleeps during the day. Added to that was Herbie's breakneck schedule, which was causing him to arrive for the rehearsal at midnight, meaning he wouldn't get to the studio until about 1 a.m. But we needed to see this thing, not because we didn't trust them, but to break it down for cameras and for me, just plain curiosity as to how these four keyboard geniuses were going to put something as complex as this together. So we forgot the fact that for the next three days we were going to be on camera from nine o'clock in the morning until eleven o'clock at night, and made our way to Stevie's studio that Saturday night at midnight.

Herbie's plane was late, Stevie played around recording a couple of other things for an hour or more, and when Herbie finally arrived and Thomas and Howard were there as well, they decided it would be fun to jam for a while before doing the piece for us. And though it was fast approaching three A.M. I can tell you sitting around this studio filled with electronic keyboards, a few tech guys, and Walter and me was an experience I'll never forget. The music that came out of eight hands was unbelievable, ranging from English beat stuff, to classical riffs, to jazz to funk. I was waiting for a polka to emerge.

They finally got down to business and started playing the medley they had put together, and I could see that it really wasn't together yet. There wasn't any question that it would be a stunner on the show, but Walter and I felt they were hours away from having anything we could probably listen to so we begged off and left. They didn't need us at that time, and we needed the few hours of sleep we could get before entering the mouth of the dragon at the Shrine the next three days.

The dress rehearsal was a world of difference. There was amazing artistry on that stage as they went through the number, and a collaborative feeling among the four men of such disparate backgrounds that you might have thought they had grown up together. And when they finished the piece, there was another one of those stunned silences where everyone in the house doesn't quite know what to do. And then they erupted in applause. But even though we thought "it was soup," it still wasn't quite finished in Stevie's mind.

After the rehearsal, he asked if he could take the master backing track to his studio, which was only a few minutes from the Shrine. He said he wanted to rehearse a bit more for the show and he'd return it to us well before the show. We gave it to him, and went on with the dress, thinking no more about it until one of our audio guys told me about twenty minutes before air that neither the track nor Stevie had shown up.

My first thought, having known about Stevie's timetable, was, "Oh well, the segment doesn't air until almost two hours into the show, we'll be fine." But not a second later I remembered that I had foolishly scheduled Stevie to perform "I Just Called to Say I Love You" as the second performance in the show, and that was only about a half-hour away. I made a couple of panic calls, including one to the hotel nearby where we had given Stevie a holding room. Somebody answered and said that Stevie had left a half-hour earlier, but when I checked with our limo person they told me that he had still not gotten into the car. I told them to go to the room and pull him out and get him into the car, as he was on the air in 20 minutes. The next thing I heard was from Ron Basile telling me that the limo was stuck in the normal pre-show traffic outside the Shrine, and that he was going out to get Stevie and retinue in.

As you might expect, the show was on the air and we were already in the first commercial when I spied Stevie being led in by his brother Milton, still half dressed. With the close-down wall down, I rushed to the stage where I helped put Stevie's tie on and with thirty seconds to spare, John Denver introduced Stevie, who performed "I Just Called to Say I Love You" with such ease and grace you might have thought he had spent a week in the Caribbean just prior to his performance, instead of being hustled onstage and into position only moments before.

But I digress. The audio truck informed me that though Stevie was there, the audio track hadn't returned. I had someone find Milton, and the track was delivered to the truck in plenty of time before the medley was to hit the stage. But the best was yet to come.

I was on the headset, listening to Walter in the truck, as the medley kicked off with an entirely different beginning than it had in the dress rehearsal only hours before. "What the fuck is this?" I heard Walter boom. "Are you sure you have the right fucking track up?" To which the answer was positive.

The number proceeded with different music, a different arrangement in some places, and a very different ending that was the same length but had a very different feel. Onstage, a confident Stevie but a bit confused Howard, Herbie, and Thomas did their best to follow the new track, and when it finished, once again, there was a standing ovation from the audience.

Until the show was over we didn't know that what Stevie had done was go back to the studio and rearrange a few parts of the number. Unfortunately, though he had planned on letting us all know what he had done, it never got to us, and we learned later, it didn't get to his partners either. It was another one of those Stevie moments that we look back to and laugh about, but the moral was and always will be: stay on your toes when you've got Stevie in the house.

And there were other terrific performances that night as well; we asked Debbie Allen (with whom I was working on the television series *Fame*) to choreograph a special version of "America" from *West Side Story* as part of our tribute to Lifetime Achievement honoree Leonard Bernstein; Huey Lewis and the News (very hot in the mid-'80s) gave us a great opening number going from a capella into a house-rocking "The Heart of Rock 'n' Roll"; and Hank Williams. Jr. got real with "All My Rowdy Friends Are Coming Over Tonight." Then we went for gospel in a big way with a medley that started with the late Pops Staples's

"Nobody's Fault but Mine" done on a bare stage with him on a chair with a guitar, went into Deniece Williams's "God Is Amazing" (Deniece is amazing!), followed that up with the Clark Sisters whirling through the audience and the stage on "Hallelujah," and finished with the great James Cleveland and his Greater Los Angeles Community Choir along with the previous performers bringing the house down to "Can't Nobody Do Me Like Jesus." It was a great tribute to gospel music, but an even greater tribute to these four incredible artists.

It's kind of ironic, as I think about it, that though gospel music represents only a small segment of total CD sales, it is one of the most beloved genres of music and has been responsible for many of the great moments on the Grammy Awards show. It has performance potential that is special, and I've found that I inevitably wind up positioning it somewhere in the show following an intimate moment. It has such a capacity to bring the crowd back into the show, to be celebratory, and why not? Its purpose is to inspire, to speak directly to the Lord, and to make a connection. Reverend James Cleveland and Shirley Caesar could do that, Kirk Franklin could do that, secular artists like Whitney Houston, Stevie Wonder, and others could do that, and at its best, there's nothing quite like it onstage.

But as strong as the gospel performance was that night, I felt that if it hadn't been Tina's night (yes, I'm coming to that performance), it would have belonged to Chaka Khan who performed "I Feel For You," a song that even today is an anthem performed by every R&B wannabe diva; but nobody can touch the original. It's only too bad that her 25-year career has been sprinkled with moments where she's been upstaged by the artists of the moment. Chaka's the one I always turn to for a guaranteed score on the air, and she never disappoints. That night was one of those moments where every singer in the house went to school, and learned something from the real queen of R&B.

So now we come to Tina.

I had worked with her a few times over the years, going back to a *Soundstage* we had done a year or two earlier for an album that didn't bring her back. And then there was the moment with James Brown on the show a couple of years previous and a few assorted guest spots on shows in between. But now it was 1985, she had come back, and there was no doubt that tonight was to be the coronation.

I had an idea for her performance. This was in the early years of the moving stage lights, called Panaspots or Vari-lites. They had been developed by Genesis for touring and I can remember being amazed at Genesis's live shows when they came around for the first time with the lights. No one had yet used them on television, and I thought they would be perfect for the Tina performance. What I wanted to do was to construct a 30-foot-wide staircase, about eight feet high, put the Panaspots on a truss behind the staircase at floor level and, as Tina ascended the staircase from the rear and came into view of the cameras and audience, bring the truss up along with her, fanning the lights in on her gradually so that by the time she reached the top of the staircase, she was almost burned out from the rear, so that all you could see was this silhouette of that famous body and hair.

When I approached her management about it, they didn't like it. She won't like it, they told me, she's wearing six-inch heels and it'll throw her. I insisted. I said we'd build the piece, try it and if she didn't like it, we'd forget about that part and just do the performance straight. Even though they were very much against it, they agreed to try it.

Rehearsal day came, and the first time through, the lighting was off and they gave me one of those "I told you so" looks. But I insisted we try it again and give our guys time to find the right timing. The second time it was magical, and it only became more magical through rehearsals and the dress rehearsal. On the show, it's a moment that's burned into nearly everyone's brain cells as the quintessential vision of Tina Turner. Not to forget that she then went on stalking the stage like a lioness on the veldt, sang her heart out, and in that performance alone earned the Record of the Year award that she received from fellow diva Diana Ross.

With tears in her eyes, she accepted the award with a simple "I've been waiting so long for this," thanked the appropriate people, and then walked offstage and into a second career that has placed her at the very top of the music business.

It was an incredible night for Tina. Not only did she win Record of the Year, but she added Best Female Pop Vocal Performance and Best Rock Female Vocal Performance to her Grammy bag, and then cheered as her friends Graham Lyle and Terry Britten won Song of the Year for "What's Love Got to Do with It." Tina even won the praise of Leonard Bernstein, who in his moment onstage told viewers that he was going to wrap it up so that they could get ready for Tina, who was coming up next.

And what of the staircase and lighting design that we had come up that "wouldn't work" according to management? No apology, no thank you, but something even better. The next day a phone call from the office; Would we be able to have the staircase for the tour that Miss Turner is planning for the summer? And that's the way she made her entrance for the next two years. Up the staircase, into the light, and into music history.

⌒

The press was warming up to the show, evolving as it was into a more responsive and special night of performances and awards. The *L.A. Times*, often critical, wrote,

> *The evening's main winner was NARAS. After years of being ridiculed by pop and rock critics for being too conservative in its choices, the academy came up this year with its most impressive set of nominees and with a ceremony that clearly elevated rock perform- ers to equal status with more mainstream artists. In fact, 1985 may go down as the year in which rock and roll was finally welcomed to the Grammy club—as such acclaimed rock figures as Prince, Bruce Springsteen and Cyndi Lauper were almost constant subjects of at- tention during the three hour-plus program.*

The New York Times added, "The production numbers covered an extraordinary range of music from Kenny Loggins and "Footloose" to Julia Megenes-Johnson slinking suggestively through an aria from Bizet's *Carmen* to a synthesizer session led by Stevie Wonder."

The ratings reflected the interest in Tina and music in general that year, not coming close to the previous year's all-time high set by the Michael show, but other than that, the highest in five years, pulling a 23.8/35 share.

And so into history went the 27th Annual Grammy Awards, and with it, career performances by Tina, Cyndi, Stevie, Chaka, Huey Lewis, and others. And for us, one more mountain scaled, with hopes for a higher peak for the next show. That's the way it goes, and no one is happier about that than me.

CHAPTER 8

The 1986 Grammy Awards

The Arrival of Whitney Houston

I t's funny how things happen when you're in the heat of battle. While the competition between the Grammys and the American Music Awards was ongoing, sometime in the mid-'80s (AMA producer) Dick Clark was feeling the heat and was making a distinct effort to beat the Grammy ratings, even if—within the musical community—the Grammys had the edge. But because the AMAs were traditionally kept out of the competitive sweeps period, while the Grammys year in and year out went up against the toughest competition the other networks had to throw at it, there were a few years where the AMAs bested the Grammys. The other factor was that at that time, while NBC was the dominant network, ABC had a strong schedule and usually finished second, while CBS was a distant third. All in all, excuses aside, for several years, the shows were neck and neck, and to Dick's credit, he used everything in his arsenal so that he could have bragging rights to "the No. 1 music show." In those days, the Academy had a certain amount of stodginess and wouldn't use the promotional devices the AMAs did. Also, the Grammys would book only nominated performers and performances for the show, and never allow an artist to introduce a new song. The AMAs did. Most important, while the rules of the Grammys inevitably stopped us from doing anything but reflecting the nominations, and sometimes the nominations were far from what we wanted to do on the show, it was rumored that some of the winners on the AMAs knew who won before the show, a no-no in the awards show world.

Even with all of that, it wasn't uncommon for highly desirable acts to do both shows, a fact that Dick magnanimously proclaimed was not a problem for him (after all, his show preceded the Grammys by four to six weeks) but was becoming more and more of a problem for us.

Whitney Houston, the hottest thing in music at that time, was a true test case for us. Because in those days we wouldn't even begin to book the show until the nominations came out (we might make exploratory calls, but the rules were no nomination, no booking), Whitney had already accepted an AMA booking by the time I called her manager at the time, Gene Harvey.

When I called to invite her, Gene somewhat sheepishly told me that Whitney was going to do the AMAs, and even worse, in his mind, she was going to sing "How Will I Know," the uptempo song off the first album. I could almost hear the conversation between Gene and the AMA people.

"Of course we want Whitney, but we want her to do "How Will I Know." It's uptempo, we can do a great production number with it, and she'll really score."

I paused for a moment after he told me about the song. It was almost as if he expected me to be angry, to tell him we weren't booking her because she was giving the "good" song to the other show.

The truth is that I never wanted "How Will I Know." I had first seen Whitney the summer before at a little private gathering that Clive Davis had invited me to where Whitney and a four-man group "showcased" four songs, among them "Saving All My Love for You." And I left that showcase thinking that I had seen an artist who had the potential of becoming one of the great performers of our era. And much of that was due to the singular performance of "Saving All My Love for You."

For Gene's benefit, I played Bre'r Rabbit to his Briar Patch. I harrumphed, indignant that he had given the AMAs the uptempo number. How could he do this to the Grammys? This was patently unfair.

I slowly "backed down," in the same way Bre'r Rabbit backed down, knowing that rabbits *live* in briar patches, and thrive there.

The payoff was worth it. When a frightened but confident Whitney Houston took the Grammy stage that night in February, four weeks after she had gotten good, but not overwhelming response to her AMA performance, it was truly *A Star Is Born* time. She lit up the house, and though the show had opened 15 minutes earlier with a powerful performance by Sting of "Russians," there's no question in my mind that all anybody saw that night was this strikingly beautiful woman who walked onstage with the presence of a star and whose beauty, if that could be possible, was overshadowed by the strength and power of her voice.

As testament to what an amazing moment she had delivered on the show, later in the year she was awarded an Emmy for her performance on the Grammy show. And by the way, when her name was announced as winner for Best Pop Vocal Performance, Female later in the show, it was for "Saving All My Love for You," not for "How Will I Know"!

One of the other moments on the 1986 show that I loved was the medley we put together built around Ronnie Milsap's then hit, "Lost in the Fifties Tonight." We had Ronnie on a number of shows during his very hot country streak from the late '70s into the '90s. He's a great live performer whose records never really captured the spirit of his live performances, and I thought this would be a perfect opportunity to show him at his best. And the song, which was an amalgam of the essence of a country performer paying tribute to the black roots of rock by using "In the Still of the Night" gave us a great chance to demonstrate how and where the two forms that gave us rock and roll merged.

We wanted to build it out as well, so the natural thing to do was to add Carl Perkins, who had never appeared on a Grammy show before, singing "Blue Suede Shoes." I also knew that Huey Lewis, who was as hot as could be at the time, had a great love and respect for roots R&B, and so I asked him to join the party and do a bit of "Flip, Flop & Fly," a Louis Jordan tune that actually predated anything else we were doing in the medley. Huey loved the idea.

So we were able to build a great nine minutes of the Grammy show that began with Ronnie's nominated hit, returned to the roots with the original Five Satins, led by Freddie Parris, the original lead singer, then moving to Carl tearing it up doing "Blue Suede Shoes" and ending with Huey and the News doing "Flip, Flop & Fly." Of course it got a standing ovation in the house, and in the mid-'80s, when techno pop was at its peak, we were able to send a message to a newer generation of music fans that pop music didn't start with Tears for Fears.

Ronnie was ecstatic. His musical range was wide, and to be on the same stage with these other performers was one of the highlights of his life, he told me immediately after the performance. And when he was announced as the Grammy winner for Best Country Vocal, Male, moments later, his face lit up with the biggest smile I had ever seen him have, and he was walked to the podium where he made a point of honoring both the black and white performers whose influences had combined to create modern rock music.

The Grammys had always had a dichotomy when it came to the jazz representation on the show. One of jazz's most vocal supporters was Mike Melvoin, a jazz pianist whose session work had included playing behind everyone from Sinatra to the Beach Boys, and whose two daughters, Wendy and Lisa, were then part of Prince's Revolution. He was also the honorary chairman of the Academy for two years, and as part of his mandate, he was determined to give jazz an even greater presence with the Academy and on the show. The same passion that Mike brought to his music as an artist, he brought to his love of jazz and desire to see it featured on the show. The production company, on the other hand, had the more basic objective of getting a rating for the TV show, and because jazz represents a sliver of the overall record sales (therefore the mass appeal) we were always looking for creative ways that would give jazz its moment but not turn off the majority of our audience, who were waiting for mainstream pop music—notwithstanding the Academy's true mandate to have the Grammy show be representative of all kinds of music. In fact, when the chips are down and we have to point to the basic difference between our show and the other music shows, that's what we point to as something that elevates the Grammy Awards, and we feel that people get it.

That year we had a rare opportunity to feature jazz and we took full advantage of it. Again, those being the days when we could stretch and create special moments on the show, we took the time to put together what might have been the greatest collection of jazz artists ever to be featured on one stage (not counting the classic "Sound of Jazz" program that was on CBS in 1954 and had Billie Holiday, Count Basie, Coleman Hawkins, and so many others in one historic broadcast).

But we did our best to match that one. The segment started with basic blues featuring B.B. King and then brought out the then young turks like Herbie Hancock (who helped put the segment together) with Ron Carter, Stanley Clarke, Stanley Jordan, and Tony Williams doing "Honeysuckle Rose;" from there is was onto "Groovin High/Scrapple," with Dizzy Gillespie, Gerry Mulligan, David Sanborn, Gary Burton, and Bobby Hutcherson, and then onto "How High the Moon/Ornithology" featuring amazing vocals from Sarah Vaughan, Joe Williams, Manhattan Transfer, Bobby McFerrin, and Diane Schuur. Finally everybody jammed on a blues turnaround that truly brought down the house. Mike Melvoin, who had shepherded the piece from day one, was in jazz heaven, and though we knew we had risked a certain segment of the audience losing interest over nine minutes, that was far outweighed by the joy and purity of the music that was onstage for that time.

The year 1985 had been a big one for Phil Collins. After an eight-year run with Genesis, Phil had broken out on his own and become a major star. His *No Jacket Required* was nominated for Album of the Year, and he had picked up several other nominations, although the frontrunner was definitely the all-star "We Are the World," which ultimately went on to win Grammys for Record, Song, and Pop Performance by a Duo or Group. But having done his first solo concert show three years earlier, I knew he was a huge jazz fan, and more than that, worshipped Buddy Rich. My plan was to bring Phil into the jazz segment and have him play with Buddy. To me it was the perfect way to pay tribute to Buddy, and at the same time, for crassly commercial reasons, add a pop star on camera. I floated the idea to Phil and he agreed, not believing that he was going to get to play with Buddy. And when I talked to Buddy's people, they agreed as well.

Putting two drummers together is probably the most difficult pairing you can do. It's not so much a clash of egos as a clash of sound. And when we gathered at SIR Studios on the Saturday night before the show for an offsite rehearsal, it was apparent that my dream was to go unrealized. It was one of those uncomfortable moments, where even Phil's presence polarized the jazz players onstage, and the outspoken Buddy Rich was true to his reputation. He straight out refused to do it.

I spent a little time (maybe too much time, in retrospect) trying to keep it together, but there was a moment that I knew that if we didn't get on with it with Buddy on skins, there wasn't going to be a jazz segment. I went over to Phil, who knew what was going on, and he graciously saved me the embarrassment by telling me he felt out of place and bowing out. It was one of those moments that we would relive several times over the coming years.

Phil's presence on the show wasn't compromised, however, as he went on to win three major Grammys on the show, for Album, Pop Vocal Performance, Male, and sharing the Producer of the Year title with Hugh Padgham, who had co-produced *No Jacket Required* with him. He also gave a virtuoso performance of one of his best live songs "Sussudio."

"We Are the World" was a big Grammy winner that year. Michael Jackson and Quincy Jones accepted several awards that night, and at one point, we even attempted to bring as many of the original participants as possible together, but it wasn't happening. It was kind like trying to catch lightning in a bottle; it only happens once. We abandoned it a couple of weeks in, and nobody was really sorry about it.

The 1986 show was also the show that brought Barbra Streisand back into Walter's and my life. We were still living off the fumes of her only previous appearance for us when she and Neil did the duet, and though we would go to her each year to either perform or present, Barbra was smart.

She waited until something made sense to her to do, and when we called and told her manager Marty Erlichman that we were presenting a Lifetime Achievement Award to George Gershwin, it appealed to her. So we began the "Barbra" drill again. Phone calls at night, agonizing over script and hair, wanting to approve the package we had put together, and so on. But once she got to the show, as with other amazing artists, it was all worth it. The segment was very special, made even more so by the presence of a woman who truly believed (and helped write for that matter) every word she spoke. Barbra wasn't reading copy off a teleprompter, she was speaking from her heart.

The other performances on the show ranged from extremely good to so so. We didn't always score. In fact, that year featured two of the weakest performances we had done to date or since.

I knew why we booked a-ha, nominated for Best New Artist that year. Every year we try and perform that category, and though Sade was also nominated that year, she didn't tour, and as hard as we tried to get her we couldn't. The other nominees were Freddie Jackson (who I liked), Katrina and Waves (remember "Walking on Sunshine") and Julian Lennon, but for some long-forgotten reason we keyed in on a-ha. Their record "Take On Me" was forgettable, but remember this was the early years of MTV, and the animated video that had been made for that track was delightful and propelled them to the top of the charts. We booked them, and to this day I regret it. They did a serviceable performance, but I can't remember what they looked like, what the set was like, or why they were there.

The other embarrassment from that show was unintentional at best, and well intentioned at worst. The Rolling Stones had never won a Grammy, and though we knew they really couldn't give a shit about it, we convinced them, through my friend Peter Kauff, to accept an award that would be presented via remote in London. And then we got Eric Clapton to make the presentation, so we thought this would be terrific.

We hadn't bargained on two factors, however. One was the degree of mild contempt in which the Grammys were held by Mick and the boys, and number two, perhaps even more significant, was the fact that we would be presenting the award to them at about three in the morning in London time, giving them plenty of time to "celebrate" their award and get good and sloshed by the time we threw it to Eric in London. Looking at the tape today, I see what the critics were talking about when they referred to the silliness of it all, but at the time, all I could think about was that we finally were having the Rolling Stones on the Grammys. Several years later, when I finally got to work with Mick, I asked him about it, and he barely remembered, putting it away with some of the other "non-moments" in their long and illustrious career. Fortunately, if not for the Stones, it was a softening for Eric, who a few years later was to become a true Grammy-honored artist, and didn't hold the incident against us.

CHAPTER 9

The 1987 Grammy Awards

The Blues Go to the Grammys

Looking back, even though a lot of the tracks nominated for Grammys this year were from the old guard, who could complain about artists like Paul Simon, Steve Winwood, Peter Gabriel, and John Fogerty in the running?

In fact, when the nominations for the 1987 show came out, the production company sat down with the NARAS TV committee and laid out a show that would have featured all four of the abovementioned performers, mixed with relative newcomers like Whitney Houston, Janet Jackson, Luther Vandross, and Anita Baker, as well as a couple of wild cards like Simply Red and the then very hot Billy Idol.

Our first major disappointments came when both Gabriel and Winwood declined our invitations. Peter was on tour and wasn't able to move any dates around, and in fact would join us a few years later for his first appearance, but Winwood just plain said no. And as hard as we tried to get him, it just wasn't going to happen. Years later, when I asked him about it on the *VH1 Honors* show, he said he really didn't have a good reason, just didn't feel as though he should be there.

Disappointed as we were not to have either of them on the show, we were excited when everyone else—Janet, Whitney, Paul, Luther, Simply Red, and Billy Idol all said yes. All indications pointed to a potentially hot show, filled with current pop stars and ready for some of the accoutrements that would turn a good show into a great one.

My first thought was to reach into the well of music which had not only served me well twice before but was the genre that I loved with a passion—the blues. Many of the acts we talked to remembered that first Blues Summit in Chicago I had done in Chicago 13 years earlier, a show that was built around Muddy Waters and featured Junior Wells, Willie Dixon, Koko Taylor, Dr. John, Mike Bloomfield, Buddy Miles, and Johnny Winter. Although there was no way we could match the depth of that show, especially as Muddy Waters had recently passed away and the list of blues legends was quickly diminishing, I wanted to do what we could to pay honor to some of those great performers before they left us.

So I made a list—Albert King was a seminal voice in blues, and Willie Dixon was certainly the blues writer whose influence was the widest. Junior Wells had been sick and hadn't performed live for a while, and of course, B.B. King was the modern-day lightning rod whose presence would make the form accessible for the widest audience. Add to that mix Koko Taylor, whose record of "Wang Dang Doodle" was covered by every young female rocker who knew and loved the blues, and then throw in some modern masters like Robert Cray, Dr. John, and Etta James—and it could be a segment to remember.

I approached Ry Cooder, another old pal from *Soundstage* days, and he agreed to help put it together, and we laid out a two-song segment that began with "When I Make Love," a Willie Dixon classic, and brought it home with "Let the Good Times Roll," featuring a roaring sax solo from Big Jay McNeely. It was one of the highlights of the show and did exactly what we had hoped; it gave some body to a show that might have been criticized for being too pop—it added some meat to the bones.

Every so often, and it doesn't happen every time out, these things take on a life of their own, and the camaraderie that surrounded every rehearsal paid off with an amazing seven minutes of television that brought the audience to its feet at the end. And my personal moment came after the show when a grateful Ry Cooder walked up to me and handed me a card, signed by all the participants thanking me for doing something special from "Ken's Blues Crew"—it was a great feeling.

And while I was to go on to work with a number of these guys more in the future, there was one man who was to find his way back into my life a lot over the next several years. His name was Mac Rebennack, although to the world he was Dr. John. And though our relationship had a shaky start, it was to last for a long time.

As a classically trained pianist, I greatly admired those guys who could just sit down at the piano and let the music roll off their fingers. I didn't know much about the New Orleans piano tradition at that time, but through Mac I was not only to learn much more about it, but also to come to love it above everything else.

In my Chicago *Soundstage* days, I would often go to the airport and pick up the talent myself. Not only was it necessary, because we had no budget for limos, but it also gave me some time outside the studio to bond with the artists and to let them know what I had in mind. So one cold September morning, I went out to O'Hare to meet Mac's plane to bring him to the studio. But when he got in the car, he handed me a rumpled piece of paper and asked me if we could stop there before we went to the studio. I looked at it and didn't recognize the address at all, but I agreed to take him there. He said it was important.

We pulled up in front of a faceless low-rise building on the north side of Chicago that had no sign on it. He got out of the car and went in, while I sat to wait for the few minutes he said it would take him. After about a half hour, Mac reappeared and as he got in the car, he apologized and told me about his addiction problem. It was the only time he ever spoke of it, but I could see that this was a man who had struggled with it, and was determined to beat it. We would work together a number of times over the years, and every time he continued to amaze me not only with his flying fingers, but also with his ability to play just about any kind of music, and play it wonderfully.

It would be 12 years and 3000 miles before the blues came into my professional life again. *A Blues Session: B.B. King and Friends* (1987) was one of the most rewarding and best-remembered shows of my career, even though I would swear to this day that not as many people saw it as talk about it. To this day, we'll get requests in the office for copies of the tape, many from the public, but just as often from musicians who have heard about it and want to see it.

Much of the credit for this show goes to Tisha, who once again came through with the bookings that helped make the show soar. This was one of those pure shows, pure because nearly everyone booked had a love of B.B., and pure because every artist was a great performer.

Imagine, if you will, the rehearsal the day before the show and a room filled with the likes of Eric Clapton, Phil Collins, Stevie Ray Vaughan, Albert King, Gladys Knight, Chaka Khan, Etta James, and Dr.

John—all there to pay homage to, but more to play with, and for, B.B. King. And because it was important to me to have the feeling of to-getherness in that show, I needed them all there for the rehearsal even though I had A&R'ed the show with all kinds of duets and ensembles.

I had promised everyone that the rehearsal would be done in five hours, but I knew better. I also knew that once everyone got in that room (a hot, un-air-conditioned space in East L.A. that dripped blues and funk), nobody was going to leave, and they didn't.

B.B. was the glue, and in the conversations we've had over the years since that show, we've both marveled at how much glue there was in that room. It was the first time that Stevie Ray Vaughan got to perform with his idol Albert King (he even said on the show that he'd never forget performing "The Sky Is Crying" with Albert); it featured a perfor-mance of one of music's true R&B anthems, "Please Send Me Someone to Love," written by Percy Mayfield and wailed by Gladys Knight look-ing directly at Percy's widow, who cried all the way through it, and it was show that has the distinction of starting with the blues ("Why I Sing the Blues," introducing all of the acts) and ending with the gospel clas-sic, "Amazing Grace," unifying the sacred and the profane of the black musical experience.

And in between: a stage full of artists, some new, some old, but all in love with the blues, singing and playing together and separately.

The highlight, of course, was the duet between Eric and B.B. on "The Thrill Is Gone," done together previously but never delivered with the purity and strength that each of the artists brought to it that day. In a breakdown "duel" at the end of the piece, while most people waited for the fireworks to begin, Eric respectfully traded bars with B.B. to show that in no way would he ever go over the master.

I love B.B. and the music he's made over the years. He makes me joyous, and he makes me cry.

The careers of both Luther Vandross and Anita Baker were on the ascent, and the good news was that in the world of R&B, both were ac-knowledged as being truly special performers. Stylistically, they were both very different from anyone else, so vocally distinctive that as soon as you heard their songs, there wasn't any question about who was singing.

Luther was the inheritor to the throne of a long line of sexy R&B singers and was being compared favorably to Teddy Pendergrass, and Anita had this Billie Holiday mystique all over her. We had booked both of them on the show, Luther to sing his hugely popular "Give Me the Reason," and Anita to sing "God Bless the Child" as part of the Trustees Award presentation for Billie. I then thought it would be great to team them up to do a Marvin Gaye/Tammi Terrell song as part of another tribute we were doing, and they both reluctantly agreed.

The rehearsal was to take place at Luther's house about a week or so before the show, and the last thing I heard was that they were both excited about doing it. Anita showed up at Luther's after I had arrived and, from the first moment, we were dealing with oil and water. They both got through the rehearsal, although it wasn't pleasant at all, and the next day both of their managers called to tell me it wasn't going to work. I did my best to try and put it back together, but to no avail.

The footnote to this (and the subject of numerous rumors about the two of them) is that several years later, after both had risen to even greater popularity, some genius decided that they should tour together under the umbrella title *The Love2Love Tour*. They should have talked to me, but that probably wouldn't have made a difference. The stories about the tour are legendary, from the gift of a cheese tray sent by Luther to Anita on the opening night of the tour (cheese is something you never send to a singer; it closes their throats), to the amazing demands that wound up in the riders of both acts from about the fourth tour date on: each artist would have a dressing room on the opposite wall from the other, and a temporary dividing wall would be put up splitting the hallway so that neither artist had to look at the other on the way to or from the stage. It was a nightmare, although when I went to see the two of them, they both gave great performances.

Years later, Luther would suffer a major stroke and his recording and performing career would be over. At the time, thinking back on some of the pretty marvelous performances he had given us over the years, including a very special performance of "A Change Is Gonna Come" on a Cinemax Sessions gospel show we did, I wanted to do something for him. Having been told he would be watching, we put together a medley of "A House Is Not a Home" performed by Alicia Keys, and the last (and biggest) hit he had prior to his stroke, "Dance with My Father," sung by Celine Dion who came in from Las Vegas to sing it for him. We had taped a brief appearance by Luther to play at the end of the medley, and it was an extremely emotional moment for us. Luther passed away much too soon, in 2005 at the age of 54, and music lost one of its most powerful and sensitive voices.

Among the other performances that year was Whitney Houston's return engagement, this time as a full-fledged star, and with a song to match. To put it any other way would be false; she came out and hit it out of the part with "The Greatest Love of All," and proved to any disbelievers that she was the goods.

As we often did, we saved both the Record and the Album of the Year presentations until the end of the show. By that time, we had performed several of the nominated songs, and our hope was always to build as much of a horse race about the winners as we could, and also to give that segment of the audience who might not have seen some of the acts a chance to weigh in.

When Record of the Year went to Steve Winwood, I looked out in the house and saw Paul Simon sitting there thinking that the Album would go to Steve as well. I also knew that Whoopi Goldberg and Don Johnson were coming out next and that Whoopi, as always, would ad lib her way through the nominations, adding to Paul's anxiety level. And she did.

But then she opened the envelope and the years dropped off his face as he took the stage and delivered one of those slow, well-thought-out speeches that spoke eloquently about the *Graceland* album and Paul's debt to the African musicians and influences which had led him to and through it.

Billy Crystal, who had led us through a show that was filled with a very diverse evening of music better than it had ever been done before, thanked everyone, said goodnight, and then introduced a rare finale that allowed me to revisit the past once more, with a twist. With Ben E. King in the lead, several of the acts who had appeared on the show, among them Whitney Houston, Mick Hucknall, Luther, and others came onstage for a great version of "Stand By Me." Was it hokey? Yeah, of course it was, but for millions of music fans it said something good about music and where we were that night. And as the now defunct *Los Angeles Herald-Examiner* said the next day:

> *It seemed as if we were witnessing something a bit more special than a mere star-studded grand finale—that in fact we were witnessing an invitation to take part in a heartfelt but risky experiment in fraternity—and with voices so lovely and rhythms so undeniable leading the way, who could resist such a call? With moments like these, clearly the 29th Annual Grammy show set new standards against which future performances will be judged.*

CHAPTER 10

The 1988 Grammy Awards

"The King of Pop" Pops Up . . . and Pops Some Ratings

It had been seven years since we had done the Grammys in New York, and it was definitely time to go back. In fact, after the 1988 show, we would begin to alternate years in Los Angeles and New York, and that pattern would continue until 1998 when the well-publicized Mike Greene/Rudy Giuliani fight would keep us in Los Angeles for the next several years.

Going back to New York, though, with one Radio City show already under our belt, we could afford to take more chances with the facility, and try to use more of what has made it "America's Showplace," the largest proscenium stage in the country, elevators that would move independently and allow us greater flexibility in setting and striking equipment, and a general feeling of space that we just didn't have back at the Shrine.

And so, as if to show our gratitude to the city, in a year when the nominations for Record of the Year included two holdovers from the previous year (Paul Simon and Steve Winwood), plus U2, Los Lobos, and dark horse Suzanne Vega, we set out to overlay a New York theme to the show for the first time ever.

As for the execution: we created two special segments, one of which was a tremendous hit and another that has become known to the internal Grammy world, kindly, as "a noble experiment."

Let's start with this: if you've read this far, you know just how much I love early rock and in particular, doo wop and the music of the street corners that gave it its name. It was the first music I listened to and loved, and the first songs we sang and played as "The Continentals," a high school group that worked various schools singing "Earth Angel" and "In the Still of the Night." It remains dear to me today for its admitted nostalgic meaning, but also because of its purity, its simplicity, and its heart.

So when we ran it by the TV committee and had an opportunity to reunite some of the great groups of the '50s, put a ribbon around it with my old friend and favorite Dion DiMucci (with whom I had done a memorable *Soundstage* show in Chicago), and then place a historical perspective to it all by booking the legendary deejay Jocko Henderson, it was just too much to resist, and we fell in love with this nine-minute segment of the show. And of course, while there were doo wop groups around the country, the fact is that whether it was Dion in the Bronx or a hundred other groups that walked in and out of the Brill Building between 1951 and 1960, this segment was all about New York.

Here's the lineup: after Jocko's rhyming intro (was he the first rapper or what?), out pranced, in this order, the Cadillacs doing a killer version of "Speedoo," the title that became the legal name of its lead singer, Earl Carroll; then a seminal New York white doo wop group, the Regents, singing "Barbara Ann," a whole different quality; next, the original Flamingos with "I Only Have Eyes for You," complete with the original "shoo bops;" the Bronx group, the Angels, doing "My Boyfriend's Back" (our paean to the girl groups); and then, as if to put the period to the sentence, Dion and friends taking the stage for a great version of "A Teenager In Love."

Legend has it that the segment bombed, but I don't agree. To a huge segment of our post-35 audience, these songs were as important as Gershwin, Cole Porter, Prince, and the Beatles—and just as relevant. Our New York audience got it, I still believe America got it, and if it's one of the few things that the critics can point to after 30-plus years of doing network television, then so be it, I'll take it.

The second special segment for that show also had its problems, but when I looked at it for the first time after a number of years I was amazed to see just how well it stands up.

The obvious premise of the piece was to sample the remarkable depth of the New York musical experience, from rock to rap, from Broadway to Latin, with a taste of a few things in between. George Benson, who had grown up in New York but now lived in Hawaii, agreed to come in and reprise one of his most recognizable hits, "On Broadway," leading directly into a classic performance of Cab Calloway doing "Minnie the Moocher." I still think about Cab's face, probably at the Grammys for the first time, experiencing just how drastically music had changed over the years and watching in wonder as Run-D.M.C. pranced across the stage rehearsing their snippet of "Tougher Than Leather." There was a great moment with Tito Puente and Celia Cruz doing "Quinbara," the first of the four or five times I would do that number with Celia over the years. Then, from one of the opera coves on the side of Radio City Music Hall, Lou Reed, with the help of two slinky background singers, gave out the most sanitized version of "Walk on the Wild Side" he had ever done. We had also booked Miles Davis to work with David Sanborn, but he took ill and we had to cancel that part of the piece, moving David into the capper for the piece, a full-out version of Billy Joel's "New York State Of Mind," with Billy and David coming up on the front elevator of the stage with a full backdrop of the city skyline behind them.

While it was by no means the quintessential piece of New York music, it went a long way to getting the house on our side, and coming as it did about an hour into the show, it lifted the place off its feet. And though I've probably seen Billy do "New York State of Mind" 20 times, and done it with him on television several more, for my money it was the best performance I've ever seen of the song, which is more of an anthem to me than "New York! New York!"

Another New Yorker, a slight girl from Greenwich Village, helped contrast the big blowout numbers of the night with an intense, personal delivery of her Song of the Year nomination, "Luka." Suzanne Vega brought the giant hall to a standstill as she stood centerstage with a guitar and made every eye and ear concentrate on the bittersweet saga of a street girl lost in the impersonal bowels of the city. It was almost breathtaking to watch, and brought the show back to its basics, performer and song united as one.

Unfortunately the mood was broken not 15 minutes later when Jackie Mason, booked because he had a hot show on Broadway at the time, came out and embarrassed the entire front section of the house, most notably a shocked Quincy Jones. Mason, who had been given a short piece of copy to read before we presented the Best Comedy Album, obviously didn't have a clue at whom he was pointing that infamous "Ed Sullivan" finger, and at one point he looked at Quincy and made a reference to "my black brother." Quincy's jaw dropped as the camera caught him, and the previous hour of the show in my mind at least vanished into space as I saw the whole spirit of the show, built upon this synergy of music as expressed by my New York segment, crumble around a few words spoken not only in ignorance, but just to get a laugh. We wrapped him up as soon as we could and tried to recover the rest of the night. Billy, very sensitive to what had happened, came back with a couple of lines about Jackie, but the horse had left the barn, and it was a long way back.

That moment wasn't the end of the surprises that came from presenters that night however. Little Richard, presenting with Buster Poindexter (he of "Hot Hot Hot" and the New York Dolls), preceded his reading of the winner of the Best New Artist Grammy with, "And the winner is . . . me," following it with "I have never received nothin! You never gave me no Grammys and I've been singing for years! I am the architect of rock and roll! I am the originator!" Shades of the piano medley when given the stage, he'd leapt on the piano to take the focus away from Ray Charles, Jerry Lee Lewis, and Count Basie. Richard had done it again. And got another standing ovation. It pays to be the bad boy.

~

Michael Jackson was on top of the world, both literally and figuratively. He had come over to Radio City for his rehearsal earlier that day and wowed the crowd. He was set to perform a medley of "The Way You Make Me Feel" and "Man in the Mirror" as the keystone performance on the Grammys that year, and there wasn't any question as to whether or not it was a stunning performance. We had laid out a number that started with him behind a 20-foot-high screen with only his silhouette visible. The screen would fly, he would bring out just a few dancers and move into "Feel" for about two minutes. And then, aided by a full 40-voice choir that would come up from the basement on one of the giant Radio City elevators, he would perform an amazing version of "Man in the Mirror."

Only Michael wasn't happy with the hour we had given him for rehearsal. I had worked with him on a few shows, and in fact had negotiated this appearance with a lot of terms. Michael doesn't make it easy. With other shows, he's been known to request, and get, special awards, huge ticket requests, and a lot of other "special" stuff. For the Grammys, there was none of that. Come, be recognized for his work, and give it up to the millions of people who would be waiting to see whether or not he could follow up his multi-Grammy win for *Thriller* with some awards this night.

The phone call came toward the end of that day's rehearsals. It was pleasant enough, from Michael himself. Could Walter and I come over to his hotel that evening and go over the rehearsal tape of his performance?

We were rehearsing late that night, but of course, if Michael wanted to see us, we knew we had to go. It's all part of the job, and I knew from past experience that if we didn't work it out then, we would have a rougher day the next day, show day.

So, tired and cold (New York in February isn't like Southern California in February), Walter, Tisha, and I trudged the three blocks to the Helmsley Palace, were guided through the flank of security guards both in the lobby and on the penthouse floor Michael occupied, and were led into a spacious living room with floor-to-ceiling southern exposure views of the Big Apple at night. It was almost surreal, played against the subdued lighting in the four-room suite, in which there was only one occupant.

Vince Patterson, Michael's choreographer and one of the most creative minds in the business, accompanied us on this journey, and it was a good thing he was there. After a few minutes of small talk (you don't talk politics or religion with Michael), we all went upstairs to Michael's spacious bedroom (also floor-to-ceiling windows) where he had a VCR set up to watch the tape of the rehearsal which we had given him when he left Radio City. He really didn't have much to say. A shot here, a shot there he thought might have been better, and for the most part, he was happy. He commented a few times to Vince on his performance, and how he could have done something here and there to have made it bigger or more dynamic.

And then, for all intents and purposes, our meeting was over. We went downstairs again, gave each other mutual thanks and good wishes for the next day's performance, and were on our way out when Michael called Vince over to him and whispered something in his ear. Vince then handed Michael something and we left together. Out in the hall, I asked him what Michael had said. He told me that Michael had asked him for the little wooden dummy microphone that Vince had with him. And then he told us something that has stayed with me since that night.

"Did you notice that little eight-by-eight-foot wooden square that Michael had put down on the floor in front of one of the windows?" he asked.

We said that we noticed it, but didn't pay much attention to it.

"That's for Michael. It's about midnight now, and my feeling is that Michael will be in front of that square and the mirror next to it for the next five hours or so plussing up his performance so that it's perfect tomorrow."

The lesson was clear to me: the next time you think about these legends and envy the life they lead, the parties they go to, the extravagances of their lives, just for a moment think about Michael Jackson, at the time the biggest-selling musical artist in history, with millions of adoring fans, spending the night before what might be his biggest night ever, sweating in front of a mirror, alone on the 43rd floor of the Helmsley Palace.

The next night, show night, all of that work paid off as Michael delivered one of the most amazing performances in Grammy memory, and his career as well. Taking the stage alone, he opened with a piece of "The Way You Make Me Feel," building to a crescendo as one female dancer and a couple of male dancers joined him as he dropped to his knees toward the end of the first part of his performance. Then, with a clean stage he launched into "Man in the Mirror" a pop song with great gospel licks that grew and grew until the rear elevator rose up from below stage level and a 60-voice choir made its appearance on cue to take the solo moment into a heavenly choir of voices, backing up a great performance from Michael. He was all over the stage, in the air, on the ground, and by the time he finished (as opposed to the dramatic breathlessness that we sometimes see) there was nothing left of him on that stage. It had all been given to the audience, and Michael stayed there, waiting for the recognition that has always been his motivation. It came in tidal waves, and though he didn't win a single Grammy that night, his Grammy came in the acceptance that he received from an adoring audience that night at Radio City.

One other performance deserves mention. Sandwiched in between a highly forgettable country medley (it has been our curse to think that size matters in country music as opposed to quality), Terence Trent D'Arby inched toward temporary stardom in the Best New Artist category with a virtuoso performance of "If You Let Me Stay." This short-lived incarnation of James Brown in another form was magnetic onstage, and I believed that he would ascend to the heights of at least R&B, if not pop stardom, over the coming years. The fact that he hasn't is mystifying to me, but then again I've picked a few others wrong as well. The lack of pop stardom, however, doesn't diminish my respect for his talent, and in some ways actually leads me to believe that some artists really are too good for the masses.

Though it would be 13 years before U2 gave their first performance on the show, the boys were there that night to accept one of the biggest awards—for Album of the Year. Bono, tongue in cheek as usual, joked about the band's responsibility as social commentators saying that it's hard "carrying the weight of the world on your shoulders, saving the whales and organizing summit meetings between world leaders, but we enjoy our work." For his part, the Edge predated his cryptic comments on the 2001 show by thanking such disparate entities as Bob Dylan, Walt Disney, Morris the Cat, Batman and Robin, and "sumo wrestlers throughout the world."

By the time the Record of the Year was awarded, Paul Simon's win for "Graceland," a year after he had won the Album award, was almost anticlimactic. And after having endured three hours of waiting the previous year, I suspected that Paul had planned a trip to Brazil that year just to avoid having to sit through the show again. He has never admitted to me that I was right.

CHAPTER 11

The 1989 Grammy Awards

Don't Worry Be Happy

I wasn't around for the 1989 show—I was grounded.

We had done a great show in 1988 at Radio City, with terrific ratings, and some of the best reviews we had ever gotten. It was a Michael Jackson year, and his performance that year was amazing, contributing of course to the ratings. But a couple of things happened that year that pissed Pierre off. From his point of view, I had gotten a little out of control, a bit cocky, and, in his mind, disrespectful. When we're working with the acts, my concentration is 100 percent focused on the act, reading eyes and body language and making sure that everything is perfect. Although Pierre and Michael Jackson had met before, Pierre asked me to bring him over to Michael for a minute to talk, and—with what was going on onstage (Michael is very high maintenance)—I forgot. Pierre logged that in his mind. He said nothing at the time, although he made it clear he was not happy about it. It took until the following spring for him to call me in for a "lunch" during which he reminded me of what happened and then told me the following: "We'll be doing the Grammy Awards this coming year, but you're staying home. You'll be back the following year, but you'll be watching this one." I was shocked, which may have all been a part of my problem, but I did stay home and hated every minute of not doing the show. It took a couple of years after that for us to restore the relationship we had had before the 1988 show.

For the 1989 show, however, Pierre decided that he and Walter would produce it together, and proceeded to do it. It would be imprudent of me to comment on that year, but Walter has since said to me that without me there to work the talent and try to keep the show from becoming overloaded with needs, I was sorely missed—and all I could say to him was that I missed him more.

This might also be a good time to provide a bit of background as to how the show comes together and who does what. It's a complex group, and has been from the beginning, and like other organizations has its functional and dysfunctional aspects. But when you put it all together, somehow every year that live show that goes out to millions of people, and it works—as I have been heard to say on occasion, when all is said and done, it only has to work once.

Although we do somewhere between ten and twelve shows a year, the Grammy Awards is clearly the big one, and it certainly wouldn't have come my way without the support of the aforementioned Pierre Cossette.

Pierre made his name in show business first as an agent handling such stars as Ann-Margret, and then he sidestepped into the music business by co-founding Dunhill Records, the home of the Mamas and the Papas among other acts in the late '60s. He has always done television shows and is the first to admit that his strength is in selling the shows and hiring the right people to do them. Despite this, he probably made his biggest financial killing in the early '70s when he came on the idea of putting *Sha Na Na* on television as an access series when the networks had come under major criticism for programming adult material early in the evening. Thus came what was known as "The Family Hour," just preceding the prime-time periods, and a frantic need for programming. I don't know how much money he made with *Sha Na Na* and its predecessor, a potboiler called *Stand Up and Cheer* with Johnny Mann, but it must have been a bundle since he owns the building (a nine-story job where he has offices) and three homes that I know of. He's a remarkable individual, and though it hasn't all been roses between the two of us, I will always be grateful to Pierre, who has now stepped into retirement from the show.

Then there's my longtime creative partner on the Grammys, director and producer Walter Miller.

Walter is a story in himself. His volatile personality has followed him all his life, and stories he's told me about being kicked out of school are only symptomatic of his ability (?) to both start and end fights with his sharp tongue, his acerbic wit, and if he is to be believed, his fists. My relationship with Walter, like that with Pierre, has gone through some rocky periods, many of which will follow in detail elsewhere, but as with Pierre, we've gone through so much together we think like a single person. Past 80, Walter continues to have a vibrancy that belies his age, and he continues to amaze people with his ability to direct a show like the Grammys year after year.

Right from the start, we gravitated toward each other, but as I've said elsewhere, both of them, all three of us in fact, have the egos that are a prerequisite of this business. You get knocked down a lot doing what we do, and without a strong sense of self, you can get eaten alive. Self-protection is important, and all three of us share that trait, in varying quantities.

In the beginning, when both Walter and I were learning our way around, Pierre was clearly in charge of the Grammy operation. As the years went by, Pierre was more than happy, once he gained trust in us, to give us our respective cred in doing the show. There have been many times over the years when Walter and I felt strongly about doing something with the show that didn't feel right to Pierre, but more often than not he was more than willing to stand with us to take the credit when it worked (a fact which has never bothered us).

The fourth longest-lived member of our team is talent executive Tisha Fein. What makes Tisha truly unique, in addition to an indefatigable capacity to come back from being turned down by one act after another, is her genuine lack of fear of criticism in coming up with a palette of ideas that range from perfect to ridiculous. I love her for it, and even though at times I don't demonstrate it, I know she'll never change. Over the years on show after show, the Grammys and many others, Tisha has been my partner in taking a good show and making it great.

John Cossette surfaced early in my run of the show as the associate producer and then left for a few years before coming back to his father Pierre's company and to the show. Johnny has what may be the toughest job of all: balancing the creative boundaries which every year we try and expand with a realistic budget for what is clearly, in terms of production, television's biggest annual music event and a show that in many minds becomes even more complex every year, whether it be in upgrading technical requirements like 5.1 and high definition, which John championed early on, or just size and scope of production numbers and performances. A few years ago when Pierre decided to take more of a backseat role in the show, he, John, and I got together and figured out a partnership arrangement with regard to the show, and I must say that the past few years have not only been smooth sailing, but also that I've grown to respect John and his role in the show more with each passing year.

In the early years, I was the sole producer of the show and, in addition, found myself writing many of the performance and presenter intros myself, even though we had a writer on the show. In those years, we also wrote the host's opening monologue, but from the year of Billy Crystal on, as we booked comics and television personalities to host the show, we would add writers they were comfortable with, and it was a blessing. In recent years, I've been very fortunate in having the writing talent (and friendship) of David Wild, whose musical knowledge is matched by a remarkable sensitivity to expressing the magic of music as well as its passion.

In terms of the Recording Academy leadership, Mike Greene arrived on the scene as the unpaid chairman of the Academy in 1986, and became its first paid president in 1989. It looked like he'd be there as long as he wanted until a series of personal issues found their way into print and he was forced to resign in early 2002, to be replaced by the current president, Neil Portnow. There's a book on Mike, some of which is pretty well known to his critics and fans, and some of which is better left unsaid.

What can't be ignored, no matter what kind of controversy he engendered during his tenure at the Academy, is that Mike took a sleepy organization, whose entire public persona was the Grammy Awards, and turned it into a financial and creative powerhouse.

Mike and I had one of the most complex relationships I've ever experienced. I had great respect for his corporate abilities, and we shared some musical tastes. But he could also be the most difficult person I've ever met at some times, while at other times he would make you believe he was your closest family member.

Our disagreements have taken place in both public and private, and although he might think differently, while he was at NARAS we shared a mutual need; I have loved the Grammy show from the minute I became involved and whatever battles ensued between Mike and me, I believe everyone always knew that I was always thinking of the show first, and any personal agenda or preferences after that.

Mike was hardheaded and so am I. Mike would never settle, and neither would I. Mike was perhaps the most manipulative person I ever met, and though I'm reluctant to admit it, I guess I'm capable of being manipulative too—it's simply protective coloration in a business such as this.

Where we differ, and we *really* differ here, is in our work styles. I avoid confrontation and would rather solve a problem with reason than with a hammer. Mike was a hammer guy, and I believe, because he's said it to me in less guarded moments, that he really doesn't give a fuck what anyone thinks about him as long as he gets what he wants.

How that played out during his tenure at NARAS was fascinating. The day the nominations were announced, the production company would meet with the NARAS television committee and Mike and would lay out the basics of the show. Those meetings used to be contentious, but became less so over the years. It became pretty obvious what most of the show bookings should be, and the real issues came out after we'd agreed on most of the show and had moved on to the possibilities that most of us recognized as the "color" of the show, which we might each prioritize differently. I'd like to think we had three camps—Mike, the committee, and the production company but the reality is that Mike ran the committee, and it wasn't beyond him to call for a vote with his hand raised, and we'd be outvoted.

And that was just the beginning of the process. The assault that comes from the labels on a year-round basis gets notched up tremendously in those last seven or eight weeks, and the pressure that we all bear, but particularly Mike and me, was all consuming. One of the things I'm most proud of is that in all the years I've been doing this show, I've never consciously played favorites. Do we play a bit with presenters and try and make people who have helped the show happy? Of course, but when it comes down to the performances on the Grammys, every artist has to fight his way onto the show based on merit, and the show proves that year in and year out.

In 2003, we did the first Grammy show without Mike's presence in 13 years, and it was a resounding success. Truth be told, it had to be, since so much of Mike's modus operandi was to divide and conquer the various elements of a group dynamic and make himself indispensable. That we succeeded with such a loud bang, increased ratings, positive reviews, and viewer satisfaction was a tribute not only to the absence of Mike's controlling personality and arbitrary nature, but to the new leadership at the Academy in the person of Neil Portnow, who walked into the line of fire at one of television's most difficult event shows and made everyone feel good about what they were doing. He, and the show, set a high standard to repeat, but there's no question that we're all up to the task.

The relationship between Neil and our production team has developed into one of trust, mutual respect, admiration, and positive thinking. None of the issues surrounding a show as big as the Grammys are easy, and Neil's presence is both comforting and positive. There's never any question about approaching him with either good or bad news, or exploring options when the first plan you have doesn't seem to be working. In a business or personal relationship, those are pretty important pluses, and I've grown to value him for his judgment and support.

The other key element on the Recording Academy [?] side is the televison committee, comprised of a group of NARAS members with whom we work closely in charting the course of the show. They bring a variety of different points of view to the process, and with the arrival of Neil, have become great partners in the shaping of the show.

Other people who deserve mention here are Bob Dickinson, our lighting designer and an idea person of the first order, and (first) Bob Keene, our longtime production designer who became an invaluable member of the team, and then his successors, Brian Stonestreet and Steve Bass.

Bob Dickinson is a genius. He thinks outside the envelope, doesn't ever think in terms of lights until he's thought in terms of performer and performance, and has come up with some of the most astounding looks for the shows we do without overshadowing the performers. That's the difference I find in Bobby as opposed to other talented lighting designers: he knows that he's there for support, and it's "not about the lighting." There's an old show business expression that fits here: "No one ever walked out of a theater humming the sets."

Bob Keene, a scenic designer who did most of the "really big" shows you watch from year to year, including the Oscars and the Olympics, took a little longer to grow on Walter and me. In the early years, we viewed him as we have looked at other support people with whom we have worked: anxious to please, but sometimes feeling as though he knew more than we did and often overzealous to sell us on his ideas rather than listening to ours. As the years passed, I think the three of us pulled back, listened to each other more, and allowed the relationship to grow into a truly collaborative one, sometimes beginning with our ideas needing to be translated into scenic realities, and sometimes coming from Bob, who developed a much more edgy approach to trying new things. His tragic death in 2003 was a major blow to the show, but fortunately his assistant, Brian Stonestreet, had gone to school on Bob for a number of years, and with the addition of a young designer I've used on a number of shows who is definitely left-brain oriented, Steve Bass, the torch was passed and creativity continues to flow from the design department.

And then there's Ron Basile, who still answers my phones 19 years after he started answering them, but in reality knows more about the details of doing these shows, from union contracts to band layouts, than the dozen other people who does what he does combined. Ron is the spine of Ken Ehrlich Productions.

In fact, it's hard for me to realize that these pages have progressed so far without special mention of Ron. He came to me in 1988 directly from a job at a flower shop, and at the time I had no clue that he would become the single most important employee, collaborator, and friend in my working life. He's truly a renaissance man, and I can walk by his desk at any given time and hear him talking on the phone to people about everything from computers to health problems, from the cost of a camera jib to the mechanics of a generator on the site of our next show, and everything in between. And beyond that, he's just one of the nicest and most genuine people I've ever met. There just isn't anyone who doesn't like Ron, and with only one or two notable exceptions, I've never heard him say anything bad about anyone. Ron would be a success at anything he ever wanted to do, and from time to time I'm confounded by the fact that he's chosen to stay here and work with me (not always an easy thing to do) for the past almost 20 years.

David Wild, who's been writing the show with me for the past several years, is another member of the team whose function goes way beyond the title "writer." David's expertise as a musicologist is vast, and though it pains me to admit it, he's probably the only person I can turn to when there's some obscure fact about a group, a label, or the day, month, and year of the release of the last Velvet Underground album . . . it's in his head. I love bouncing some of my more out-there ideas off David, and either he'll confirm or deny their reality or attractiveness, more often than not adding something that I'd never thought and making the idea better.

So that's the group that gathers on Los Angeles' West Side every year to put together "music's biggest night." A psychologist would have a field day with this group, and I've often thought we ought to have a staff position for one on some of these shows.

⤳

Now that you know the players, let's take a look at the 1989 show, which opened promisingly enough with a great performance by Whitney Houston of "One Moment In Time" and ended three hours and twenty minutes later with Bobby McFerrin winning the Grammy for Record of the Year for "Don't Worry Be Happy," a novelty song which, given the benefit of time and distance, in a year with offerings from U2, Metallica, Eric Clapton, Luther Vandross, Anita Baker, and Sting, seems a bit out of place.

Metallica delivered one of the strongest performances of the night with "One," but then suffered the indignity of being bested in the newly introduced Hard Rock/Metal category by—and this was a rough one on the Academy for years—Jethro Tull. In a year when the Academy added two new categories in response to industry outcries about both rock and rap categories, the awarding of the Metal Grammy to Tull was compounded by the list of nominees in the new Rap category, ultimately won by D.J. Jazzy Jeff & the Fresh Prince—Will Smith to those of you living in a hip-hop–free cave all these years.

As a student of the Grammys, if an outsider that year, I was thrilled that George Michael received two nominations, fewer than I thought he would, but when he lost both of them, I thought the Academy had missed a bet. George, who would go on to work with us a number of times in the '90s, was one of those artists who was exactly right for the times, creating pop masterpieces like "Freedom," "Faith," and others. Years later he was a part of one of my favorite combinations of any show we did when I had him join Stevie Wonder and Steve Winwood in an incredible opening number that blended "Superstition" with "Gimme Some Lovin" on a *VH1 Honors* show.

You probably want to ask me by now: So, Mr. Smug Grammy Producer, how did it feel to be like one of the regular people, sitting there at home, remote in hand with ample opportunity to tune away from the Grammys and check out the rest of Wednesday night television? Well, I've got some answers, but not necessarily the ones you might expect.

First and foremost, the temptation to channel surf is definitely there. With an awards show like the Grammys, if (even for a moment) you lose interest in the awards themselves, which is fairly easy to do, or a performance comes on that you just don't care about, boy is it easy to push the button and go elsewhere. From years of looking at what we call "minute-by-minutes"—graphs that show us at any given moment if viewers are coming or going, I've seen it happen.

But being a part of the audience with choices is very different than looking at it on a chart. Event programming for the most part is non-linear, meaning that there really isn't a beginning, middle, or end as there is in dramatic or even reality programming. If the awards don't drag you along to the end, then the music is the only thing you have to hook into, and as music awards show have blossomed, chances are that by the time you reach the Grammys, you've seen several if not most of the acts that you'd expect to see on our show elsewhere. Granted, that has changed in recent years as we've gone to more and more special segments, and tried to change up the show, but of necessity, the major nominees have already won or been nominated for AMAs, *Billboard*, and other awards, and usually for the same songs. We'd love to think we do them better and differently, but maybe sometimes those differences are too subtle for you the viewer.

As I sat watching the show, realizing that none of the nominees had achieved the legendary status of nominees in other years, and thus were less known to me than the Springsteens, the Whitneys, the Stings, and other horse race possibilities, I knew I would continue watching because the opening billboard of the show promised a different value—artists I hadn't seen a lot of, but who had made some interesting, if not compelling music that year. Metallica was not a television staple, and I looked forward to seeing what they would do. Likewise, Sinéad O'Connor, who had not yet achieved the "enigmatic" style she would later aspire to. But few others promised any intrigue, and in retrospect, I think I kept watching because of my curiosity to see what they would do without me more than from an abiding interest in the show itself.

In a room with a few other people (most of my friends were at the show and I certainly didn't feel like being there), I noticed the same kind of reactions, although a certain politeness or deference to me hung in the air. It didn't stop them from being critical, however, a quality that from that day on I would imagine when I was backstage watching each show unfold. I've always been reasonably self-critical, or at the very least incapable of accepting compliments very well, and when few were coming from the group watching with me, I realized that part of me watching the show enjoyed a strong feeling of *schadenfreude*. I tried to avoid it myself that year, but it's a pretty strong human quality, and whether I expressed it out loud or not, it was there.

I can't tell you how happy I was when the show was over, and I no longer had to squirm in my seat sharing the experience with others. I probably should have done myself more of a favor by watching the show alone, but I think that my friends feared that I might do something dangerous to myself and shouldn't be left by myself. But when it was all over, a feeling of relief came over me, and knowing that I was going to be back the following year, I made a pretty good show of trying to be generous about the show itself and demonstrating some compassion for what I was certain Mike Greene had put Walter and the rest of the crew through on this one. I know I saw some things on the show that had to have come from Mike, and that Walter would have known better than to do on his own.

The ratings were the lowest ever that year, coming down 24 percent from the previous year to a 16 rating with a 26 share. I felt sorry for what Walter had gone through on any number of levels. In future years, when in the midst of some major crisis or looming threat, he'd turn to me and say with a very knowing look, "I'm glad you're back."

CHAPTER 12

The 1990 Grammy Awards

Bonnie Raitt; Love in the "Nick of Time"

As anyone involved in what we all do for a living would tell you, you often have to bury the past to move on with the future. The up-and-coming act that you wouldn't book five years ago because of the lack of name recognition is now a big star, and you hope that they don't remember how you treated them then. Conversely, the big name whose star has faded and who is now looking at you to help gives you pause, and while you want to help if you can, your first obligation is to the show. It gets hard to balance all of that, and there have been numerous occasions over the years where both of these situations have made for very difficult decisions.

One decision that was easy to make came as we were putting together the 1990 show. It was probably, from a pop music point of view, one of our bell wether Grammy Awards, complete with pop stars that included Billy Joel, Linda Ronstadt, Bette Midler, Gloria Estefan, Don Henley, the newly emerging television star/rapper Will Smith, Stevie Wonder and Ray Charles paying tribute to Paul McCartney, and (yes) a Michael Bolton and Kenny G duet. It's easy to say, looking back on it from a 2007 perspective, it embodied all of the elements that have made the Grammys the target of criticism for being too pop, but I can tell you that in 1990 we looked at it and thought, this is going to be a big show for us. And from a ratings standpoint, it was, out-rating the previous year's show by far.

But even with all of the pop music on that show, one artist emerged that year who would be more responsible for the turnaround in negative attitudes about the Grammys than any other—and she may just have been the most unlikely person in Grammy history to do so. Her name is Bonnie Raitt.

Contrary to popular lore, she was not an automatic booking on the show that year. As you might imagine from the wealth of pop talent that was present, she was nowhere near the top of the list when we sat down with the Academy TV committee to lay out the show the day the nominations came out.

But she had two major champions on our side: Pierre—who for years had been close with Bonnie's parents, John and Marjorie—and me. I had stayed close to Bonnie from our first *Soundstage* experience in Chicago in 1975. Bonnie was always better than her chart positions. The Warner Brothers albums she had made until the late '80s had gems on them, and as a person she was one of the purest and most honest people we had ever met and worked with. The business loved her, pockets of people who "got her" loved her, and it was simply a matter of time until the world got her. And after the Grammys that year, everybody got her.

Her performance on the show was magical. I had positioned her to perform directly after the Best New Artist performance, the long remembered and ill-fated Milli Vanilli (more about them later), and just before the highly anticipated Paul McCartney tribute, shortly before the end of the first hour of the show. Of course I had hopes that she'd win some Grammys that night, but she was certainly not the favorite by any means, so I scheduled the Best Rock Female Grammy, the award I felt most sure she'd have a chance to win, right after her performance.

As in love as I was with the title song of the album *Nick of Time*, she sang "Thing Called Love," an uptempo rocker that showed off her guitar playing and sexy side off to their max. When the standing ovation came, as it did within seconds of her finishing her performance, I knew she had a chance to sweep that night, and a minute or two later when her name was read, I thought that this was going to be a very big night for Bonnie. She slowly walked to the stage, and nearly 20 years of dirty clubs, bad buses, album sales disappointments, and insecurities aplenty were lifted from those strong shoulders as she graciously acknowledged her win in the Rock category. But that was nothing. Thirty minutes later, after the nominations for Album of the Year were read by Natalie Cole and Ella Fitzgerald, she returned to the stage with an even more emotional speech that once again brought the house to its feet. You would have thought that her third award, for Best Pop Vocal Performance, Female, would have been anticlimactic, but it was met with the same outburst from an audience that was clearly bringing her into their hearts that night. And even though the final award of the night, for Record of the Year, went to Bette Midler, who had just given a great performance of her nominated song, "Wind Beneath My Wings," it was clear to everyone there and at home that the night belonged to Bonnie. Even Bette looked at Bonnie sitting in the third row (even that said something about her chances) and said, "See Bonnie Raitt, I got one too."

Of the four speeches that Bonnie made on the air that night, though they all have blended into one, I still remember some of her words, which only serve to speak to her humility, her surprise, and her appreciation. After saying she had been "transported," and crediting "divine intervention" and admitting that *Nick of Time* had been her first "sober album," she told the audience, "My sobriety means I'm going to feel great tomorrow." After winning Album of the Year she added, "I can only take so much of this! Wake me when it's over."

Though the effect on the business was immediate, no one really knew how big an effect on the entire music industry this one win would have. They found out quickly over the next month as Bonnie's album jumped from 40th place to first and stayed there for weeks, more than doubling sales the album had seen in its entire release time before the Grammys. Although the show had had impact on careers before, this was clearly one of the first times that the Grammys had been responsible for "making" a career. And I don't say that solicitously, Bonnie reminds me of it nearly every time we're together. And graciously, though I am appreciative of her comments, I remind her of the years before spent on those buses, on those stages, and, more than that, of the great music that she had been giving us for 20 years before February 22, 1990.

Bonnie's win that night set the stage for the emergence of the female rock artist which led to the domination of the charts by women, which led to the creation of an entire generation of "divas," a concept I've been credited with inventing, via the VH1 *Divas* shows that I created and produced, as long as they were relevant (I left once I felt they weren't anymore). It was truly amazing for me to see what one night, a group of significant Grammy wins, and an absolutely untouchable Grammy performance was able to do not only for an artist, but also for the music business itself.

Another of my highlights that night was the award we gave to Miles Davis, who had been booked previously and not made it. This was to be one of his last appearances, and it has led to another Grammy legend of suspicious origins. Everyone associated with the episode claims to have been the person to whom Miles was talking, but believe me, I was the person who was stared down with the now-legendary statement to come.

We were rehearsing with Miles, an enigmatic performer to say the least. As part of the tribute, he would perform "Big Time" before being presented the Lifetime Achievement Award by Herbie Hancock, who had not only played with Miles, but had been discovered by him at the age of 20 and asked to join perhaps the most influential voice in jazz at the time. We had been warned: Miles ain't easy, and he's just as likely to walk out as play, so be gentle. The rehearsal had begun easily enough with Miles coming to the stage without so much as a hello, putting trumpet to lips, and playing. But now the 3:30 minute version of "Big Time" was at five minutes and counting, and Miles showed no sign of stopping. I sat at my production table in the front of the house trying to figure out what was going on, and quietly walked to the stage and asked my friend Herbie what to do.

He looked at me like I was crazy. He said there's nothing to do but go out and tell him to stop. If you don't he'll either play all night, or he'll leave without knowing what you want. Sound advice, except that even after my years of working with talent, this seemed to be a potentially explosive situation.

I pulled myself together, went out in the middle of a drum solo, walked up to Miles and told him that we had put this number in for 3:30 minutes, while waiting to find out what a trumpet feels like when it hits your head, or perhaps worse.

Miles stopped the band. He did a half turn on me, facing upstage, not unusual for either a discussion or a performance from Miles. He took a moment. He looked up at the front of the stage, but said nothing.

Finally, he turned toward me and pointed. When he raised his arm, I think I did a visible move backward, but I don't remember.

"Hey," he said. "How long was I playing?"

I responded that it was over five minutes and counting.

He took another beat.

"See that wall up there?" he said pointing to the hardwall curtain that we would bring down to stage level after each performance so that we could turn the stage around for the next performer.

"Yeah, I see it," half expecting him to tell me to cut it down right then and there, it was in his line of sight.

"Well, when I've played long enough for you, just drop that wall."

That was it. Plain and simple. Miles would play until the wall came down. So easy, so simple, so Miles.

And that's what happened. He played, his back to the audience half the time, but always in range of the handheld camera that Walter had placed in the rear of the stage, and when we hit 3:30 minutes, we brought the wall down, Miles hit a little arpeggio, and the music stopped.

He got his award, we got a great story. Sadly, Miles passed away the following year.

<hr>

The Paul McCartney tribute contained surprises of its own, one of which had nearly the mystery of Miles Davis. It concerned whether or not Paul would agree to perform on the show at the conclusion of the segment.

We knew we had a winner already. Stevie Wonder came and did a killer version of "We Can Work It Out," and Ray Charles even improved on his recorded version (if that's possible) of "Eleanor Rigby." Meryl Streep, a huge McCartney fan, read some wonderful copy around a clip piece that we had put together, but the payoff would have been Paul playing something.

Paul's representative at the time and a friend of mine, Ron Weisner, did about everything he could to make it happen. Paul's then manager, now gone, was totally uncommunicative about whether Paul would play or not, and so we were left in a will-he-or-won't-he position that we had only one solution for.

We put a piano onstage that sat there waiting for Paul when he arrived to accept the award. He was coming in on a flight from San Diego that evening, and with some bad weather, wasn't even scheduled to arrive at the Shrine until we were about 30 minutes away from the presentation. Forget about playing, we weren't even sure he was going to make the show, and we were juggling fast to move it later in the event the flight was diverted to Ontario Airport. But he did get there, and with only a few minutes to spare, I gently asked the question of the manager, who shrugged his shoulders as I knew he would. There was nothing left to do but to face another Miles Davis moment and ask Paul himself.

I walked up to him, said hello (we had met a few times before), and welcomed him to the show, telling him what a terrific segment it was going to be. I swallowed and asked him if he thought he wanted to play. This was obviously the first time he had ever heard the request. He paused, and then said that if he had known, he would have.

Of the 14 performances we did that night in addition to Bonnie Raitt, Bette Midler, and Miles Davis, one remains very special to me.

One of the artists who had eluded me for a long time was Don Henley. I was a big Eagles fan and had always wanted to work with them, but up to that time television had been anathema both to the Eagles and to Don as a solo artist. There was very little Eagles footage at all, and until their reunion in the '90s, no real concert footage existed. Don (and his longtime manager Irving Azoff) were very skeptical, even in the MTV generation, about television, feeling that rock guys needed the mystery and shouldn't be unmasked. On the other hand, there was no question that MTV had a lot to do with breaking Don's solo career, and that the videos for "The Boys of Summer" and "The End of the Innocence" were very instrumental in making him a viable solo artist. Don agreed to do the Grammys after much coaxing, and the staging for "The End of the Innocence" was very true and very simple, matching both the eloquence and the elegance of that song. It was my favorite song of the year, and though Don won a Grammy that night for Best Male Rock Performance, I was very disappointed that it didn't win for Song of the Year.

The performance was electric, and placing it before the Male Rock award was fortunate, since Don was able to come to the stage and give exactly the sort of speech that I expected from this curmudgeonly character who has a hidden warmth that he doesn't show very much. In a backhanded compliment that said so much more than its few words, he said, "Oh I get it, you perform a song, you win an award."

On his way out, he gave me the Henley eye, which was enough for me to know that he was both being consistent with who he is and also appreciative of the honor and grateful for what we had done to support the performance. Over the past 15 years, which have included numerous times with Don, I know I'm OK when I get "the eye."

Billy Joel saw his first taste of Grammy defeat that night, after opening the show with "We Didn't Start the Fire." We had painstakingly visualized the song by obtaining clips of nearly all of the 200 names that he mentioned in the four-and-half-minute song, and though the performance was hot, and Billy's band was hot, that was as hot as he got all night. It obviously didn't affect his career any, and later that year when he toured with Elton John and I went to two of the shows, he was as exciting onstage as he's ever been, maybe even better.

Billy wasn't the only one who suffered at the expense of Bonnie's victory. The progressive music media were all over Fine Young Cannibals as the logical choice to win Album of the Year as well as Record. There was a lot of support for Tom Petty, who was a longtime Grammy shutout, and I've already said how much Henley's record and album meant to me. It was an adult record, just as Bonnie's was, and there was a pocket out there that said that this would be Henley's year. When he didn't win for Song of the Year, it should have told me that it wasn't, but "Wind Beneath My Wings" had been a huge hit for Bette and in fact was probably more of a "Grammy song" than the introspective "Innocence." And then there were the Traveling Wilburys, nominated for Album of the Year, and the last live recording by Roy Orbison, who teamed with George Harrison, Bob Dylan, Tom Petty, and Jeff Lynne to create a pretty sensational offering. A number of critics had named that album the best of the year in their year-end polls.

In other words, we had a horse race, and a horse race is always a good thing. It not only made for a better show, and we played it for that, it also brought viewers who were as interested in the nominations as in the individual performances. That was borne out by the ratings, which rebounded 18 percent from the previous year (which I sat out) to an 18.9 rating and a 31 share.

I'd like to think that some of that bounce was credited to Garry Shandling, who came in to replace Billy Crystal, when Crystal had been asked to "move up" to the Oscars. That Crystal went on to become one of the most beloved Oscar hosts of all time, ranking right up there with Bob Hope and Johnny Carson, is a good thing; that he cut his teeth and came to the attention of the Oscar producers from his role on the Grammys has somehow been lost, and that's not a good thing, as far as I'm concerned. It would happen time and again with some of our choices, among them Ellen DeGeneres and Rosie O'Donnell, who went on from the Grammys to host other shows after being with us first. Shandling was admittedly not a music fan, and he played that to his advantage in his host role. Although we asked him back, he certainly couldn't live up to the standard that Billy had set.

By this time, the competition between the American Music Awards and the Grammys was pretty intense, heightened by the unstated but not totally denied belief on the part of mutually desirable acts that they would not get an offer from the Grammys if they did the American Music Awards. As Dick Clark became more defensive and ultimately went public and threatened a lawsuit against the Grammys, it was strange that he was simultaneously proclaiming how much better his show was doing in the ratings. If in fact that was true, I kept telling myself, then why was he worried about what he perceived as a "Grammy booking policy?"

To soften the situation, Mike, in what he called a "gesture of good faith," but what I felt was one of his rare moments of weakness, decided to give Clark a Trustees Award and to present it on the Grammys. I think Dick was probably stunned to hear about it, and he accepted our invitation to come to the show and receive it. What had started out as Mike's show of goodwill turned sour however when Dick, who had prepared an acceptance speech and given it to the teleprompter operator himself (surprise!) walked onstage and discovered, as did we, that there was a problem with the prompter and the speech was lost. He had to deliver it without the aid of the prompter, which he felt was something we had purposely done to him—I can state without equivocation we had not. Remember, it's a live show where things like this happen, and no one should have known that things like this can happen more than Mr. Clark, a veteran of hundreds of hours of live event television. In any case, rather than easing the situation between the two shows, it only exacerbated and intensified it for a good many more years until the AMAs made their move to the fall of the previous awards year.

Although much of the enmity between the two shows had begun with Mike (and I admit to being a very willing participant), Dick held me personally responsible, a feeling that would last until the Emmy broadcast of 2006, which we produced, when I proposed giving a special award to Dick a year after his serious stroke. When we saw each other for the first time at the Shrine Auditorium for his rehearsal, we both got teary, and I told him how much I admired him and what an inspiration his career had always been to me.

~

This was also the year of Milli Vanilli.

Milli Vanilli was an example of pop at its worst, although none of us, including me, said so at the time. Performing the Best New Artist category is sort of a mandate at the Grammys, and though we looked at the other nominees, including Neneh Cherry, the Indigo Girls, Tone Loc, and Soul II Soul, Milli Vanilli were easily the most accessible and were riding high on the pop charts. We went ahead and booked them without ever seeing them live (a rarity for us), and it wasn't until we showed up at their rehearsal two nights before the show that we first knew a joke had been played on us. And we were about to play one on our audience, which wasn't fair.

The rehearsal was ridiculous. Walter and I saw from the minute we walked in that Milli Vanilli couldn't dance, and though they were playing a backing track for their vocals, that wasn't unusual for a dance rehearsal. What we didn't know was that it was their plan to use the backing track for the show itself, something we never did (with the exception of the one Janet Jackson performance a few years earlier).

We battled with management over them singing live and decided on "mixing" the tracks, something we have occasionally done when the performance is more dance and less vocal. In this case, as our audio people told us, "they couldn't fucking sing their way out of a paper bag."

The performance was a joke, but the bigger joke came moments later when they were awarded the Grammy for Best New Artist, and despite the Academy's recall of the Grammy the following year, there was egg on our collective faces that would never be scraped off.

On balance, though, as much of a cop-out as it seems, if it takes one Milli Vanilli every 20 years to have the Bonnie Raitt moment, to have had Miles Davis perform for one of his last performances, and to have experienced the grace and beauty of Don Henley singing from his heart on "The End of the Innocence," then I'll take one of those . . . but once every 20 years is enough.

CHAPTER 13

1991 Grammy Awards

*"Another Day in Paradise" at Radio City
as Quincy Comes "Back on the Block"*

The enigmatic Bob Dylan came into our lives once again on the 32nd Annual Grammy show we did from Radio City Music Hall.

Our special segments on the show, instituted after the show went to three hours, were working pretty well, even after the much-maligned doo wop segment of 1988. It gave the show an opportunity to look back into the vast history of music, and book some people who were either overlooked by the nominations or were, to be frank, just too cool for the Grammys.

The 1991 show contained two such segments, the first a tribute to John Lennon, following on the heels of the previously aired McCartney segment, and the second, a Lifetime Achievement Award presented to Bob Dylan, which would be hosted by Jack Nicholson and feature a performance by Bob. Bob agreed to perform through the efforts of my longtime friend and attorney, Jeff Ingber, who had also gotten Neil Diamond to do the Streisand duet on my first Grammy show. It was not an easy thing to get Bob's consent, and up until about ten days before the show, Bob had not given a final OK to performing. But suddenly we got a call saying that he had thought it over and wanted to perform.

Rehearsal day came around, and Bob showed up with his band. As usual, other than a casual hello, he stayed very much upstage prior to and even during his rehearsal, and generally eschewed the hangers-on around the stage who wanted to say hello or chat. Bob's not big on chat. The rehearsal went reasonably well, and with Jack Nicholson in the house, he felt pretty safe.

It was a rainy night and for the first time at Radio City, rather than have our offices in the bowels of the place, we were working out of a trailer just outside the stage door of the venue. Though we had rehearsed

Jack's speech about Bob, which was a collaborative venture between a couple of writers and me, when Jack showed up an hour or so ahead of the show, he wanted to do some changes. Since the dress was over, I took a few minutes with him in the trailer.

I had met Jack before, and on previous occasions he was very clear to let me make sure I knew that "I don't do TV" (you can imagine how that sounds Jack-ized). But he was psyched about introducing Dylan, and wanted to be meticulous about his intro. As we sat there reviewing the copy, I started to read it for his revisions. At one point, I heard myself talking, and—Christ if I wasn't doing a bad Jack accent. I looked up from the script page and saw this sly grin come over his face as he watched and listened to me. I gave him this sheepish grin, as if I knew what an asshole I was being, even though until that moment I didn't even realize it, and he put his hand on my shoulder, looked at me, and said, "Don't even think about it, I've heard a lot worse…sometimes from myself."

We laughed, cleaned up a few words, and then I took him inside where he found himself the center of attention in a sea of music stars. He took his seat in the audience, and I wondered if he'd make it until midway in the show when the Dylan segment was scheduled.

The time came, and I walked him to the offstage position, where he paused, peeked through the curtain to see the faces in the front row, and then ambled out to set up the first clip package, a brief retrospective of Bob's career. And then it was time for Bob.

I think he was a good minute into the number before any of us realized just what was going on. Whatever song he had rehearsed in the afternoon had vanished and in its place was a nearly unrecognizable (for that first minute) version of "Masters of War." Now, granted, the weeks leading up to the Grammys were the first weeks of the Gulf War and in the midst of America's longest peacetime experience, there was a great deal of concern that this limited attack to keep Saddam Hussein in check might spread into an all-out war. There were nightly bombing missions that were carried live on American television, and news bulletins had become a regular part of primetime programming.

For Bob, whose ideology had not only followed him through the years but had made him an even stronger presence as he added years, this was an opportunity to make the flip side of the statement he had made nearly 30 years ago about our increasing involvement in Viet Nam, and to make it to a worldwide audience. And he did just that, although this version of "Masters" bore little resemblance to the classic version that appeared on his earlier album.

But that was only the beginning. When he finished and Jack brought him to the stage to accept his award, Bob gave one of the most enigmatic speeches that had ever been heard in the midst of an award show. He thanked Jack, took a few beats, and then looked out at, no, actually *over* the audience, and slowly spoke the following words:

"It's possible to be so defiled in this world that even your mother and father won't know you. But God will always believe in your own ability to mend your own ways."

Was this a statement about American foreign policy? Was it a comment on the transitory nature of people in general and in particular the music business that was being celebrated that night? Or were these the studied words of one of America's great poets adding to the considerable compendium of words and thoughts that separated and yet connected him with generations of fans? Simply put, I don't know, and though our paths have crossed several times since, I've never had the nerve to ask him what it meant. But it put a period to one of the most interesting twelve minutes of a Grammy show ever.

The John Lennon segment, which was positioned a bit earlier in the show, had its own share of drama, but for entirely different reasons. Tracy Chapman had been named Best New Artist two years before, and the combination of her sensitive vocals and rich material had made her a strong contender to be an artist who would be around for a while. There was a parallel in our minds at least to Lennon's quiet side, and I was anxious to book her to sing "Imagine." When I called her management, they were thrilled and told me that in fact she did play the piano, and would love to do it.

But when we got to rehearsal, it was obvious they had neglected to tell me the whole story; yes, she played the piano, but she was just learning to play. And she was no Rubenstein. Even at the dress there was pressure to pull her from the show, but her manager assured me that between dress and show she'd do nothing but sit at the piano and learn the chords for the song. Which she did: with that plaintive voice accompanied by those very simple chords ringing through the house with honesty and emotion, she scored.

To make sure we scored, however, I scheduled Aerosmith, huge Lennon fans, to close out the segment. They brought a whole new life to "Come Together," and eleven years after John's death, I wondered how the irony of their performance in tribute to John would play against their Grammy nominated, and eventual winning song, "Janie's Got a Gun." Several writers, in their review of the show, got it and commented on the reality of the ensuing years between the two songs.

But there were still plenty of thrills to come, and one of them was right around the corner when Garth Brooks made his debut appearance on the show. To this day, we don't talk about it, but I know Garth, on his part, has never entirely forgiven us for coming up with a set that contained a faux barroom look and had him commenting on a stageful of extras acting like "country folk" while he sang about a raucous Saturday night in the South.

Although the segment scored, Garth's feeling about it and the fact that he lost out to perennial Grammy favorite (and all-around good guy) Vince Gill kept him from coming to the show from that time on. It's a shame, because while I've worked with him on other shows, the fact that he won't come back to the Grammys hurts us, and it hurts him.

↝

One of my favorite Grammy stories—one that feels a lot like payback—happened during this show, and although I'm not quite sure what the lesson is here, perhaps you can figure it out.

In the late 1980s, maybe as a backlash to the lack of "musicality" on the music scene, two events occurred that were considered anomalies in the music business.

After years of playing to an adult audience that was growing older along with him, longtime pop stylist Tony Bennett found himself with an adoring base of young people who seemed to discover him for the first time. Forget that from 1951 to the middle '70s, he had a string of hits that ranged from the anthemic "I Left My Heart in San Francisco" to the totally forgettable "In the Middle of an Island." Through it all,

Bennett never stopped making records, touring more than half the year playing nightclubs, and making consistently beautiful music.

At almost exactly the same time, a young New Orleans musician from a famous Crescent City family (his father had been the District Attorney of N.O. for many years), Harry Connick, Jr., had begun to break through big due not only to his handsome classic face, but also to his homage to the big band singers of an earlier time, most notably Frank Sinatra (with some Tony Bennett thrown in).

I had first met Tony in the middle '60s when he was a regular (when he was in Chicago to perform) on the *Marty Faye Show*. He was one of the truly nice guys in the business, and nothing made me happier than to see his resurgence.

I wanted to book him on that year's Grammy Awards knowing that his appearance, based largely on his comeback, would trigger a great crowd response and probably give us one of those hoped-for moments.

The Grammy TV committee wasn't in favor of the idea, going through one of its seasonal "let's get hip" periods, which occurred with mysterious regularity over the years. Their understanding of hip was questionable.

My suggestion of pairing Tony Bennett and Harry Connick, however, met with universal approval, particularly after I pointed out that to book them as a performing pair would show a timeline and demonstrate that having moved on, music sometimes had the capacity to revisit itself and do it well. I was somewhat of a Connick fan, although there was a part of me that felt that he was exploiting what had gone before for his own benefit. Despite that feeling, the opportunity of having them together on the show, as hot as they both were at the moment, was attractive. The committee agreed, but insisted that I book Connick first so that we weren't "stuck" with Tony.

My first call was to Connick's manager with the offer that they perform separately and then finish off together. I said further that I wanted Harry to open the set, to finish and then to introduce Tony with something like "if it weren't for this next man, I probably wouldn't be here tonight." The manager agreed, not wanting to lose the opportunity of such a significant performance.

I then called Tony's son and manager, Danny, who was thrilled and told me that Tony would do anything we wanted, and was grateful for the booking.

As the show approached, it became clear that Harry's manager was re-thinking the plan. Her first backpedal was that Harry would perform on his own but didn't want to perform with Tony. Even though I had told the TV committee that I would try and get a joint performance, and hated losing that, Harry's manager prevailed, and I accepted that there would be no duet.

Next came a call from Connick's manager about a week before the show saying that she had reconsidered and that Harry would not perform unless he followed Tony's performance. As much as I disliked this plan, I knew that it wasn't impossible that if I lost Harry Connick, I might have to "unbook" Tony, and I didn't want to risk it. So once again, I accepted her decision, and we moved on to the show rehearsals, reversing the order of the set.

But before I confirmed it, I once again called Danny Bennett and told him what had happened: that Tony would have to open the set and that, as before, he wouldn't be performing with Harry. As I often do, I tried not to put it on the other act, instead saying that it was a show decision, even though it wasn't and I suspect that Danny knew it was coming from the Connick side. I might mention at this time that both artists were on the same record label, Columbia Records.

Danny didn't agree to this right away, but the next day called me and told me that Tony was OK with it, and to proceed. I was relieved, although I honestly felt extremely uncomfortable that I had put Tony Bennett in this situation.

Radio City Music Hall is a great place to work. But because of the complex stage elevator system, once you have a plan in place, it's nearly impossible to change. We had set Tony's trio on the pit elevator, closest to the audience. When he finished singing, the pit would go down and the next elevator upstage toward the back would rise with Harry and his 16-piece orchestra on it for his performance. Once that was decided and all the departments knew about the plan, it was locked and couldn't be changed.

We got through the first rehearsals just doing the two songs without a problem. Very few people around to react, and all business. But the next day was the dress rehearsal, and with its organized chaos, a place where nearly all the talent were in the house along with a few hundred other people, spending the five hours it takes to get through the show on show day.

Garry Shandling introduced Tony and he was revealed with his little trio singing a song from his Grammy-nominated album *When Will the Bells Ring For Me*. The response was thunderous from the people seated for the rehearsal, so big in fact that though Connick's elevator had brought him up to stage level, there was no way for him to start until Tony's applause died down. He then went into his big band number, which was certainly a good performance, if not a great one.

The rehearsal hadn't been over for more than five minutes when I got a call from Harry's manager, who was ill and couldn't make the trip from Boston for the rehearsal. Harry had "reconsidered." I was right, it would be best for Harry to credit Tony with being an influence, and he should precede Tony on the show, which was now two hours away from live broadcast.

But the ship had sailed. Had I wanted to, the technical requirements were so complex that there was no way we could reverse the stage set-up and put Harry on first. And to be very honest, after what she had put us through, I had no great desire to please the manager.

The show went on, and as expected, Tony got a great standing ovation, and though we delayed the cue to bring Harry's elevator up, he still wound up waiting a bit before he could begin his song. Tony had scored a major Grammy performance victory, and Harry Connick's performance seemed like an afterthought. I remember wondering whether Harry knew that had he not agreed to appear on the show, Tony Bennett wouldn't have been there that night to accept this most deserved recognition for 30 years of surviving the music business.

The irony of course, is that in the category in which they both competed that night, Harry Connick won the Grammy. But Tony won the night.

CHAPTER 14

1992 Grammy Awards

Natalie Cole Is Truly Unforgettable

I guess if I had to miss any Grammy show (and I was genuinely disturbed at missing the 1989 show), this might have been the one to miss, owing to a number of factors, not the least of which (as has been described to me) was the dictatorial way in which Mike Greene overpowered the entire organization, to the point of adding bookings after the show had been loaded into Radio City and was beyond the breaking point. That, combined with the seven-Grammy sweep by Natalie Cole (though well received that night) made for a critics' target when combined with wins by Marc Cohn (for Best New Artist win) and Michael Bolton, both considered lightweights.

Watching from a distance—I was not on set due to a commitment to produce *The Dennis Miller Show*—I saw some outstanding performances, including Seal's version of "Crazy," Bonnie Raitt returning with one of my all-time favorite songs, "I Can't Make You Love Me," Paul Simon's "Cool Cool River," and a rare Metallica appearance for "Enter Sandman." But so much about a Grammy show is about pacing, and had I been around, I doubt that I would have opened with Paul Simon and then gone to Michael Bolton and then into Mariah Carey. Not the strongest material from any of the three of them. Seal brought the show alive again, and the Commitments doing "Mustang Sally" was a moment all its own, but it took a dive again with a couple of performances until Metallica hit the stage followed by Bonnie.

In a four-hour-plus show, though it would seem that you've seen and heard a lot already, it was barely halftime, and the show had already seen its best moments. L.L. Cool J did a hot version of "Mama Said Knock You Out," but Color Me Badd's "I Adore Mi Amor" followed by Boyz II Men's "Motownphilly" seemed too much of the same thing, and it was left to Vince Gill to light up the crowd with a beautiful version of

"Pocket Full of Gold" followed by Alan Jackson doing one of the biggest hits of the year, "Don't Rock the Jukebox."

Aretha Franklin was joined by Michael McDonald in a surprisingly tame version of "Ever Changing Times," surprising because each of them individually is a vocal and performance powerhouse, and it seemed as though they were both a bit lost in this song. Such was not the case when Luther Vandross came out to sing "The Power of Love" with Aretha. That was strong and reminded everyone why she was the Queen of Soul, and he was the Prodigal Prince.

After six trips to the stage, it was pretty much a given that Record of the Year would go to Natalie, and it did. She continued to be a class act to the end, thanking all the right people, and giving her father the credit he deserved. I kept thinking back on that day a decade earlier at the New York recording studio when a less-than-lucid Natalie showed all the signs of a person about to take a long and difficult ride. As we have talked about since, and as she has publicly stated, you have to really be down to realize just how high you can fly. And she has flown.

Not too many people know the true story of how she came around to agreeing to sing her dad's material, and in particular, to sing *with* her dad. That's because not too many people watched the first Grammy Hall of Fame show that we did from New York in 1981, a show that honored her father Nat King Cole, Count Basie, Ray Charles, and others.

Natalie's career actually began with a great track "This Will Be" that took this girl right out of college and jumpstarted a career that as of this writing is going on 30-plus years. We met quite early while I was producing the *Midnight Special*, as Natalie was not only a regular guest, but, because of her background, a terrific guest host, able to convincingly deliver introductions of other artists as well as singing duets with them. I loved her for that, and we did a number of shows together in those few years before the Grammy Hall of Fame show.

For that show I had this idea of having her sing "Unforgettable" with her father, and had gone to Kevin Hunter, her manager at the time, with the thought of doing it. He told me in no uncertain terms that she did not want to "trade" on her father's name, and though someday she might do that, it wouldn't be for many years. I understood, but didn't accept it and continued to be dogged about getting Natalie to do this. She finally relented, and I arranged a pre-recording session in New York where we would re-record the parts of the song that she would sing, dropping her father's vocals out of those parts. She showed up for the session and I could see that she wasn't in good shape. In fact, she had begun her troubled period, a period that would see her career spiral downward and the hits stop coming. She would commit herself to re-hab before re-emerging in absolutely great shape.

That had been ten years before her incredible Grammy night, and yet I knew something was wrong. We talked about how we were going to do this, using a split screen with her father on one side and her on the other, and then we said goodbye until the rehearsal the next day at the venue. She came, she did it (I don't think she really wanted to) and it would be a number of years before she'd revisit her father's material.

Going back to pacing, I think the show might have fared a bit better with a few changes in the routine. Giving out the Song of the Year at the top of the show (granted, not knowing that "Unforgettable" would win) allowed a 75-year-old composer, Irving Gordon, to take the stage and, in a long and rambling speech, undo a great deal of the progressive steps the Academy, and the show, had taken in the past several years. Adding to it was the fact that the award was presented by Michael Bolton, not the coolest guy in the house.

All during production, I was hearing the stories of how Mike was out of control and listening to no one. I'm not arrogant enough to think that I could have controlled his every demand, but I had developed a working relationship with him, and a directness that, if nothing else, made him aware of being accountable. Unfortunately he had no sense of that in 1992.

There were some significant winners that year that affirmed Mike's outreach program, among them three Grammys to R.E.M., and another Grammy for Metallica, now three years removed from the Jethro Tull embarrassment. Luther Vandross continued to be a Grammy favorite, and Will Smith (as D.J Jazzy Jeff & the Fresh Prince) won his first Grammy in the still new Rap Duo or Group category. While Will was considered kind of "rap lite," the fact that L.L. Cool J won the Rap Solo category took a bit of the taint off the other award—still it would take a few more years before the Academy would really get hip-hop right.

Whoopi Goldberg hosted the show and ranged from extremely funny to mildly embarrassing. The problem with comics and comic actors on award shows is reasonably obvious; these shows now take place in huge theatres or arenas, venues that work for hockey, basketball, or spectacular rock acts that fill the stage. By and large, however, they don't work for comics. They're just too vast, and for the audience in the back half of a theater or arena, comedy just doesn't work. And what happens then is that the comic gets nervous, frustrated, or just plain scared and tries too hard, going for jokes that he or she ordinarily wouldn't have done. And it becomes a vicious circle, one that is hard to dig your way out of. And that's what happened to Whoopi that night. And though I know how much Whoopi loves music, she's a lot more comfortable introducing Luther Vandross than Garth Brooks.

In the end, the low ratings and lukewarm reviews that the show received that year were due more to the fact that it ran four hours than how good or bad the host was. Many of the reviews used a similar word, "endless," to describe the TV show, and the reports from the 6000 attendees at Radio City was that it reached a point of pain somewhere in the last hour.

Though I wasn't around to experience it directly, the fallout for us the following year was significant. The CBS executive on the show was replaced, the network sent very clear signals that the show was to "get off on time," in no uncertain terms, and for the first time ever, notes of our timed dress rehearsals had to be sent "upstairs." So much for the freedom of going over "a little" that we had enjoyed for so many years. It was a bit ironic that eight years later the network would come to us and ask us to expand the show from three to three-and-a-half hours.

Interestingly, the huge win by Natalie Cole, preceded the previous year by six wins by Quincy Jones, and then the Bonnie Raitt sweep the year before that, really upped the power of the Grammys, and in particular Grammy performances, in the marketplace. The show and the award had always had a certain sales effect in the ensuing weeks, but in the past three years, perhaps because all three CDs had not been huge sales successes prior to the show, they had become monsters at retail. And while we reveled in the ability of the show to make such a mark, out at the labels and among managers and agents, the fight to get on the show was to become even more intense than it had ever been before.

CHAPTER 15

The 1993 Grammy Awards

Eric Clapton's "Tears," and Peter Gabriel's "Steam"

Because my short-lived stint as producer of the Dennis Miller debacle kept me away from the 1992 Grammy show, it also allowed me to avoid the fallout of a Grammy show that was the longest in history, though I am certainly not arrogant enough to think that I would necessarily have made a difference in the length of the four-hour show, dictated by an over-zealous Mike Greene.

But I was certainly glad to be back for the 1993 show, and as he's told me time and again, so was Walter. He had a tough time the year before, and it also took a tremendous toll on Pierre.

The 1993 show was shaping up to be terrific, both in terms of potential performers as well as the nominations. In addition to Eric Clapton's *Unplugged* CD, which was an odds-on favorite, there were Annie Lennox, k.d. lang, and U2—all nominated in the Album of the Year category, along with a long shot, *Beauty & The Beast*. The Record of the Year category had at least two excellent contenders in addition to "Tears in Heaven"—k.d.'s "Constant Craving" and Vanessa Williams's admittedly syrupy but appealing ballad "Save the Best for Last." Long shots, in my mind, were Celine Dion and Peabo Bryson's "Beauty and the Beast" and the anomaly, "Achy Breaky Heart."

The safe bet was "Tears in Heaven" and for good reason. Eric Clapton's growth from a guitar god into one of music's most evocative ballad singers had been tipped throughout his career, but with this song, so personal and delivered with such passion, he set a new standard. The record, fuelled by his appearance on *MTV Unplugged* had made it a huge hit, but beyond that it was the story behind the record that made it so resonant with fans. Eric had written it following the tragic death of his son, Conor, who fell from a New York apartment window hours before Eric had been on his way to see him. It had put him into a major depression, and as I knew from our brief encounters over the years, Eric is an extremely intelligent person and a very introspective thinker. He's very analytical about himself, and very aware of the world. I couldn't begin to imagine what this was doing to him.

The question that came to my mind was, Would he come to the Grammys and perform this song at a celebration of music where he might be rewarded for writing such a personal song? Or would he remain private about his feelings and think that to receive an award for this might be self serving, and counter to its purpose?

Early on, it looked bleak. I had worked with Eric before the show, but he was certainly not a Grammy favorite before this album. For his amazing body of work, he had only been awarded two Grammys prior to 1992. So he had no love for the Grammys and compounding the issue were the yearly shows he did at Royal Albert Hall (usually about a week's worth) that always managed to be held around Grammy time.

It took a lot of pleading, the help of his then manager Roger Forrester, and all of the efforts of the record label, Warner Brothers, to convince him to come to the Grammy show.

It was too late to change the Albert Hall dates, so I had to settle for one day with him, that day being show day. And he couldn't be there in time for the dress rehearsal, so I'd have to rehearse him between dress and air, and at best get one pass at the song in rehearsal before he performed it live on the show.

Fortunately his plane was on time, he reached the Shrine at 3:30 (the show was scheduled to go live at 5 p.m.) and we ran the song in front of a full house of performers and presenters, not the ideal first rehearsal situation.

It was then that we learned that he would not be performing the song as he had on the record, but with a different rhythm. For the first 30 seconds or so, we all held our breaths, not certain that he was going to sing "Tears in Heaven" so different was the instrumental intro. But then he went into that first lyric, and we all knew we were witnessing something very special. Eric had stayed true to his principles once again, changing the tempo of the song to give some hint that, in fact, though Colin's death was still very much in his mind, he was making an attempt to move on with his own life, as we all must, and the subtle changes in the song were his way of beginning that journey.

But there was still the performance that night, and an extremely exhausted Eric retreated to his dressing room to rest and ready himself for the performance that mattered.

We approach every Grammy show as if it is a movie. Unlike other shows, we don't know the winners in advance, so our show structure has to be based on our instincts, our hunches, and our luck as we try and factor in who will walk away with Grammys. And of course, it doesn't take a genius to know that if you can build the excitement until the end, you can keep viewers involved.

So, I had scheduled Eric's performance last in the show. But I also wanted to make sure that the audience knew he was there and would perform, so I scheduled two of his other categories, Song of the Year and Pop Male Vocal earlier in the show. He won both of them, and we knew we had successfully set the stage for his moment later in the show, wondering only if by some quirk he might be aced out for Record of the Year, the last award of the night.

His performance—with only that award left to present—was more magical than it had been in rehearsal. There was one of those rare silences over the house at the end of the number, a silence usually reserved for those moments when you know that something much more meaningful than an artist singing a song has taken place. Then the crowd broke loose into one of the biggest ovations in Grammy history, and Eric made his way toward me offstage to wait for the on-camera shot that went with the nominees for Record of the Year.

We didn't miss a beat. I asked Tina Turner, a friend of Eric's of many years, to present the Record of the Year award, knowing that would heighten the emotion if he were to win. And as she read the nominations, I watched his face tighten with perhaps a bit more intensity than the hundreds of other faces I've watched over the years. Maybe in fact this award would mean something more than "winning a Grammy," that in Eric's mind this would be one more significant remembrance of Conor.

And then she read the name, Eric Clapton, and I took one step away to be out of camera range. But he found me anyway, and as he made his way to the podium, I looked around and, to a person, everyone backstage was in tears.

Of course, as usual the press turned everything upside down, choosing to focus on the length of time it finally took the Academy to properly award Eric instead of reporting on the touching moments that he provided throughout the show, and in particular, at the end. As if his rendition of the song weren't enough, his acceptance speech brought a silence to the house, and I suspect in living rooms everywhere.

In his usual self-deprecating manner, after thanking the appropriate people, Eric said, "I was convinced that this [album] wasn't worth releasing. I'm very moved, and very shaken, and very emotional. The one person I want to thank is my son for the love he gave me and the song he gave me."

⌢

I continued my quest for U2 to perform on the show, and once again I was thwarted, even though a few weeks before the show I had produced *MTV's Inaugural Ball* for the first Clinton inauguration at which Larry Mullen and Adam Clayton had teamed with Peter Buck and Mike Mills to create a very special one-time-only performance of "Losing My Religion, Baby" an agglomeration of "Losing My Religion" and "Achtung Baby." It was fabulous, and though I talked to them at the show about the Grammys, it was too late and I was to wait nine more years before the Grammys would see U2 rock on "Beautiful Day" on the 2001 show.

But even though U2 wasn't to rock on this particular show, there were two amazingly outrageous moments that more than made up for the lack of excitement that the Irish lads bring to every one of their shows. The first was a balls-out performance of "Give It Away" that teamed L.A.'s favorite sons, the Red Hot Chili Peppers, with George Clinton's P-Funk All-Stars.

That one came about after a meeting I had with Anthony and Flea of the Chili Peppers, at which they announced that they wanted to do something on the Grammys that had never been done before. Now that's often said, and once in a while results in something special, but not always. I asked them if they had any thoughts, and further, if there was anyone in particular they had always wanted to perform with. Spontaneously, and in one voice, they said George Clinton, and having been a

P-Funk fan from the beginning, I got very excited. Nowhere near as excited as I was to become when Clinton's diaper-clad, muumuu–wearing tribe showed up in full regalia for the first of the two rehearsals we scheduled. It just got more and more absurd as it went along, and the rehearsals were pale versions of what actually happened once they hit the stage for the actual show.

The Academy has its review session on the morning following the show, a time during which they look at the tape of the show and evaluate what we at the production company have done to elevate or shame them the night before. It's interesting in that in all the years I've done the show, we've not only never been asked to attend one of these sessions, but we've never officially ever heard the results of it, so if their purpose is to cause some change for the future, so far it hasn't reached us.

Anyway, unofficially I heard that there were cries of "never again" with regard to the five minutes of madness that occurred on the Chili Peppers/Clinton segment. Interesting since to a person, the comments and reviews from the show all highlighted the outrageousness of that particular moment as one of the defining moments in Grammy history. It showed that we could finally have fun with the music, and let it all out. I loved it, the audience went crazy, and if there were opportunities to do more things like that, I'd do them in a minute.

In fact, George Clinton and his band of wandering gypsies were to return to the Grammy stage nearly ten years later in an anthemic "Tribute to Funk" segment in which we filled the stage with Earth, Wind & Fire, Outkast, and Robert Randolph in addition to the unpredictable mayhem that was the trademark of the inimitable Mr. Clinton. And again, though we weren't there to witness, I was told that this time the TV committee loved it. And they should have.

The second moment that scored big was the opening of the show in which we teamed Peter Gabriel with members of the Cirque du Soleil troupe in a great version of "Steam." Acrobats, strangely dressed "little people," and an assortment of Cirque folk traipsed across the stage as Peter rendered a fine version of a classic song that would go Grammy-less that night. But it kicked the show off in a way that nothing else could have that year, and even lifted lethargic host Garry Shandling to new heights.

The 1993 show also marked the first time I worked with Celine Dion, who performed "Beauty & the Beast" with Peabo in a cut-down version with no set to support them. I was not a big fan of the song, and by this time was developing even more of a thin skin about the criticism of the show as too bland. I knew this performance was going to be a field day for those and other critics, but as early as the first rehearsal we had with Celine, I recognized that here was an artist with not only a great instrument, but also a sense of herself and the songs she sang. I became a fan, and remain one to this day, a fact that has only been strengthened over the years by the professionalism, commitment to her art, and warmth I've been fortunate to experience with both Celine and Rene Dion (her husband and manager). They are special people, and deserve all the success they've achieved.

In fact, since that first meeting, we've gone on to do several solo artist specials with Celine, and each one has been more of a joy than the previous one. Celine is a professional, Rene has always had the confidence to give us some room to be creative with Celine's presentation on television, and we've delivered every time out, both creatively and in terms of ratings. However, the first meeting for Celine Dion's second network television special was not a happy one. I had made the trip to Montreal in May 1999 to meet with several of Celine's management to discuss a fall special when we learned that Rene, was being operated on in Florida for throat cancer. The meeting would take place without him, and there had been a major change internally on her side, which meant that for the most part we were working with people who had not been very involved in our previous shows with Celine.

Ironies in show business abound. From the beginning, we had planned the show as a benefit for Celine's pet charity, cystic fibrosis, which took the life of her niece years ago. It was very important to both her and Rene that this show be something of a "giveback" for all of the success they had had in the past several years. This show was her first special following the tremendous success of "My Heart Will Go On," the song from *Titanic*, which appeared both on her album and on the soundtrack, and was the culmination of five years of No. 1s for her.

And we had decided on doing the show at Radio City Music Hall, which was undergoing an extensive remodeling, and would re-open with Celine's show as its first concert event. But before it would settle, something came up on the Radio City side which almost threatened to derail the show altogether.

A high-ranking executive in the Madison Square Garden organization, (the corporation that owns and runs Radio City as well as the Garden) Marc Lustgarten, was stricken with cancer and as a tribute to him the powers-that-be at MSG decided that they wanted to open the Music Hall with a benefit that would set up a charitable foundation in his name. And they were committed to that.

So there we were. Here was Rene in the hospital recovering from surgery and soon to undergo radiation for his cancer, the Dion organization committed to doing this show as a charity for cystic fibrosis, and Radio City committed to a charity show of their own. Could it be saved?

Rob Prinz, Celine's agent at CAA, stepped in and performed a miracle. Celine would have her show to open the Music Hall for concerts, a second Radio City re-opening show would take place (that we would do with Pierre), and the terms of the rental for Celine's charity show would be favorable, a concession made by MSG because we had already concluded a deal for the show as the official re-opening of the Music Hall.

But there was still the show to do, and the question of whether Rene would be in good enough shape to be there, and be contributory.

The show came together remarkably well. There was a new album to promote, an album of Celine's Greatest Hits so we knew several of the songs on the show would be both hits and contained in the new album (that's why record labels love television so much; it can launch albums like nothing else). To augment Celine's appearance, we had booked 'NSync and Gloria Estefan, who had recorded "Music of the Heart" together, and who were extremely compatible in my "duets and ensembles" philosophy.

And best of all, Rene was getting better and stronger.

He stayed in Florida while we all worked to get the show together. He limited his phone calls, his involvement, and his input, speaking only through Dave Platel, Celine's new "manager of record" (Rene was still the "manager"). I finally saw him three days before the show when they all came for rehearsals, and I held back my tears of joy at seeing him in good shape.

But I still had a problem. I knew Celine wanted to address his illness, but even though I knew them both well, I didn't know if I felt right putting the words into her mouth that could express her feelings. I've written for her on a number of shows, and she's pretty good about telling me when I'm right or wrong. I appreciate that.

But then I heard her duet of "All the Way" with a track from Frank Sinatra. I knew the two of them loved Sinatra, and that in fact "All the Way" was their great love song together (they're very romantic people). The words rolled off the computer, and brought me to tears when I read them back.

But that was nothing compared to the way she said them the night of the taping at Radio City. Rene was in the house, healthy. Celine had announced that at the end of the year she was going to stop and take some time to stay home with him. It was nearing the end of the live tour for her band and staff, most of whom had been there from the beginning. And all of that combined to create another most emotional "moment."

And then she started to sing, and the 6000 people in the house all melted away and all that was onstage was Celine and the film footage of Sinatra singing with her.

Because the show was taped, we had a moment to regroup after we did the number, and it was a good thing. I went out to see Mego, Celine's musical director, and we embraced. Celine was offstage getting it together, and out in the house, Rene's head was down so the crowd couldn't see his tears.

We had a show to finish, however, and finish it we did. And when we gathered after the show at a party Sony music chairman Tommy Mottola held at a New York restaurant, the joy of the evening, mixed with the emotion of it all, made for one of the warmest post-show celebrations ever.

An unexpected Grammy moment occurred on the 1993 show when we turned to the Gospel category to perform a contemporized version of Handel's *Messiah*, put together by Take Six's Mervyn Warren. It rocked the house, and counterpointing it was a classical performance of the same piece, which preceded it and set it up beautifully. It was an amazing blend of two disparate types of music, coming together to make the point that great music really knows no boundaries, and by inference it said that popular music, which was to become even more polarized, shouldn't be!

You didn't have to be a genius to see that whenever Michael Jackson walked onto the Grammy stage, the ratings took off. And even though *Bad* didn't reach *Thriller* sales, and the bloom was falling off the rose with each passing year, we demonstrated that we had no shame by using Michael once again as a "Legend" recipient and bringing him back one more time. This time, however, we did have a switch, having Janet make the presentation to him long before the MTV "kiss," triggering the still-famous line from Michael to the world, "I hope this puts to rest another rumor that has been in the press for too many years. Me and Janet really are two different people."

CHAPTER 16

The 1994 Grammy Awards

The Highest Whitney, the Lowest Sinatra

The 1994 Grammys remain as one of my favorite Grammy shows of all, due in large part to Whitney Houston's sensational opening number of "I Will Always Love You," sung as one of the elevator lifts at Radio City Music Hall rose up out of the basement and revealed her on our version of a Busby Berkeley birthday cake. The set alone was spectacular, but I've heard Whitney sing that song dozens of times over the years and it was never better than that night. That wasn't all—returning to the days of special segments, we put together a fitting Curtis Mayfield tribute with Bonnie Raitt, Bruce Springsteen, Vernon Reid, the Impressions, Steve Winwood, and B.B. King all saluting the Chicago R&B master who had suffered a paralyzing accident while onstage the previous year. And of course, I had a personal interest in making this segment great, since I had known Curtis since the *Curtis In Chicago* PBS show we did in 1973.

On the other hand, the very same show gave us one of Grammy's most embarrassing moments, the ill-fated ending of our tribute to Frank Sinatra, but more about that later. To this day we have carried the taint of having been the show that "took Sinatra off," and that's hard to live with.

But getting back to Whitney Houston—I guess, looking back at the tape of the show now, I took the easy road out. As I've said, we always like to follow a performance with a category we think the person who just performed has a good chance to win. I know that we've been accused of knowing the winners, hell—even Don Henley joked about it on the show itself—but the fact is that both Walter and I believe it's great to follow up a performance with a win. With Whitney, nominated all over the place, the sure thing was Pop Female Vocal, so once she stood the place on its ear with the song, we scheduled that award next, and the room went wild when Whitney walked out from backstage to accept the award from the song's writer, Dolly Parton, and the song's producer, David Foster. It was a little risky—had it not won—having these two people out there to present (we rarely took that kind of risk), but it was an amazing moment when it happened, and it was just the beginning for Whitney, the song, and the album from which it came, *The Bodyguard*.

Now of course you want to know about Whitney and drugs, about Whitney and Bobby, about all things Whitney. All I can or will say is that yes, I've been around Whitney when things aren't alright, and it's very sad to see. Is she the same Whitney Houston that I first put on a stage in 1985? No, she isn't, but then again, I've watched a lot of performers change over the years. Is Whitney the performer the same as she was in the beginning? That's a complicated question with an even more complicated answer. Although right from the start Whitney had the stage presence of a person twice her age (she was only 19 when we had her on the show the first time), she's gained even more poise and presence over the years. But, and it's a big "but," that's been tempered by the some of the behavior I've been witness to in recent years. Can she still deliver a performance capable of making the hairs on your neck stand up? Of course she can, and does, but the difference is that you once *knew* that was going to happen, and in recent years you hold your breath waiting.

Moving to one of the next most memorable events of that year's Grammy show, the Curtis Mayfield segment was something that exceeded everyone's expectations, which were high to begin with. Trying to cover a lifetime of memorable music with a stage full of superstars in seven minutes is nearly impossible, but in this case we did it. The segment opened with Bruce Springsteen and Bonnie Raitt doing "People Get Ready," moved on to B.B. King and Steve Winwood (his first Grammy performance) doing "Woman's Got Soul," followed with Tony! Toni! Toné! doing "Freddie's Dead," then back to Bonnie for a smoking "Look into Your Heart" followed by Bruce's "Gypsy Woman" and then concluding with everyone sharing "It's Alright." It was at that moment that Curtis in his wheelchair was brought to the stage, and this once strong, soulful voice struggled to deliver some equally soulful chosen words that evoked the spirit of his greatest songs.

Speaking of artists who carry with them a sense of history, Bono seemed the perfect choice to host the Sinatra tribute, marking the first time he would ever appear on a live Grammy show (ironically, before the show moved to a live format, Sinatra had been the first-ever person to appear on a "Grammy" show, explaining what a Grammy was to viewers of the 1965 compilation pre-taped show which introduced the Grammys to the television audience).

Bono was a quick "yes" when we asked him, although he asked if he would be permitted to write his own speech, which was fine with us. As the day of the show grew near, we were still formulating the segment as Bono and I talked, but there was no script from him. Our communication with the Sinatra group came through Eliott Weisman, who I knew from the first Liza Minnelli show we had done together in New Orleans in 1979.

Also involved was a long-time television producer, George Schlatter, who had been involved with much of Sinatra's television work over the years.

Though we had left the details of the Sinatra segment very open, including the possibility of a performance by Frank, Schlatter told us that the best we were going to do was to have Bono make the presentation and Frank give an acceptance speech.

What we all knew was that Frank had moments of absolutely normal behavior and other moments in which he was not very lucid at all. To be ready for whichever Sinatra we got that night, we had arranged with Schlatter that he was to be the person in the truck with Walter to make the call. If he felt during Frank's speech that he was losing it, he would tell us and we would, as gracefully as possible, go to commercial.

The moment arrived, and of course Bono was spectacular. I still have a framed and signed copy of his remarks hanging on a wall. He compared Sinatra to an epic hero, to a man who had seen it all and done it all, and of course had done it "his way." It was masterful, and all that was left was for Frank to come to the stage and accept his award. But just before he took the stage, someone came up to me and told me that a couple of bottles of liquor had been delivered to Frank's dressing room, and that they had been consumed, although I didn't know by whom. I idolized Sinatra myself, and was committed along with Walter, who had done several shows with Frank going back 20 years, to pulling this piece off.

Frank came to the stage and shocked us by announcing right off the bat that if he had been asked to sing, he would have loved it. We *had* asked him to sing—everyone in his camp knew we had asked that. We were told no several times, and in no uncertain terms. As he continued, it was clear that whether alcohol-related or not, Frank was genuinely touched by the tribute. Knowing how he had been venerated so many times over his career, I was amazed that this honor would have so much meaning for him, but it did.

It was shortly after this pronouncement that he began to go. His eyes got a bit glazed and he asked for his wife Barbara. Schlatter had told us that that was the key point; if he asks for Barbara, it means he's in trouble and doesn't know where to go next.

In the truck, Walter looked to Schlatter for help, and George, true to his word, made the call.

"Take him off. He's gone," he said in a voice loud enough for me to hear through my headset. Walter waited for the second, and even longer, as Frank searched for the words which wouldn't come, and then he pulled to a wide shot, cued the music for the commercial bumper to come on, and we left the venue for a commercial.

Unfortunately, that music played to the house at the very moment that Frank momentarily regained his composure and decided to say more. But the music in the house added to his confusion, and we very quickly sent a stage manager out to help him off the stage. Bono, standing there with Frank, pre-empted that move and, putting his arm around Frank, was the consummate professional, and walked him off the stage as if everything were fine.

And it might have been, at least to the people watching at home, save for Garry Shandling's next move. Obviously, we would have taken heat from people in the house, and perhaps even the press in their press room, for what had happened. But we only did what Sinatra's people asked us to.

Backstage, in the little host area we had set up for Garry and his writers to watch the show, come up with one-liners, and stay a bit removed from it all, things were happening fast. By the time I got there to explain exactly what had happened, Garry's handlers had convinced him that he had to go out and respond to the situation. Pierre and I were both there and explained that Sinatra's people had told us to take him off, and that we shouldn't make it worse by commenting on it. The clock was ticking, and before I had a definite answer to my question to Garry of whether or not he would say something, he walked past me and moved to his host position onstage.

We returned from commercial and Garry Shandling proceeded to bury us.

"Well," he said, and not without some attitude, "if I were the producers, I certainly would have let Mr. Sinatra finish his speech."

We were dead.

Not that we had done the right thing, but in fact we had done the *only* thing. To this day, even Schlatter agrees that if Frank had gone on any further, it would have been disastrous. He had lost track of what he was saying, and didn't have a finish. It was tragic, terrible, but the last thing that we wanted was to have been involved with what might have been Frank's last-ever television appearance, one that potentially embarrassed one of the world's greatest artists.

Shandling is another matter. I had really enjoyed working with him, and had gotten to know him reasonably well. He was never the best host we had, but his style and lack of musical knowledge actually worked for him on the show. He was a civilian, like the audience, caught up in the music business for one night a year and having a good time with it. But what he had done that night was unforgivable. Although others at the Academy were willing to forgive him for his momentary lapse of judgment, what he had done to exacerbate the situation made it impossible for us to recover. I made up my mind at that moment that it would be a long time, if ever, before I could accept him as a host of any show I would do. I respect his talent, and I've seen him go on to modest success as an actor, but he burned us and that wasn't right.

And as if what Garry said weren't enough, our humiliation continued when Billy Joel paused in the middle of his song, "River of Dreams," looked at his watch, and not knowing the real story of the Sinatra "goodbye," referred to the passing time as "valuable advertising time lost." The whole affair had nothing to do with show time or commercial time lost, it had to do with trying to mitigate the embarrassment of one of America's greatest musical icons looking foolish in front of millions of people—something that my friend Mr. Joel has done on his own several times over the years.

⌐

In addition to the performances already mentioned, Aerosmith rocked for their second time in four years with a version of "Livin On the Edge" that even outshone their "Come Together" on the Lennon tribute. Steven Tyler was in rare form, and Joe Perry delivered a sizzling guitar solo that echoed through Radio City and brought the crowd alive. Sting entered his more introspective period with "If Ever I Lose My Faith In You." The latter was nominated for Best Pop Male Vocal, and took the prize, continuing what was to be a pretty long string of Grammys for him. We continued our efforts to present more Latin music by having Gloria Estefan back, but this year performing for the first time in Spanish. "Mi Tierra," a number that featured an all-star group of Latin musicians produced by (her husband) Emilio Estefan, Jr., was one of the hottest numbers of the night, and looked great onstage. There was no surprise when *Mi Tierra* won a Grammy for Best Tropical Latin Album.

What *was* a surprise however occurred later in the show after Garth Brooks's performance. He rocked with "Standing Outside the Fire," and standing backstage with him I felt sure he was going to get his first Grammy. He was already selling millions of records, had crossed over, and was on his way to becoming one of the real musical phenomena of the '90s. I was shocked when Dwight Yoakam's name was read, but probably not as shocked as Garth who must have said to himself that this was his final Grammy appearance.

Garth was to give me one of the truly high moments in my career, however, the next year when he appeared on the first *VH1 Honors* show that we did, in another famous "one time only" duet that I had put together that created some incredible stage magic of its own.

It had rained that spring morning in Los Angeles, so I gave myself a little extra time to get to the Shrine Auditorium for the first of the four *VH1 Honors* shows we did starting in 1995. I wanted to get there early on show day for a number of reasons, not the least of which was that I had scheduled an early morning rehearsal with Garth and James Taylor.

This was the first time they were meeting each other. Garth was at the top of his game, selling millions of CDs and becoming the hottest thing in the music business. He had said no to the show earlier in the year, but I called him back and asked him what I could do to change his mind about coming. He told me that if he could get to work with James Taylor he'd do it. You see, James was Garth's idol, and in fact, Garth had named his first child, Taylor, after James.

When Garth and James greeted each other, there was a kind of restraint that I perceived as the mutual shyness that both men have offstage. I tried to help a bit, but the thought obviously crossed my mind that I had made a mistake and this hoped-for magic might not happen. But then they sat down next to each other, Garth took out his guitar and they began to rehearse the medley of "The River" and "Sweet Baby James" that I had put together. The two songs blended together beautifully on paper, and I only hoped that the two of them would bring the warmth and affection that I sensed from speaking with each of them on the phone.

Well, I had nothing to worry about. As the song progressed, even though neither man looked at the other, I could see that this was going to be something special. After taking solo verses, their voices merged in the choruses and I got that tingle that I pray for each time we put people together to sing.

I looked at Jack Sussman, the VH1 exec who had asked me to do the show, and just like James and Garth, we were too into it to speak. But the payoff came at the last chorus, when I looked at Garth and saw tears pouring down his face. They finished, and without a word to James, he stood up, walked over to me, and embraced me.

"Ken," he said, "I apologize for losing it. It's just that I've admired this man all my life, and in the middle of the song, I looked over and saw little Taylor listening"—Garth had brought his son along—"and I realized that this was the man he was named for, and it got to me."

Later that day, I brought them to the stage and they rehearsed the number twice before I stopped it. You can't over-rehearse these things, they lose the spark.

And then that night, in front of 6000 people and millions more on television, Garth and James earned a standing ovation from a crowd who found the same "moment" that we had seen only ten hours earlier that day.

While Garth's Grammy performance was one of the highlights of the show, we didn't do hip-hop or the show any favors by having Digable Planets perform. I had loved the record "Rebirth of Slick (Cool Like Dat)" very much, and they had been named to a number of critics' "Best" lists at the end of the previous year, but they were an act that I should have seen perform live before I booked them. They did a reasonably credible performance, lost the Best New Artist Grammy to Toni Braxton right after, and within six months to a year, disappeared. Every once in awhile when I listen to a classic hip-hop station, the song comes on and I wonder whatever became of the act. I'd like to think their influences are felt in acts like Outkast and the Black Eyed Peas, but I doubt that those acts would agree.

Aretha Franklin showed up and despite the fact that we gave her 2:15 to perform "Natural Woman" as part of her Lifetime Achievement Award segment, lit up the house. Her acceptance speech, as usual, was Aretha at her best, thanking all the right people for all the right reasons. Later in the show, the world-class string trio of Itzhak Perlman, Pinchas Zukerman, and Lynn Harrell gave us one of those rare audience-appealing classical segments with a Beethoven String Trio. It came close to earning a standing ovation, but it might have just been too much for some of our guests to get up again.

It was all coming down to the last award, which we had decided would be Album of the Year, rather than Record, to accommodate Sting's performance near the end of the show. We had performed three of the nominees, Sting, Billy, and Whitney, but the R.E.M. album and the Steely Dan albums were also in the running—albeit long shots. Bonnie Raitt and Lena Horne read the nominees and to no one's real shock, America and the world heard *The Bodyguard* for the eighth time. In true Clive

Davis fashion, he came to the stage in what will undoubtedly remain one of the highlights of his life. He had fashioned the album with a patchwork of artists, producers, arrangers, and writers, and—with Whitney at the top—had created one of the great soundtracks of all time. It has gone on to be the biggest-selling soundtrack ever, and though a number of the artists on it have not followed up with anything to match it, it remains a great record with this fragile combination of uptempo R&B mixed with power ballads.

It was Whitney's year—hell, it was Whitney's decade, and my only hope is that I'll be able to say that again.

CHAPTER 17

The 1995 Grammy Awards

Bruce Reunites with the E Street Band

If anyone were to ask you to name the Record or Album of the Year Grammy from pretty much any year, you'd be hard pressed to do so. Although the award is certainly the most important honor one can receive in the record industry (have you ever heard anyone introduced with, "Please welcome American Music Award winner") the simple fact is that careers are made or enhanced by *performances* on the Grammys, at least as much as the awards themselves. That is not to downplay the importance of winning, but whenever we find ourselves out with people talking about the Grammy Awards, it's often about the performances and the moments that surround them.

The 1995 show was no exception. Nominated for Album were old friends Eric Clapton, Tony Bennett, and Bonnie Raitt, our new friend Seal (of whom I was and remain a great fan), and the Three Tenors. The Record category included Sheryl Crow, Boyz II Men, Bonnie Raitt, Bruce Springsteen, and Mary Chapin Carpenter—all people with whom we had worked in the past year. So I was beginning to be torn not only about booking, but also about which of these acts I really hoped would take home the Grammys. The job calls for objectivity and mindfulness of what's best for the show, and I'm proud of the fact that over the years, I've never let my personal choices get in the way.

Except when it comes to Bruce, that is. We had finally succeeded in warming him up to the Grammys the previous year when he took part in the Curtis Mayfield segment and had a great time, and now with five nominations, most of which were for "Streets of Philadelphia," from the Tom Hanks picture. It was a great song, certainly one of Bruce's darkest, but also one of his best. And I can't tell you how surprised I was when Bruce's manager, Jon Landau, called me before I reached him to tell me that Bruce was ready to sing. It was the call I had been waiting

20 years for, and the irony of it occurring two decades after the John Hammond show I had done in Chicago that Bruce had wanted to be a part of was not lost on me.

I was sort of torn as to whether to open or close the show with Bruce's performance. There's an unwritten television law that you open these shows "up," and whatever you might say about "Philadelphia," "up" doesn't come to mind. As much as I try to keep the Academy people out of the sequencing of the show, when they heard my plan to open the show with the song, they weren't happy. But over the years we had built up a certain amount of trust, and they went along with it.

When the show opened that night and revealed Bruce, Roy Bittan, Garry Tallent, and Max Weinberg from the E Street Band (in itself a coup since Bruce had not yet decided to go on tour with them as he would a few years later), there were gasps in the house. The audience knew that Bruce would perform, but no one expected us to open the show with that performance. And Bruce delivered. If the record contained so much of the honest emotion that few artists other than Bruce can capture in his recordings, then the live version, the first time it had ever been performed before an audience, was electric.

When Annie Lennox and George Michael read Bruce's name moments later as the winner of the Grammy for Song of the Year, it was the first of three awards Bruce would win that night for "Streets of Philadelphia." His acceptance speech, as every speech Bruce ever delivers, belied the kind of gruff, raw rock 'n' roll image that he projects onstage. It was eloquent, introspective, but most of all honest.

"This is for the folks who have come up to me in restaurants and on the street who have lost their sons or their lovers or their friends to AIDS and said the song meant something to them."

Nothing more needed to be said, but I was certainly looking forward to seeing Bruce return to the podium a couple of more times that night. And he came back once more, but not to claim the big prize of the night, the Grammy for Record of the Year.

That honor went to Sheryl Crow, a singer/songwriter whose career I had watched since she sang backup for Don Henley, and whose manager, Scooter Weintraub, had asked me to come and see her at the Club

Lingerie one rainy night in 1993.

She was next up on the show after Bruce, and her performance set up the two Grammys she would win on the show almost too perfectly. After the nominations were read by Adam Sandler, Paul Reiser, and Liz Phair, Sheryl heard her name read for Best New Artist, rushed from backstage to the podium and gushed her acceptance speech with tears in her eyes.

Nearly three hours later, Sheryl's name was read once again for Record of the Year, and she came to the stage once more to deliver the final acceptance speech of the night. Earlier, we had performed four of the five nominees, Boyz II Men, Bruce, Bonnie, and of course Sheryl, and after she and Bruce had ping-ponged wins, it looked as though one of the two of them would take the Grammy for Record. Personally, I was torn. I loved "Streets of Philadelphia," and thought that "I'll Make Love to You" was a great pop song (and it had set the record for the longest time at No. 1 on the charts), and I really liked both the Bonnie and Sheryl songs.

The choice of Sheryl echoed through the music industry for weeks. Bruce was clearly the favorite, and even though he won four Grammys that night, the big one had eluded him once again. The same criticism, but perhaps even stronger, followed the Album of the Year choice.

We had performed Bonnie's "Love Sneakin Up on You," the title track from her Album nomination, immediately preceding the category, but I didn't feel as though she would win. Seal's performance earlier in the show was great, and there was a lot of heat around him. He was also a "Grammy type," musically accessible and personally very appealing. Tony Bennett was also nominated, and had performed an appealing version of "Moonglow" with k.d. lang earlier in the show. I didn't give that album much of a chance at all.

The fourth nominee was the Three Tenors, and I just couldn't imagine a classical album winning for Album of the Year, even though it had racked up huge sales. And finally, Clapton's *From the Cradle*, which we had done two shows about late in 1994, was nominated and I felt it was not only a great album, but also a strong contender for the Album of the Year award.

When Vince Gill and Anita Baker read the nominations, I was standing backstage with Bonnie, who had already told me that she was rooting for Eric's tribute to the great bluesmen of the past, and didn't expect to hear her name called. But I don't think she ever thought she'd hear Tony Bennett's name read.

Looking back these many years later, it made some sense. The combination of Tony's performances on two previous Grammy shows, coupled with the MTV embracing of him with an *Unplugged*, and the masterful work of Tony's son Danny, had created a threshold that was unique in the music business to that time. Here was a 70-year-old classic singer, whose career had begun in the '40s and whose appeal now crossed over every segment of the music business, strolling to the stage to accept the highest honor of the year. His speech was touching, and when he came offstage, we embraced and he whispered something to me that I'll always remember.

He never forgot about *The Marty Faye Show* in Chicago in the '60s where we had met, and though Marty was gone, Tony knew what he had meant to me, and obviously to him.

"This would have made Marty very happy, Ken. It's a good time to think about him now."

⌐

As we approached the end of the show, everything seemed to be going well. The winners were popular favorites, the performances were scoring, and though Paul Reiser wasn't the best host we had ever had, he was carrying the load well. And then it began to unravel.

Staging any of the multi-artist shows we do, but particularly the Grammys, is tremendously difficult and complex. Lighting has to be changed in between numbers and sets need to roll on and off to support the performers—sometimes entire groups of musicians, from four-man rock groups to full symphony orchestras. And while the microphones and amps are all pre-cabled and linked to their proper sources to feed sound to the audio truck, the movement that takes place with stagehands rushing them on and offstage sometimes takes its toll on those connections. We usually use the time during commercials to do one quick sound check to make certain that everything is connected and the truck is getting the sound that must go to three separate places: the back of the house for sound in the house, the monitor mix position to feed the right things to the artists, and the audio truck, which does the final mix for the live show on television. All of these things are critical, and though that's what rehearsals and the dress rehearsal are for, as I've said before, the one time it all needs to work is the final performance on the show. Sometimes the gods are with you, and sometimes they're not.

The acts move onstage on platforms, "wagons" we call them, with the instruments and amplifiers and monitors placed so that all that needs to be done is for them to be plugged in, tested, and then played. During the commercial before Bonnie Raitt's performance, everything moved on in its allotted four minutes, we did a quick sound check, and then Paul Reiser moved to his host position to introduce Bonnie. But from my offstage position, I saw that something was wrong. Bonnie's amp, a relic that had seen thousands of hours of playing time, went out, and though I watched our audio team—looking like a team of surgeons doing brain surgery—no matter what they did, they couldn't get it to work.

Paul jumped in and tried to vamp to cover the delay, but he was fast running out of material. Though he had been a stand-up comic, to stand out in front of those millions of people and hold the audience was tough, even though we always had material standing by. Although it was only a three-minute delay, it seemed like hours, and by the time Bonnie started, the show was already about four minutes over the three-hour allotted time.

Having something like this happen early in the show is bad, but having it happen near the end of the show is a disaster. We pace ourselves over the three hours, losing time in some presentations, picking it up with others, trying to stay within two or three minutes on either side of being right on time. And there's no one with a more masterful sense of the clock than my friend Walter Miller. But now we were way over, with very little show left to pick it up. And to make matters worse, though Bonnie's performance was the last category to be performed, we had done something that we seldom do on the show: we had scheduled a finale that featured Luther Vandross with Crosby, Stills, and Nash doing "Love the One You're With." Luther had been nominated for the song that year, and of course it seemed like a great idea to have them perform it together as a tag to the show.

I had laid out the number so that it began with CSN doing a couple of minutes on their own, and then surprising the audience by having Luther come out and join them, singing his own two verses and choruses at the end.

All Luther had asked of me was to make sure that he got on the broadcast, and I had assured him that whatever I had to do, he'd make it. And until Bonnie's amp went out, we were in good shape.

We even skipped the goodnights, trying to buy ourselves another minute of show time, and got right into "Love the One You're With." CSN were great, singing perfect harmonies with Stephen delivering a great guitar solo. But as I looked at my watch, we were dangerously close to going over, and we had been getting ever-increasing pressure from CBS every year about not doing that. Luther walked onstage, got about four lines of his verse out, and the CBS network left us to go to local news all over the country.

There was nothing to do but to go out onstage and tell Luther what had happened, and I did. I have a great fondness for Luther, and he's been there for me on countless shows. He's also a very sensitive human being, and I knew this was not going to sit easy. And it didn't. He stormed off, ran to his dressing room, and wouldn't speak to me. It took nearly a year for me to get back in his good graces, and I still feel awful about what happened. It's the only time in over 20 years that a performance didn't make it on the Grammys.

Probably the most important thing to come out of this particular Grammy show was less related to the show and more related to the Academy. Though few could quibble with the Springsteen nominations and the Springsteen win, and the Clapton *From the Cradle* Album nomination was widely recognized, the nominations for the Three Tenors, the Tony Bennett win for Album of the Year, and the Sheryl Crow win for "All I Wanna Do" raised a furor among critics, labels, and the fans alike.

The New York Times article was typical of those written around the country and said that the Grammys had long been accused of being out of touch, but this year, many top-ranked executives in the music industry "have also turned against them." *The Los Angeles Times* was even rougher. There were rumors of labels threatening to withdraw support for the Academy, and stories about them trying to push the other awards shows as opposed to the Grammys, and it really hit home.

Not unmindful of this criticism, Mike Greene came out publicly and quickly—answering the criticism by saying that the Academy was going to respond by looking into a new process that would be more responsive not only to public taste but also to the Academy's basic mandate to recognize excellence. At the production company, we had similar reactions as we talked to friends within and outside the industry after the show, but we had been limited to no input into the nominations process. All we could do was echo what we were hearing on the street, and hope that the Academy would be able to correct what for years had been a flawed process.

Soon after the show, Mike announced a process whereby the general membership would submit works for the top four awards, but that the final list would be chosen from the top 20 contenders by a blue-ribbon committee that would review the nominations and decide which five would become the final nominees in those categories. Those five would then be voted on by the full membership. My belief was that this was more than just a stopgap effort to stem the bad press the Academy had taken, and that time would tell as to whether or not the new process would result in a more responsive and more critically acceptable group of nominees. And as the years went by, and the committee became more of a factor, there's no question that it would make a big difference in the Academy's credibility, and by virtue of that, the credibility of the television show.

Maybe the competition was especially rough that night, maybe there just wasn't a great deal of interest in the music of the year, and just maybe it was because late in the show we featured both a jazz and a classical performance (two categories always lobbied for by their respective proponents), but whatever the reason, the show had the lowest ratings of any Grammy show to date, racking up a lame 11.8 rating with a 19 share. To that point, no Grammy show had ever reached less than 22 percent of the viewing audience, and however we chose to spin it, the simple fact was that this show just didn't have the appeal to viewers that we thought it would.

It's so hard to quantify the numbers for any given show. The simple fact is not that the show didn't hold over its three-hour time slot, which is usually consistent from year to year, but that the viewers just didn't come to the party when the show opened. In retrospect, when two of the five nominations for album of the year skew as old as they did (Tony Bennett and the Three Tenors), you don't have a lot going for you youthwise. This was even one of the few years in the entire Grammy/AMA competition where the American Music Awards beat the Grammys—a figure Dick Clark would hold up to us for years.

CHAPTER 18

The 1996 Grammy Awards

A Special Night for Alanis Morissette

One of the things we do on occasion on the Grammy show is to take a major category and perform all five nominees in an attempt to set up the "horse race" that can carry us through the show and keep viewers around for three hours. Unlike dramatic shows or situation comedies that have a beginning, middle, and end, award shows are non-linear, and running the category is our way of creating tension and hopefully sustaining interest in the show from beginning to end.

Since we had no clear frontrunner for the 1996 show, having all the performers for Record of the Year seemed like a great idea, particularly since all five nominations represented different types of musical experiences. "One Sweet Day" by Mariah Carey and Boyz II Men had recently passed BIIM's "End of the Road" as the longest-running single at No. 1 on the charts, and it was a huge teen favorite, combining two of the biggest acts in music on one song; Seal's "Kiss from a Rose" was not only a big single, but it had come from one of the biggest soundtracks (and movies) of the year, *Batman Returns*; TLC's "Waterfalls" captured a great urban feel with a message that was universal to all teenagers and had enjoyed more airplay than nearly any other song that year; "Gangsta's Paradise" was a powerful statement about gang violence that not only masqueraded in an accessible ballad form but also sampled an old Stevie Wonder track "Pastime Paradise," thus connecting with several layers of music fans; and Joan Osborne's quirky "One of Us" had become an MTV/VH1 favorite among mid-to-late-20s listeners, an elusive and extremely desirable music audience.

All of the elements of a great race were there, and we set about booking all five nominees, knowing that we could spread them out over the three hours of the show and, if the stars were right, we'd have a great story to tell about the music of 1995.

Each performance was different and compelling in its own way.

We opened the show with Mariah and Boyz II Men, and the extraordinary vocals of the Philly-based group blended so beautifully with Mariah's amazing range that our initial risk in once again opening the show with a ballad turned into a plus—a number that scored both in the house and at home. It was also a song whose simplicity connected with an audience on a number of levels, a fact we had learned while watching it several times several months earlier when we had shot a Boyz II Men concert special that aired right at the end of the previous year.

The second Record of the Year performance took place almost an hour into the show when TLC performed "Waterfalls" in the middle of an elaborate set that hid rather than highlighted the tentative vocals of the three girls, who had found themselves as much the subject of tabloid stories as stories about their musical accomplishments. This was also a rare performance where we allowed the use of backing tracks and "mixed" vocals (in which prerecorded vocals were mixed in with live onstage performance vocals). It was more or less against Grammy policy to do so, but we made a special provision when the number was essentially a dance number, and this one was ostensibly more dance than vocals. Remember, this was at the very beginning of the time when major acts began going out on tour doing the very same thing. Although it wasn't right, we briefly convinced ourselves that we were doing the right thing. We don't do it anymore. In any event, the performance seemed to score with the house, the girls were adorable, and we got away with it.

For the second year in a row, Seal delivered a solid performance of a solid song, and got a standing ovation for "Kiss from a Rose," the third Record of the Year nomination of the five we performed. And Joan Osborne's performance of "One of Us" was effective, if not electric.

The dazzler, and the one least expected on a Grammy show, was Coolio's "Gangsta's Paradise." Not only was the staging sensational with Coolio being suspended above an ever-changing scene of humanity staged to follow the song on the deck, but Coolio's lead vocalist, L.V., backed by a gospel choir, elevated the track to greatness, and by the end of the number the vast majority of the Grammy viewers, who had probably never seen Coolio, were converted. It was also the most interesting song of the five nominations, and there was a time leading up to the show where I seriously thought it might win for Record.

By the time the names of the five nominees for Record of the Year were read near the end of the show, there was no runaway winner, and in fact, upsets galore made predicting Record and Album almost impossible.

Mariah and Boyz II Men had been shut out, as had Joan Osborne; TLC had only won one R&B award, as had Coolio, and Seal seemed to be the big winner, with both Song of the Year and Pop Male Vocal Performance already in his pocket. Joni Mitchell, who had pulled off one of the major surprises of the night earlier by winning Best Pop Album, a new category, presented the Record of the Year award with Vince Gill. They recapped the category, opened the envelope, and announced Seal's name, who joyously came to the stage for his acceptance speech. His was a wonderful and warm speech, and although he alluded to his background, he never talked about his homelessness or his rough road to success over the previous ten years.

And if the Grammy for Record of the Year was an unpredictable contest, it was matched by the race for Album of the Year. The Academy's new policy of having a blue-ribbon committee take the top 20 vote-getters in the major categories and reduce them to the five finalists seemed to be paying off in the quality of the nominations. Pearl Jam had its first nomination in a major category, Joan Osborne picked up an album nod, Mariah's *Daydream*, as poppy as it was, demonstrated great vocals and some strong arrangements, and Alanis Morissette's critically acclaimed and very popular *Jagged Little Pill* made the list. Only the Michael Jackson anthology *HIStory* was suspect as a nominee for Album of the Year, but because of Michael's history and mixture of old and new on the album, it could certainly qualify.

If there was a standout performance on the 1996 show, it was Alanis's "You Oughta Know." For a short while after the nominations came out, it looked as though we might not have her at all. Although it barely exists today, for many years those artists who cried "integrity" were often torn about performing on the show. As hard as it is to believe (people in the business are constantly telling me how "easy" it must be to book the Grammys because everyone wants to do it), we still encounter Grammy backlash, and Alanis was one of those artists who agonized over whether or not she should perform on the show. (I must publicly thank Bruce Springsteen, Madonna, and Eric Clapton, all of whom went through the "too hip for the Grammys" period, for agreeing to come on the show and break down those barriers over the years.)

Alanis ultimately agreed, and we set about the very difficult task of trying to satisfy her very real feeling that we should be true to her as an artist. It involved numerous conversations with her people and was never really resolved until she came in for her own rehearsal two days before the show.

And it didn't finally end until viewers actually saw her onstage on the night of the show.

Normally, when an artist agrees to do the show, and we've collectively decided on the performance, we work from the CD to design a look and break the music down for cameras. It nearly always follows, although there are numerous times when arrangements change, the form of the song changes, and we rethink things. But none of us were prepared for the version of "You Oughta Know" that we saw for the first time when Alanis came in for her rehearsal.

Instead of the intense angry version of the song that had become a huge radio and MTV hit, Alanis brought a passion to her live performance that, without in any way compromising the meaning or message of the song, added a whole new spin. It was now done slower, sparer, almost empty—and when it was quiet, it was a whole new quiet.

The set that we had constructed to support the performance had an intensity to it that no longer worked with the new arrangement. There were colors on the set, not bright, but certainly no match for the drama that accompanied the performance. We knew it, and Alanis knew it.

We stood at the side of the stage during the rehearsal, knowing that the look needed to change. Scott Welch, Alanis's manager, stood with me and watched my face drop as I watched the first time she sang the song. He looked at me, I looked at him, and within ten minutes we had figured it out.

No more bright colors, no more lit towers. Instead, we asked our scenic designer to go out find some candelabras and some muted oriental rugs, and to drape the set with them, bringing the light levels down to a minimum.

Bobby Dickinson took most of the front light off Alanis and her musicians and replaced them with subtle back and side lighting that added to the drama of the look. And Walter adjusted his shooting pattern to stay much tighter and closer on the performer instead of featuring the other musicians who had been present on the track but were now very secondary to the performance.

We took a significant step closer to what went on the air at the dress rehearsal, but there were still tweaks to make, and the only time left to make them was on the air on show night. The song became even more about the woman and her song, and with a single spot highlighting her from one side, the performance went up another notch.

Coming as it did as we crossed the first hour of the show, it seemed to have even greater impact on the audience, and the whole tenor of the show for that matter, and no one was surprised or unhappy when a Grammy goddess, Bonnie Raitt, announced Alanis as the winner of the Best Pop Female Vocal award moments after her performance.

But if no one was surprised at Alanis's win in the Female Pop Vocal category, there were plenty of surprised expressions when she took the Album of the Year Grammy. In retrospect, it was a win waiting to happen, and if there were any non-believers before the show, her virtuoso performance dispelled nearly all of their doubts.

⌇

Hootie and the Blowfish performed and were then named Best New Artists, thereby continuing a jinx that has claimed the careers of more than half the Best New Artist winners over the years. A second album, lower sales, a third still lower, and then, other than the occasional charity golf tournament in which we see Darius Rucker, *off the charts*. And the truth is that they were a pretty good bar band who had catchy sound who had caught a couple of hits at a time when there was a dearth of pretty good bar bands making records. But then again, who lost that year? Well, starting at the top: Shania Twain and Alanis Morissette, who would go on to become two of the top-selling female artists of the decade. Then there was Brandy, who had a pretty good career going for a number of years, and finally Joan Osborne, a hippie throwback who probably would have challenged Joni Mitchell for some pretty introspective songwriting and musicality if she had been around 20 years earlier. But that's kind of the way it is with the Grammys, not to mention the music business. You don't exist in a vacuum, and the tabloid shows and public awareness of the music charts put it all on a competitive level, and it always seems to be related to sales and not creative output.

A curious phenomenon, that Best New Artist category. Over the years it had undoubtedly had a positive effect on artists like Christina Aguilera, Sheryl Crow, Mariah Carey, Natalie Cole, Carly Simon, and Bette Midler, but the flip side were acts like Paula Cole, Arrested Development, Men At Work, the Starland Vocal Band, and A Taste of Honey who never recovered from being named Best New Artist. I never like to generalize, but it certainly seems that unlike some other Grammy categories that not only propel sales but also have an influence in career building, the BNA win is a more fleeting thing.

If we missed any beats that year, it was a shortage of great rock performances. In a year that saw nominations for U2, the Eagles, Nine Inch Nails, Pearl Jam, and Alice in Chains, we saw fit to celebrate rock with Hootie, and it was a big miss for us. We'd try and make up for it in coming years, but we were also seeing the end of an extremely fertile period in rock and the arrival of one of the more fallow musical periods, a trend that always seemed to me to be like the waves on the ocean—with us continually waiting for the big one. And it would come, but first we had to go through some reasonably bad hip-hop, some teen pop divas, and some overly choreographed and underwhelming boy bands.

Before I close the chapter on this particular Grammy show, I should mention Ellen DeGeneres. We had booked Ellen the year after she hosted the first *VH1 Honors show*, primarily because her show on ABC was beginning to generate some heat, but for me, it was more because she got the music. She was a fan, had a real love for everything from rock to rap, and brought a real feeling of the fan to her role as a host. Additionally, we did some very clever backstage pieces with her, pieces that later found their way onto the Emmy show, which she hosted later that same year. She was terrific, and she helped make this show a big score. The ratings were up 24 percent over the previous year, scoring a 14.6/23. The reviews were good as well, declaring the show "the best telecast in years," an homage that I was getting tired of hearing, since it seemed to reflect on the previous year which was usually also called "the best telecast in years." I began to figure that by calling the show "the best telecast in years," they could praise with faint damn, as opposed to the alternative.

But even before the final playoff for the Record of the Year had echoed into history, I was already thinking about the coming year, and the challenge that lay ahead in taking the show from theater-sized venues like the Shrine and Radio City Music Hall, and lifting it into the most important arena in the world, Madison Square Garden. As we made our way from party to party and folks complimented us on many of the performances, my mind was already thinking about the playground we'd have in New York just 12 months away.

CHAPTER 19

The 1997 Grammy Awards

The Grammys Go to The Garden

Minute for minute, the 1997 Grammy show, the first award show ever to come from a venue as large as Madison Square Garden, was one of our greatest triumphs. From the opening performance, Eric Clapton and Babyface's duet on "Change the World," to the final one, a soaring full-stage medley of songs from *Waiting to Exhale* with Whitney Houston, Mary J. Blige, Brandy, and Cece Winans, we rocked the rafters of the Garden and put an exclamation point to the fact that the biggest music show of the year belonged in a venue that seated 15,000 people.

And it probably would have been the perfect show for Walter and me were it not for what we have come to call "Ellen's Grammy Song Incident" that nearly derailed the proceedings, and made for one of the most uncomfortable live experiences we've ever had. Looking back on it, it was all so unnecessary.

I had worked with Ellen DeGeneres on the *VH1 Honors* show we did in 1995, and she was great. She had a great love and knowledge of music, and brought a fan's perspective along with a great sense of comedy. On the VH1 show, prior to her hosting the Emmys later that year (I got a call from Don Mischer, the producer of the Emmys, about two days after the VH1 show aired, looking for Ellen's number), she came up with a series of backstage bits that were self-deprecating and hilarious, including one that involved Stevie Wonder.

On the VH1 show, before going to commercial, the camera found her backstage standing next to Stevie, who on cue "looked" down at Ellen's shoes and casually remarked, "Those shoes don't go with that dress," a line fed to him by Ellen. Her look of surprise broke up the live audience who saw it on a big screen in the house, and that piece, coupled with a scene in which she went into Melissa Etheridge's dressing room and broke her guitar, were hysterical. She was a huge hit and an easy choice to host the Grammys the following year, particularly since her sitcom had become a ratings hit for ABC.

Her first year as host was a success: she steadied the ship, fit in well with all the talent, and moved the show along with wit and personality. It was a no-brainer to sign her up to come back again this year.

Ellen put her heart into the show, just as she had done the year before. She even helped pull together Bonnie Raitt, Shawn Colvin, Melissa Etheridge, and a couple of other "girls" to perform an opening number, generously called "Ellen's Grammy Song." And though she was very open about what she was doing, the number didn't come together until a rehearsal the day before the show in a rehearsal room at the Garden, and because Walter and I were in the middle of on-camera rehearsals, neither of us saw it then.

Had we known what we were in for, and had we had an opportunity to see it earlier, we might have asked her to change the number. It was a very different opening from the normal comic monologue that is common to these shows, but because it had a musical base, I really liked the idea even without having seen it. As is customary, it really couldn't be rehearsed until she had all the women together, and since Walter and I both share an abiding faith in talent, we didn't see any problem with what she was doing.

This time out, however, our judgment was marred by Mike Greene's negativity about the concept and what we felt was his lack of faith in both our production team and Ellen. When it finally hit the stage during the dress rehearsal on show day, even though it wasn't the greatest number I'd ever seen, it was definitely a step aside; people love Ellen, the talent pool was impressive, and I didn't really have any question but that she'd pull it off. Was it Prince and Beyoncé? No, but it was an attempt to do something a little different on the show, and I felt that was a good thing.

Mike and the Grammy TV Committee felt otherwise. After it was rehearsed, right at the top of the dress rehearsal, I found myself surrounded by Mike and certain committee members who—with the pressure of the dress rehearsal hanging over me—wanted to know right then and there what I was going to do about the number, which they hated. I told them that my priority was to get through the dress, after which we'd have a rational discussion and I'd think about what we should do. Both Walter and I knew that this was a number that we could live with: it had certain values, and it was a much safer solution to let it go on the air than to confront Ellen three hours before a live show and possibly shake her up. It just wasn't worth the risk, I had already decided during the dress, but I waited until we finished to meet and discuss this with Mike.

I had already decided that it wasn't worth putting the rest of the show in jeopardy over this number, but I wanted to wait until the dress was over and Mike saw the balance of the show, and how great some of the other numbers were. In my mind, I thought maybe this would blow over by that time, and we could just move on to making a great show.

But at the dinner break, two hours before air, it resurfaced, with a now-enraged Mike telling us that the number had to go, and that "someone" had to go to Ellen right now and tell her that she should replace it with a monologue. I kept looking around for some support to fight this callous decision, but no one did, so Walter and I left the production office and headed down one flight of stairs to where Ellen's dressing room was, knowing this was not going to be pretty. The reader might reasonably ask why I didn't just stand up to Mike and tell him no. The simple answer is that Mike was not the kind of person you could reason with. Threatened, he would lash out, and the situation could have become even more dire.

When we walked into Ellen's dressing room, it was filled with her people, and Ellen was already doing hair and makeup. We had to stand under the harsh light of the makeup table and tell her that the song was out, and that either she should do a short monologue or, sensing that would shake her even more, we would just do a couple of paragraphs at the top and then proceed to the first award. The next thing I knew we were asked to leave the dressing room and wait outside, that her manager would have an answer for us.

Not two minutes later, they came outside with this simple statement.

"We're going to tell the press that Ellen took sick and couldn't do the show in our press release, what are you going to say?"

I was stunned, but not altogether surprised. And in a perverse way, I was happy that she had stood up to this. I knew that at the end of the day, what Walter and I could never have accomplished with Mike, would be accepted when coming from talent. As we walked back upstairs to deliver the news, I said to Walter, "Don't worry, this is now a done deal."

We walked into the production office armed with Ellen's decision, and we convinced cooler heads to prevail. We returned to Ellen's dressing room, asked to see her but were denied, and delivered the news that in fact, "Ellen's Grammy Song" would open the show.

Traditionally, during the show I divide my time between the performing talent—giving them last-minute face-to-face thank yous and a few comforting words before they perform—and the host, going over copy. But that night, Ellen surrounded herself with "her people," and I knew I wasn't welcome anywhere near her. And I knew that even if I could talk to her, it would only have been a reminder of a most unpleasant situation. So I stayed away.

To her credit, she went out and did a terrific job, funny, on target, hosting a show in a comic's nightmare, in front of a packed arena.

But after her goodnights, she walked straight out of the Garden into a waiting car and was gone. It would be almost two years before we would talk, and though in recent years we've become friends again, she never again accepted our invitation to come back and host the show. It's a shame, because she was so good at it and would have been a great permanent host for the show.

And though the show went on to become an extremely memorable one for viewers, unfortunately whenever I think of it, it's hard to get past the drama of one of the most difficult few minutes in my Grammy career.

⌒

The show itself was filled with performances that reflected the year's somewhat predictable nominations, but added colors and layers that reached beyond them. Of the fourteen performances on the stage that night, three remain with me as examples of the kind of things we can do on the Grammys that just can't be done on any other show.

The first, and probably the most newsworthy, was a five-minute medley that ended with an amazing dance-off between Savion Glover from "Bring in 'da Noise Bring in 'da Funk" and Colin Dunne, the principal dancer from *Riverdance*. The story of how it came about and how it played is interesting in itself.

I had seen both shows earlier in the season and loved them both. U2's manager, Paul McGuinness, was a backer of *Riverdance* and had been telling me about how remarkable the production was, not to mention the dance itself. When we saw it for ourselves, we realized how indescribable it really was, and why Paul was unable to convey the look of the show. Knowing that we were going to be doing the show at the Garden where we needed the size and scope of filling the stage gave us even more incentive to move toward putting a number from it on the Grammys. The company was excited about performing, and within days of the nomination, we had firmed up the booking.

"Bring in 'da Noise" was another thing entirely. The Grammy committee would have been happy with just the *Riverdance* performance, but it was clear to both Walter and me that the juxtaposition of the precision dance of the Irish show played against the street feel of "Noise" would make for an incredible piece on the Grammys, and we set up a meeting downtown with the show's producer, George Wolfe, to talk about it. Initially, he was not positive, but he came around and became very supportive as we laid out the number that would bring the two shows together at the Garden.

We had worked with Savion previously on a couple of projects, and would see him again later in the year when we would do his ABC Special, *Savion Glover's Nu York* (still one of my favorite unwatched TV specials).

I knew he'd relish the idea of a dance-off with Colin Dunne, but also knew his work ethic wouldn't sit well with Dunne, whose feeling about rehearsals and preplanning everything to the second matched the style of dance in the show.

It became one of the stranger pairings I've ever done, and it wasn't helped when Savion showed up two hours late for the pair's only off-site rehearsal ten days before the show. Although the *Riverdance* people had agreed to the short, two-minute dance-off, they put numerous conditions on the performance, insisting that Colin lead it off and Savion follow, and further, that they would have approval over everything in the number, including Savion's dance.

I reluctantly agreed, feeling that once the two principals got together, they would find the common art of dance as something that would bond them. I was wrong. Savion's free style and desire not to repeat the same steps twice in the duet seemed to throw Colin off kilter, and even in the dress rehearsal, I had the frightening feeling that the *Riverdance* people were going to come to me and call the whole thing off.

Fortunately they didn't, and the fireworks of the little duet, coupled with great performances from each of the two companies, created one of those rare moments that exemplify the Grammys. Colin's polite entrance at the top of the number only seemed to challenge Savion's street savvy even more, and his entire first routine was directed totally at Colin, watching off to the side. Colin finally got it, and fought back in his second routine, and by the time they reached the pre-arranged 45 seconds of dancing together, it was a catfight. Who won depends on who you ask, but if you ask me, everybody was a winner—especially the Grammy show.

～

Beck, along with Smashing Pumpkins and No Doubt, were three acts that probably wouldn't have even been nominated in their categories, let alone asked to perform on the show, prior to the institution of the Academy's new screening committee, which took the top vote-getters in the major categories and then "judged" them to reach the finals. In the years since it was instituted it has allowed the show, which is reflective of the nominations, to move miles ahead of what it had once been, simply a reflection of popular taste with a mandate to include classical and jazz every year. For all the criticism that Mike Greene has received over the years, it will probably prove to be his greatest legacy not only to the Academy, but for the betterment of the music industry as a whole. It's allowed artists who have achieved a certain measure of credibility as well as popularity (like Beck) to reach the final voting process and in several cases, receive the acclaim that accompanies Grammy recognition.

The Pumpkins scored with a great version of "1979" complete with a set that looked 50 years ahead of its time. Although in past years we had begun to add more and more production to the show, the vastness of the Garden almost demanded that we surround some of the acts with looks that gave them more size and scope. With Billy Corgan and D'arcy

Wretzky-Brown stalking the stage like animals, the performance had a great feel to it, although it was bittersweet for at least one of my favorite Grammy people. Mike Melvoin, who was not only active on the television committee but also involved nearly every year with some of the musical issues—playing occasionally and working on the jazz segments each year—had lost his son Jonathan, a Pumpkins member, earlier in the year. It was a very difficult moment for Mike and his wife Sandi to accept our embracing of the band to perform, and I paid particular attention to Mike as we moved through the show with the band.

The '97 show was filled with other standout moments, not the least of which was Clapton's opening number "Change the World." Three years after "Tears in Heaven," Eric had returned with the haunting song, produced and featuring a great guitar accompaniment by Kenny "Babyface" Edmonds. Babyface was nominated in 12 categories, including Producer of the Year, which he was to win. And "Change the World" would be honored with Record of the Year, Eric's second win in that category.

The performance was haunting, and marred only by Eric's speech following being awarded Best Male Pop Vocal Performance, which we put right after they appeared. As he approached the podium he said, in his usual dry, English manner, "I feel this is kind of rigged. I sing the song and I get the prize." The audience laughed, but I couldn't. Our handicapping, which in earlier days was based on the belief that viewers wanted to see a win after a performance, was beginning to wear thin, and even though we didn't know the winners, our track record was beginning to look a little too good. I began to think it was now time to start mixing up the categories rather than have the perception that we knew the winners, which we never did.

⌐⌐

As you've learned earlier, for many years Bruce Springsteen was not much of a believer in television, and not just the Grammys. He was one of the lone holdouts during the pre-MTV years, and it took a number of years for his manager Jon Landau to convince Bruce that MTV could help bring his music to a younger audience and still maintain Bruce's identity and integrity.

His virtuoso take of "Philadelphia" in 1994 was memorable, but it was his return visit to the show at Madison Square Garden in 1997 that joins my top ten. Not so much the performance, which was great, but the events surrounding it.

Bruce had recorded what he acknowledges to be one of his best albums, *The Ghost of Tom Joad*, a folk-oriented record that was filled with very personal material. It had not done particularly well saleswise, and when the Grammy nominations came out, it was only nominated in the Folk category, not a category which has found its way onto the performance side of the show very often. But Jon had the idea to appeal to Bruce on the basis of the Folk nomination. According to Jon, Bruce hemmed and hawed, jumping back and forth for weeks until about a week before the show when he made the decision not to perform.

On the Friday before the Wednesday show, we were already in New York for rehearsals and I joined Sheryl Crow's manager, Scooter Weintraub for a Sheryl show at Roseland. Standing downstairs in the crowded hallway stood a rather preoccupied Bruce with his wife Patti. There's kind of this unwritten rule that you don't talk directly to talent about business in social situations, and particularly in a situation where you could upset the manager, in this case one of the good guys. But the proximity was too inviting, and I took the moment and casually walked up to Bruce, made about two minutes' worth of small talk, and then said, "C'mon Bruce, I know you said you weren't going to do the show, but it's so important to present the Folk category, and it would be so amazing to see and hear "Tom Joad" that night. Think it over, I've still got a slot."

Well, number one, I didn't have a slot; the show was packed. Number two, I knew I had violated a rule by talking to talent without the manager present. And number three, there was no way Bruce was going to stand there with all of these people around and say, "Ken, that's a great idea. Why didn't I think of it first?"

And he didn't. I left thinking I had not only blown a relationship with Bruce by putting him in an awkward position, but also blown one with Jon, with whom I have a mutual trust to this day.

The next morning I got the call. Jon's sense of humor didn't let me down.

"So you talked to my client about doing the Grammys, huh? Ken, you know better than to do that, don't you?"

Vamp. Vamp. No right answer, but before I made an even dumber reply, Jon jumped in and said, "Ken, he'll do it. He told me he had this very pleasant conversation with you last night, and he thought about it. He'll be there."

We hastily scheduled a rehearsal time for him on the night before the show (see how things keep happening the night before the show?), and then Walter and I met with the various production departments to see how we could support Bruce's performance.

On the lighting side, I knew we were in great shape. Bob Dickinson is one of the true geniuses of our business, and all he had to hear was "Bruce Springsteen…ballad…alone on a stage with a guitar." He'd come up with something brilliant.

Bob Keene, our late scenic designer, was also brilliant, but sometimes his zeal and his commitment to support the show led him to do too much.

Now, with only three full days to pull something together, there wasn't much he could do, but he came up with a large circular ceiling piece that in years since has affectionately been called everything from "the Alka Seltzer" piece to Bruce's favorite term, "the spaceship."

I saw the drawing of the piece and both Walter and I questioned it, but Bob was very insistent that it would work. Some things are learned and others are instinctive, and I had that instinctive feeling that this wouldn't work, but also wanted to give Bob room to succeed or fail.

Cut to Bruce's arrival for rehearsal, and his walking to the stage to work. I saw his eyes turn skyward, but to his credit, nothing was said and the rehearsal went off in his usual professional manner. It was only afterward that Walter and I were called to Bruce's dressing room and he let us know with a mixture of humor and concern that he didn't like the piece. He was such a gentle man about it, and he was so right, that it only took a moment for us to turn on our friend Bob Keane, and dump it right then and there.

The performance the next night, minus the "spaceship," was compelling, and in that huge cavernous space, with dancers, bands, lights, and a lot of walloping stuff, Bruce Springsteen again demonstrated why he didn't need any of that to get the message across—when it comes right down to it, it's about the singer and his song.

Of course, it didn't hurt that he walked from backstage to the podium to accept his Grammy after the performance.

If there was any other major score for the show, it was the fact that an award show could not only be pulled off, but even pulled off with flair and style, in an arena. Various press releases referred to the scale of the show as utilizing 100 tons of equipment, over 100 stagehands to do the work, a million-dollar set, and other facts and figures with which they tried to quantify the effort. But the fact is that dozens of technical minds who handle audio, video, staging, lighting, and so on had all worked together with our creative group to bring a show to viewers that had size and scale, but also felt intimate when it wanted to be. A lonely stage with Bruce Springsteen alone singing "The Ghost of Tom Joad" could be as compelling as forty dancers who filled the same stage to perform a number from *Riverdance*. That's the beauty of the Grammys. It may have production galore, but when it comes down to it, we're still about the music, and if the music is right, it makes no difference how big the stage, how massive the venue, how distant the farthest person in the arena.

So the evening that had begun as a personal disaster for Walter and me (not to mention what we did to poor Ellen DeGeneres's psyche!) turned out to be a triumph. We had not only pulled off a giant show in a giant venue, we had delivered on our promise to create at least several moments that would become part of the Grammy legend, and, most significantly, had broken down some of the stereotypes about the Grammys old-ageism by performing and honoring some of the most exciting young acts around, and doing it well.

And as a postscript, when our turn came around to do the primetime Emmy Awards in 2005, and I went to Ellen to host a show other than the Grammys, she accepted our invitation and did a great job. It was great to work with her again after several years' absence, and I was thrilled that after the Emmys they called her to do the Academy Awards, fulfilling the dream that she had mentioned to me many years before when we first worked together on the *VH1 Honors* show.

CHAPTER 20

The 1998 Grammy Awards

Aretha Sings Opera; Soybomb Sings Dylan

"**O**K, if that's what you want."

Those words, spoken very quietly by Aretha Franklin in a cramped, hot, fourth-floor dressing room at Radio City Music Hall, on the night of the 40th Annual Grammy Awards, are the closest I can come to answering the question that I am most frequently asked—"What was the most tense moment in your career as a television producer?"

This is a tale of terror, unpredictability, and ultimately, the truly amazing grace of a woman whose anthem song "Respect" took on a new, and eternal meaning for me as a result of this one day in Grammy history.

Here's the situation: that afternoon at the dress rehearsal for the show, a tired but seemingly cooperative Luciano Pavarotti had worked his way through "Nessun Dorma," the operatic aria that we had all hoped would be the high point of a Grammy show that also contained performances by an amazing number of superstars, including Bob Dylan, Fleetwood Mac, Will Smith, and Stevie Wonder.

But now it was showtime, and Pavarotti hadn't returned from his Central Park West apartment. He was scheduled somewhere in the middle of our three-hour show, so although my unwritten rule is that all talent is in the house before we go on the air, I wasn't overly concerned. There were plenty of other things to worry about.

We were about an hour into the show when my assistant Ron Basile rushed up to me offstage with a hastily scrawled phone number for Pavarotti at home. I found a quiet phone deep in the depths of Radio City, took a breath, and made the call.

You know what's coming.

"Ken, I'm sick. I can't come and sing. I will sing for you next year, but what will you do now?"

"First, Luciano, I will get off the phone and try to figure out how to fill four-and-a-half minutes of the Grammy Awards when we're already a half-hour into it."

Said with less harshness than the words indicate in print, it was still a critical situation that needed to be dealt with—and fast. And I might add, in my 20-plus years of doing live television, though we had faced artists dropping in and out of shows prior to their airing, this was the first time I had ever faced an act canceling after the show was already on the air.

My first thoughts were random. You don't work with people for 20 years without creating some long-term relationships in the business—and the Music Hall was filled with many of those folks that night. Should I go to Sting (who was introducing Pavarotti, but not performing that night) and ask him to perform? Among the performances still left in the show was one by Fleetwood Mac, and I thought about going to Lindsey Buckingham and asking him to extend their medley, which I had already trimmed to a tight five-and-a-half minutes. But how could I go to them after we had delicately negotiated them down from nine minutes in the beginning? Or should I think about going to Stevie, my old friend and someone who was always ready with something and ask him to do a second performance, in addition to his duet with Babyface?

One thing was certain, however. Though Kelsey Grammer was hosting the show, his strengths as an actor did not include ad-libbing—and I couldn't put him in the position of "stretching" for up to five minutes without material.

And then it struck me. Three days earlier Aretha (with whom I've worked for nearly 20 years) had sung the aria "Nessun Dorma" at the Musicares benefit dinner...in another key, with another arrangement, without a full orchestra. She had told me numerous times over the years we've worked together that she always wanted to sing opera, but to ask her to sing it in front of millions . . .

She was scheduled to perform about 30 minutes from the present moment in a brief, but fun Blues Brothers medley with Dan Aykroyd and John Goodman, doing "Respect" as only she could.

I called for my long-time friend and coordinating producer Tisha Fein and Phil Ramone, who had produced the Musicares event, and we raced up the four flights of stairs. We had about fifty minutes before we got to the highly anticipated Pavarotti performance (the nonperformance). When I got to Aretha's small, overheated dressing room, complete with vaporizer and hangers-on, she was fanning herself, quietly waiting to go on. And then we hit her with this lightning bolt of a statement.

"Aretha, we have a problem. I know it's short notice, but how would you like to sing twice tonight? Go out there and do "Respect" and then 20 minutes later, supported by a 65-piece orchestra and a 20-voice chorus, do "Nessun Dorma?"

And that's when she uttered those words. I knew she would, even before I had taken the first steps up the heart-attack stairway in the bowels of Radio City Music Hall. I will always love the Queen of Soul.

And though to many people, that was the Night of Soybomb disrupting Bob Dylan's triumphant Grammy performance, and Ol' Dirty Bastard storming the stage to interrupt Shawn Colvin's well-deserved acceptance speech, for me the 40th Annual Grammy Awards will always be the Night Aretha Franklin Saved the Grammys—and not incidentally, my professional life.

⌒

It was probably the wildest Grammy ride in history; in the space of three short hours (and a couple of minutes running over), we had to cross Luciano Pavarotti off our playlist, pull two intruding entities—one named Soybomb and the other Ol' Dirty Bastard—off the stage, deal with an ailing Barbra Streisand who ultimately begged off her highly anticipated duet with Celine Dion; manage a longstanding siege trying to soothe the egos and the feelings of three female performers whose nominations totaled more than ten and who couldn't understand why we had lumped them together in a "woman's segment" on a Grammy show that was all but boycotted by the New York political establishment because of a power struggle between Mike Greene and Mayor Rudy Giuliani.

Some shows are joys to do, and some . . . well . . . they're just there to do.

This was one that called up everything we had in our playbook. Other than scoring huge ratings after a lull of a couple of years, this was one show that we can look at fondly—only, as they say, in retrospect.

I think enough time has passed to tell the whole "Soybomb" story, and not to cast blame, because there is none to cast. Still, it serves as a lesson in why the term "control freak" isn't always so bad.

Working with the Dylan crew, which included co-managers Jeff Kramer and Jeff Rosen as well as a very involved label person (Larry Jenkins) is always an experience; an experience that contains equal parts joy, angst, worry, and suffering, but ultimately redemption. That's why you do it.

Bob wanted a performance that looked different from anything else on the Grammy show in 1998. His Time Out of Mind CD was certainly one of his best efforts in years, and with a relatively weak field, had every chance of winning the Grammy for Album of the Year. He agreed to perform, but right from square one, there was talk of how we were going to make Bob's performance special. Not an unusual request, and one that we sometimes tire of hearing because we like to think that every performance is treated differently.

This started with a couple of "Bob" consultants, including a European lighting designer who came in and built a light box that would float above Bob's head, providing evenly distributed downlight from some height. It then grew to include a sparse and minimal set that was basically Bob and the band grouped a little further upstage than we usually set performers, and nothing else. Then finally came the idea of putting a variety of fans, mostly young and mostly dressed in dark colors, on three sides of the stage to respond to Bob's performance of "Love Sick."

All doable, and all seemingly good thoughts to create a "vibe" for Bob's performance. But in our desire to please the performer, a fine line to begin with, we let ourselves down—and probably Bob and his crew—in one area. Instead of holding firm to our policy of booking "extras" ourselves and delivering them to the show for use in the segment, we allowed the Dylan group to pull the extras and to people the set for the performance. And that's where Soybomb came from, and that's the moment that people remember from that show instead of what happened later in the show when Bob's CD was named Album of the Year.

To his credit, Bob has never brought it up to me, and we've worked together on projects since. His management, all good people, had some questions to answer afterward, but looking at it in the long term, it certainly made his appearance at the Grammy show memorable.

In fact, there are so many stories from that year's Grammys that the awards themselves became as secondary as they ever have over the 43-year history of the Academy.

In an occasional lapse in judgment, the Grammy TV committee, at our meeting the day of the nominations, suggested we do a "woman's segment" tying together three of the multi-nominated female performers, Sarah McLachlan, Paula Cole, and Shawn Colvin. I recall saying at the time that in my experience with these and other women (Bonnie, Sheryl, Whitney, Mariah), they resented being labeled as "women artists," since men have no such stigma in the music business. No matter, that's what the committee wanted to do, and I set out to make it work. Shawn Colvin is a lovely person, an adult who was thrilled with her nominations, and although I know she had the same feelings, she agreed to be a part of the number. Sarah McLachlan was more problematic, but ultimately, for the good of the show and my explanation that in a strange way we were really honoring the remarkable things women had accomplished in the past few years, she too agreed to be a part of it. Paula Cole held out, and only after her management realized that it was the only way she would get on the show did she relent and join the other two women.

But then, as fate would have it, we took one step too far, and I knew it would come back and bite us in the ass. Both Mike and I were impressed with the waiflike appearance and strong writing of Fiona Apple, and after most of the show was booked, we found a solo slot for her. When the other women heard about this, they became understandably upset, and the entire segment almost fell apart. But as I said, certainly Shawn and Sarah are adults, and they stayed with the program, so Paula had to as well.

The medley, truncated versions of Shawn's lovely "Sunny Came Home," Sarah's "Building a Mystery," and Paula's "Where Have All the Cowboys Gone" was good, but not great. It really didn't give any of the artists enough time to establish their songs, and it's one of the things that pains me when we have to condense for the sake of time on the show.

For Paula Cole, redemption came in the name of winning Best New Artist, a mixed blessing for the future of artists on the Grammys, and in this case, not a good sign. She failed to follow up and, although she still makes interesting music, has never surpassed that particular year in terms of public acceptance.

Sarah McLachlan survived, winning the Best Female Pop Vocal Performance that year for "Building a Mystery," and has become an artist who will most likely be around for a long time. She's a sweetheart, and we've done several other shows together, all successful, and the most touching a performance on the Fourth Annual Blockbuster Awards where she did "I Will Remember You" surrounded by candles in oversize candelabras.

Shawn Colvin had a great night, winning both Record and Song of the Year. Shawn is also a great person, and one of the only people who could've handled the interruption of an acceptance speech by Ol' Dirty Bastard's call to his homies.

I think we could have weathered all of the above had we not been recovering from another crisis, one that happened the previous night that extended our rehearsal schedule and almost took us into the toilet.

We had scored a coup: Celine Dion and Barbra Streisand had been nominated for their duet "Tell Him" on Celine's album. With Rene's help, Barbra had agreed to come to New York and sing the duet with Celine, and it was to have been one of the highlights of the show. We had scheduled their rehearsal two nights before the show, and it was sometime midday when I got the call from Barbra's manager Marty Erlichman that Barbra was ill and wouldn't be able to make the rehearsal. But, he added, she's taking care of herself and will be fine for the show itself if we could reschedule the rehearsal. Without much time to move things around we did something very rare for us. We kept the first rehearsal and Celine graciously came and worked with a stand-in for Barbra so we could block the song and work out the kinks, and we scheduled a slightly shorter rehearsal at the end of the evening before the show for Barbra to come in and work with Celine, who would come back for that.

With the "women's segment" all being rehearsed on the day before, it would be a hellish schedule, but hell was worth going through to have Barbra and Celine on the show, so we moved through the day before the show as best we could, with hourly calls from Marty updating me on Barbra's condition. At about four in the afternoon, he made the dreaded call that in fact, she was no better, and would not be able to perform with Celine on the show.

Concerned but not panicked, I called Rene and we discussed some options. Celine is a resilient performer, and obviously had other numbers rehearsed, but nothing else that had been nominated. Though it was a definite bend in the rules, with Mike's cooperation, we agreed that the only thing to do was to perform "My Heart Will Go On," a song that had not yet been released, but would accompany the release of the film *Titanic*. We still weren't out of the woods since the charts for the song were in Montreal, and it was already mid-afternoon. Someone from Rene's office jumped on a plane with everything, landed in New York at 9:00 and at 10:00 we were rehearsing "My Heart Will Go On," restaged to fit the set we had built for the duet, but without Madame Streisand.

With the rehearsal complete, and with the disappointment of not having the duet as part of the show beginning to fade, we closed up shop that night and readied ourselves for the typical madness of show day, with its dress rehearsal, last minute curveballs, and then the show itself. But we were in for one more fire drill the next morning.

I'm always up early on show day, since there's a lot to do even before the four-hour dress rehearsal begins around noon. There are always last-minute script changes from the presenters, production problems that haven't been totally solved, and myriad other details that usually come up once we walk into the venue around 9 a.m.

But this day, it would begin a couple of hours earlier when my hotel phone rang at seven o'clock with a frantic call from Marty Erlichman, Barbra's manager. Barbra had had a good night's sleep, was feeling better, and really wanted to do the duet. Could we revise all of our plans, try and schedule one extra rehearsal within the dress, and put the number back together again?

Of course I wanted to do it, but I didn't know whether or not the change would throw Celine and Rene. I told Marty I would call Rene immediately and see what he felt and then get right back to him.

In most cases, a call to the manager wouldn't involve waking up the artist, but in this case, I knew the operator would ring the room and Celine would answer the phone…which she did. I didn't even want to bother her with this, choosing rather to discuss it with Rene to avoid possibly shaking up Celine. Rene came to the phone, and as I expected, agreed that we should try and make the duet happen, even if it meant a couple of extra run-throughs of the number.

I called Marty back to tell him, he said he'd start putting everything through, and I quickly dressed to walk the one block from the hotel to Radio City to start shifting everything that needed to be done to reinstate the Celine–Barbra duet.

But when I got to the Music Hall, Marty was on the phone with the final change in plans. Although Barbra was up for it, the hair and makeup people she had brought in from L.A. to see to her had already left on flights the night before. With no one available to do those critical jobs, the number was off. After I said that the ship was sailing after this, Marty and I had nothing left to do but to confirm with each of our people that, in fact, there would be no duet that night.

Celine gave a compelling performance of the song which would go on not only to be one of the biggest-selling records of all time, but would win a Grammy for Record of the Year the following year.

⌒

With all the drama, several planned other musical highlights seem almost secondary in comparison to the unexpected events of that night. Immediately after Will Smith's opening number Vanessa Williams came out of the wings with Chris Rock to present the first award, and the close-down piece that we use to mask the changeover of sets from performance to performance caught her right between the legs . . . and I do mean between the legs. On camera it didn't look like a serious injury, and being the trooper she is, she walked to the podium with Chris and went on with the award category.

Because it didn't seem serious, and because it was the top of the show and I didn't get any report from any stage manager, I assumed she was all right, so didn't get over to that side of the stage to check on her. It was only months later when we were doing another show with her that she pulled me aside backstage, pulled her dress up "to there," and showed me the aftermath of the welts she had to have gotten from this set piece hitting her. She made light of it, but it must have hurt like hell.

She's a trooper, though, and never made me feel as though I had ruined any part of her personal life.

Certainly one of the high spots of the show was the Stevie Wonder–Babyface duet of "How Come, How Long," a rousing pop number that would have felt completely at home in any church in the land. With the help of Hezekiah Walker and the Love Fellowship Choir and one of the most inspired harmonica solos in Stevie's long and varied career, it brought the house to its feet within the first minutes and it stayed there for the rest of the number. Of all the numbers that I've done with Stevie over the years, this one is very close to the top, and that's saying something.

In the "Where Are They Now" department, Hanson made its only Grammy appearance doing "MmmBop," which I assumed would sometime soon find its way onto the marquee of a Holiday Inn in Davenport, Iowa, under the two lines; "Tonight, One Night Only: Hanson." Nice, likeable guys, but you just knew it was a year and out for these guys, Grammy nomination or not.

And then there was R. Kelly.

This Grammy show was the only time I ever worked with him, and the fun was truly in the getting there. We had several conversations with management, none of which resulted in anything more than a desire on their part to have a cornfield as the set for "I Believe I Can Fly." It was mystifying, but because Robert had been described as such an enigma, we went along and had Bob Keene construct a representational cornfield in and out of which would pop Robert at various times during the number. There were some levels, a choir of voices that would come in on cue halfway through the song, and then there was the song, which I liked very much.

To back us up—because although we might have believed he could fly, we didn't believe much in the cornfield—we took a couple of extra steps.

Bob contacted one of the people with whom he had worked on the Los Angeles Olympics and built several flying "birds" which, when swung around connected to a long pole, seemed to fly through the air unaided. They looked like they would be beautiful, and we were all ready to put them in the number until Bob demonstrated them to Walter and me on the stage of Radio City. As he launched one, holding the pole at one end and sending the other end into the air, the bird took one or two turns in the air, swooped once more, and then took a dive right into the floor of the stage, breaking into a dozen pieces. Walter and I looked at each other, and then broke up hysterically, thinking about what a moment that would be in the middle of our "cornfield" as the birds came crashing to the ground around Robert Kelly. So much for flying birds.

The second backup idea, however, scored big. Although Robert wouldn't consider video backup for the number, we had gone ahead anyway and had Ron Andreassen create a magical montage of flying aerial shots, all as if they were the point of view of an eagle soaring a thousand feet up, and all breathtaking. When Robert arrived at Radio City, even before I took him inside, I asked him to come to our trailer office outside the venue to look at the footage. He came, he loved it, and it made it so easy to 86 the corn. I still don't know what happened to the fields, but if you're in New York one day and walk into a restaurant and see some rows of corn brightening the place up, thank the Grammys.

This was also the show in which I first met Sean Combs, aka "Puff Daddy," "P Diddy," etc., etc. a pleasure that would come back to haunt me in future years. Benny Medina had hounded me for weeks about his new client who was going to revolutionize the music business, and I reluctantly agreed to spend some time with Puffy on one of his visits to L.A. When we met, I was struck with his ease in talking and ability to get across ideas, and I actually liked him until I began to analyze what he was talking about. Though he professed to be in the music business, it was easy to see that the business part was really all he cared about. Benny had certainly set it up right in telling me that Puffy was an entrepreneur, but as a person who cared deeply about the music, I was left totally cold with all his proclamations about the empire he was going to build and the power he would one day have. I tried to look inside myself to see if I would have felt that way if I was hearing all of this from a white guy, trying to give him the benefit of the doubt that way, but it didn't help. I had gotten to know L.A. Reid reasonably well, had had dealings with Russell Simmons, and knew that as competitive and driven as they were, they were still very much about the music and the art of it. Puffy was not, is not, and I don't think ever will be.

⟜

And then there is the Mike Greene/Rudy Giuliani drama.

The story that went around was that Mike verbally abused one of Giuliani's key staff people at the nominations press conference, and that the Mayor had responded by saying that he wouldn't participate in anything that had to do with such an abusive person.

Mike can be volatile, and he's prone to flying off the handle from time to time, but it's usually for effect. I was with him at the press conference when the woman from the Mayor's office came up to him and told him that the Mayor would be late to the conference but just wanted to make sure that he was going to get a presenting slot on the live telecast. Mike had already decided that no political official from any city where the Grammys were held would be on the air, and this was no exception. Well, when Mike's answer was not what the Mayor wanted to hear, and Giuliani saw an opportunity to get some print out of a relatively safe situation, he went for Mike's throat.

It would be five years before we went back to New York, and by that time both Mike and Rudy were gone from their respective seats of power. And we would return with a show that opened with as perfect a love song to a city that had undergone such sadness as possible; how much more appropriate to have two favorite sons of Manhattan like Paul Simon and Art Garfunkel, who had both performed in venues large and small all over the city, in the middle of Madison Square Garden singing about the "whores on Seventh Avenue"? But that's another story, so as we say in television, stay tuned.

CHAPTER 21

The 1999 Grammy Awards

Ricky Martin Starts a "Revolution"

As we moved toward putting together the final Grammy Awards show of the twentieth century, I don't think any of us realized that although over the years we had played extremely important roles in furthering the careers of a host of performers and Grammy winners, this show would be pivotal in launching the career of one of the last stars of the century, Ricky Martin.

It would be 18 months before we were to do the first-ever Latin Grammy show, but we had been setting the stage over the years by presenting at least one artist in a Latin category every year, and our fears about presenting a performance in Spanish, once thought unimaginable, were lessening each time out.

Ricky had already established his credentials as a bona fide pop superstar in the rest of the Spanish-speaking world, not to mention just about everywhere outside the U.S., but he had never gone beyond his Latin base here. That is until February 24, 1999, when he electrified the live audience and millions of home viewers with an amazing performance of "Cup of Life," the song he had performed on the Olympics two years before.

The story of how that performance wound up on the Grammys, and what happened to Ricky (and the Grammys) as a result, is a fascinating study in pop music marketing.

Even prior to the nominations, it was obvious that Ricky was the hottest thing in Latin music that year, and knowing that he would be nominated in several categories, I flew down to Miami to meet with his two principal managers, Angelo Medina and Ricardo Cordero. At the lunch meeting we had, it was clear that they had a plan to launch Ricky's new single on the show, the song that was to become his biggest hit ever, "La Vida Loca." But when I listened to the advance copy of the song as they played it for me that day, I didn't want to perform it, and in fact, because it was not even out at that time, by our rules he couldn't perform it. I also felt that while it was destined to become a big hit, it was much poppier and a bit less Latin than "Cup of Life," and that Ricky would benefit more by performing the other song.

As if by magic, in the middle of our lunch Columbia Records president Don Ienner called and when they put me on the phone with him, we had a long and unresolved conversation where I stuck to my guns about "Cup of Life" despite Donny's protestations about wanting to do "La Vida Loca." I stood my ground, and it was obviously more important for them to be on the Grammys than to hold out for a song that was not going to be performed.

During the meeting, they asked me if I knew any choreographers they could talk to about working with Ricky, wanting to get a more American feel to the staging of what he did for this audience. I suggested a young guy we had worked with on several shows, Jamie King, and hooked them up. Jamie would go on to work with them for the next two years, and bring something remarkable to every performance and tour he did with them.

Jamie would then go on to choreograph nearly every major artist in music, among them Madonna and Janet Jackson, as well as doing a hit Las Vegas show that he conceived, choreographed, and directed. His price went up, up to the point where we could no longer afford to use him.

That's not to say that Ricky needed that much production. Over the years, in the numerous times we've worked with Ricky, it always seems to start with production, but the reality is that while he may not have the strongest voice in the business, or even be the best dancer in the music world, he is one of those rare performers who is a quintessential entertainer. He works as if every person in the audience is the *only* person in the audience, directing himself to that one person. He connects in a way that is rare among young performers today, and I am fond of telling Ricardo and Angelo that he is almost reminiscent of a previous generation of performer, a Sammy Davis, Jr., or a Sinatra, in his desire to please a crowd.

In any event, along came Jamie and production galore, and as the mid-point of the show approached, those of us who had seen the rehearsals had a sense we might be making history that night and were anxious to see what would happen when Ricky took the stage.

It was everything we had hoped for and more. I've never seen a Grammy audience get up off their collective asses faster following a performance, and from host Rosie O'Donnell to Madonna to Sting, everyone loved Ricky, and the next morning it was all about him. Sting invited him to perform on his Rainforest show, Rosie had him on her show several times, and the CD and his subsequent tour took off like a shot.

And as thrilled as Pierre, Walter, and I were about what the Grammys had done for this young star, there were two people even more thrilled. One of course was Mike Greene, whose desire to do the Latin Grammy show took a giant step closer to reality because of the sensational performance. The other was Sony Music President Tommy Mottola, who had an abiding faith in the Latin market as the next "big thing" in pop music, and who had not only been instrumental in the launch, but was about to benefit from a raft of other artists who would follow in Ricky's footsteps.

In fact, the "Latin Revolution" became the talk of the industry from that night on, and artists from Marc Anthony, Shakira, Jennifer Lopez, Enrique Iglesias, and Christina Aguilera were all beneficiaries of Ricky's explosion on the Shrine Auditorium stage that night.

Even Madonna, who had opened the show that night and whose performance was nearly forgotten in the madness that followed Ricky's turn onstage, spoke about nothing but him to the press that night and went on to record a duet with him for his next album.

Madonna had always said no to us. She hadn't really been nominated a lot, and when she was, it was not in the best of categories, and she felt that she was doing just fine without ever having set foot on a Grammy stage.

But in 1999, once again at the Shrine Auditorium, she accepted our invitation to perform, and we agreed to open the show with her. It wasn't a real give for us, because she had had a great year and was nominated for both Album and Record of the Year. And, hey . . . it was Madonna!

Putting together the performance was quite another thing. We met with artistic directors, choreographers, designers, all good people with instructions. We made it all work, and after a couple of brief conversations about our approach, the booking was confirmed and we were on the road toward a great opening performance.

"Ray of Light," the song we agreed would be performed, isn't the traditional opening number for a Grammy show. It had dynamics, but its tempo was sort of in the middle, and it certainly didn't have room for great vocalizing. On the other hand, I've never felt that the Grammys, or any show we do, needs to open balls to the wall. The reality is, starting a show off right is more about a performer's ability to hook an audience than about the dynamics of a song, and certainly that year, Madonna was the one to do it—not to mention the inside industry and fan press that could be made out of Madonna's first appearance on the show.

Rehearsal day was one of those traditional days from hell. We got through everything up to her rehearsal fine, and then set up the stage for her.

She had cloistered herself in a dressing room and so I didn't see her until she hit the stage, and unlike a lot of accessible superstar performers, it was clear she was focused on her performance and wasn't into small talk. So we ran the song a few times for cameras to get their shots, and for her to work the stage, which featured an intricate Asian bridge and wooden screens as support.

Then it hit. She asked to come to the truck to look at the video of her rehearsal, something we seldom if ever do. It's one thing to give the performers a tape to look at and let us know how they feel, but coming to the truck in the middle of a rehearsal is one of those situations that can turn into a train wreck.

And this one was. I brought her to the video truck. She immediately moved the associate director out and sat next to Walter, and we started looking at the tape.

Walter is the youngest "old guy" you'll ever meet. He's been in television since he started as a cable puller for a cameraman in 1951, and there's not much he hasn't seen. And as a senior statesman, he's earned the right to be treated with respect. He's worked with everyone and has the vaunted reputation of putting his head down and getting through anything and everything with his eye on the prize. He's seen power go down in the truck, talent walk in drunk, lights fall from the grid, and artists refuse to go on—all in the course of a show day, these things happening on live shows, Walter's first love and greatest area of expertise.

While underneath he is one of the most sensitive, gracious human beings I've ever had the honor of working with, he is also one of the most potentially explosive. And Madonna in the truck would prove to be Walter's biggest test ever.

It didn't start well. From the first shot, Madonna had something to say. "This is too wide." "This needs to be tighter." "Why are you on the dancer when I'm working here?" "That shot is terrible."

Now I've seen Walter tear into talent and co-worker alike just for asking him if he liked his breakfast, but I had never seen anyone confront him this way, and with such insensitivity. The truck got very quiet. There were about seven or eight of us and about seven or eight of them. I stood right behind him, not knowing whether to break the silence and risk having Walter blow up because I was trying to mollify the situation, or to just wait and see what happened. It became interminable . . . and then Walter spoke.

"Well, if that's what you want, then that's what I'll give you."

At that moment, I didn't know what to do. Part of me said, Don't let her get away with this. Jump in and fight for him. And the other part of me said Walter's just faced one of the toughest moments in his professional life and survived it. Let it be.

Which is precisely what I did.

The truck emptied of Madonna's people. I put my arms around Walter and told him that in all the years we had worked together, I was never more proud of him. He had faced the firing squad and come away unscathed.

A footnote: the performance went on, with most of Madonna's suggestions listened to, but with several of Walter's shots from the rehearsal intact. The next day we got the call from her people; Madonna loved every minute. Her sexuality oozed on the stage, just as Ricky Martin's had.

But for all the machismo and sexuality that Ricky and Madonna brought to the stage that night, they weren't the sexiest moment of that year's Grammy show. That honor went to Shania Twain, whose thigh-high minidress on a raised stage left almost nothing to the imagination, and whose performance of "Man I Feel Like a Woman" did nearly as much for her career as Ricky's "Cup of Life" had done for his.

Sheryl Crow's "There Goes the Neighborhood" is a sexy song, filled with innuendo and direct references. She had asked us to come up with something special to support it, and though late in the game, I had booked some female impersonators to come down to the Shrine on the off-chance that we could fit them in as some "color" or as extra backup singers for the number.

They didn't make it for Sheryl's rehearsal, so the first time we were able to rehearse with them was for the dress rehearsal on show day. They were great looking, and more than a few men in the audience during the dress couldn't take their eyes off the "girls," and I thought we had hit a small, but very cool, home run. Following the rehearsal, the word came back that either Sheryl or her management wanted them out of the number. Though it wasn't that important to me, I thought we had done something that was very hip for the show, and I stood up for our decision. It never became a heated argument, but ultimately, when I felt it might affect her performance, I backed down, and she performed impersonator-less. I still think it would have been great fun, but I've never done anything that I thought might take a performer's concentration away from their main job, to deliver a song with conviction and commitment.

The range of the music on the 1999 show was pretty diverse, and three of the segments that we did went a long way to once again proving that the Grammys ventured into musical areas that would never be found on the other music award shows.

The first of these was a return to the gospel segments we had done so successfully in years past. Kirk Franklin had broken through as a huge gospel act, but had also crossed over to pop with his gospel cum hip-hop style. He was also a master showman who had put together an amazing group of singers who could move as well as they could sing. And when I heard his song "Lean on Me," I felt there was a great opportunity to open up the song and feature guest turns with other artists, some of whom he had worked with as well. I asked Bono, who was a quick yes, went to Mary J. Blige, who joined the group, added the great voice of Gerald Levert, and then put them all together in what would be one of the best-received numbers in the show. The staging, a box that opened to reveal each of the performers and then the full choir, was a remarkable design by Bob Keene, and it provided the visual drama to a great musical grouping.

Next up, we had long wanted to salute the music of the movies, several categories of which were Grammy categories, but which we had never performed on the show. I had originally wanted John Williams, the most Grammy-winning film composer; James Horner, whose work I admired a great deal, and whose *Titanic* score was fast becoming the all-time best-selling soundtrack album; Ennio Morricone, whose music I idolized going back to the Clint Eastwood westerns of the late '60s; and of course, my favorite, Randy Newman, whose evocative scores as well as catchy end title songs were magical. I felt we could probably do this whole segment in 11 or 12 minutes, longer than most of the special segments we did, but compelling because of their musicality, not to mention their familiarity to viewers. Mike and I had a series of major arguments about the segment, and by the time it hit the air, Randy Newman and Ennio Morricone were gone, with only token performances by John and James remaining in the mix. The segment was pretty spectacular with a full orchestra onstage, and though it was clear it followed the show business tenet of "always leave them wanting more," I really felt that we missed a great opportunity by not having Randy and Morricone as a part of it.

The final special piece that we did was an Ellington tribute, arranged and conducted by Wynton Marsalis. The combination of Natalie Cole performing "I'm Beginning to See the Light" with Wynton's Lincoln Center Jazz Orchestra doing "C Jam Blues" warmed every jazz fan's heart, and featured some pretty virtuoso performances. It was a great example of honoring jazz in a way that was accessible, and it not only became one of the best critically reviewed acts on the show, but also elevated the tone of the whole show with its presence.

For whatever reason, getting presenters that fit and could deliver lines had begun to be a much more difficult task, and while music people aren't actors, they usually do a credible job of trying to make artificial dialogue sound real. For the 1999 show, we actually did pretty well. We kicked the show off with Jerry Seinfeld and Jennifer Lopez, and then proceeded through a pretty good list of presenters including Will Smith (who's always great); Eric Clapton paired with B.B. King, playing and singing together before they presented the award for Best Female

Rock Vocal Performance; Gloria Estefan with Jimmy Smits, who did a great job bringing the crowd back into the show after Ricky's incredible performance; and Sting with Whitney Houston and Rosie O'Donnell (this a year before Rosie would go on the show and trash Whitney in front of millions of people).

In retrospect, Rosie O'Donnell was the perfect host for a show whose musical range was about as disparate as any Grammy show in recent years.

Rosie has a genuine love and appreciation for all kinds of music, and her introductions of each performer reflected her knowledge and respect for each of them. Rosie, and the show, deserved the high ratings the show got that year, and we knew as soon as the show was over that we wanted her back the next year—if only we had known. But more about that later.

Although we weren't sure of it at the time, the 1999 show was also the last we would do at a venue other than an arena. The following year we would move the show to Staples Center, then take it to New York to Madison Square Garden, and never again return to a venue that held fewer than 14,000 seats. Given the history of the show, which had begun less than 30 years ago in places like the Hollywood Palladium and the Felt Forum (now gone) that seated fewer than 3,000 people, the move was a significant one, and one that would impact the show and the Academy in a major way.

The ratings for the show were the best in five years, scoring a 16.6/26 for the three hours, and bringing home the February sweeps for CBS. Equally important, the stories about CD sales in the weeks following the Grammy show all pointed up the value of the show to the music industry.

And of course, it was about the performances, led by a huge sales increase for Ricky Martin, but with major sales increases by nearly every artist who took the stage that night. The Grammys, challenged again by the other music award shows nipping at its heels, had demonstrated its reach and importance to the music-buying public. It would continue to be the show for the music industry to support and for fans to watch.

1 Neil Diamond and Barbra Streisand performing "You Don't Bring Me Flowers" at the 22nd Annual Grammy Awards. Photo by Sam Emerson.

2 Going over copy with host John Denver for the 1980 Grammy Awards show, my first as producer.

3 Tina Turner performs "What's Love Got To Do With It"—and reignites her career at the 1985 Grammy Awards show. Photo by Sam Emerson.

4 Tony Bennett and Harry Connick "talk it over" with me, prior to their segment that highlighted the 1991 Grammy show at Radio City Music Hall in New York City. From author's collection.

5 Dolly Parton presents the Grammy for Record of the Year for "I Will Always Love You"—the song she wrote—to Whitney Houston, who sang the Grammy winning song. Photo by Kevin Mazur/Wire Image.

6 Aretha Franklin and Luciano Pavarotti at the rehearsal for the 1998 Grammy show. Pavarotti shows no signs of what was to come several hours later. Photo by Rick Diamond/Wire Image.

7 Aretha creates one of Grammy's most unforgettable moments when she steps in for Pavarotti to perform "Nessun Dorma" at the 1998 Grammy show in New York. Photo by Rick Diamond/Wire Image.

8 Celine Dion performs "My Heart Will Go On"—with one day of preparation after Barbra Streisand's illness caused her to cancel their planned duet on the 1998 Grammys. Photo by Rick Diamond/Wire Image.

9 Bob Dylan catches "Soybomb" in the corner of his eye—but keeps on singing. It was almost a full minute, an eternity in TV time, before show security carried the intruder offstage at the 1998 Grammy Awards show. Photo by Rick Diamond/Wire Image.

10 Shania Twain performing. Photo by Kevin Mazur/Wire Image.

11 A star is born on the Grammy stage as Ricky Martin electrifies the Grammy audience—and millions more at home—with his version of "La Copa De La Vida" in 2000. Photo by Rick Diamond/Wire Image.

12 Eminem and Elton John share a moment with me during rehearsal of the 2001 standout performance "Stan." Photo by Frank Micelotta/Image Direct.

13 Elton and Eminem create Grammy history with their controversial duet at the 2001 Grammy Awards in Los Angeles. What followed was one of the longest standing ovations in Grammy history. Photo by Frank Micelotta/Image Direct.

14 U2 accepting the award for Record of the Year at the 2002 Grammys. Photo by Frank Micelotta/Image Direct.

15 Alicia Keys, who would go on to win Best New Artist as well as win the Grammy for Song of the Year for "Fallin," going over her performance with me at the rehearsals for the 2002 show. Photo by Kevin Mazur/Wire Image.

16 After being apart musically for ten years, Paul Simon and Art Garfunkel join together for "Sound of Silence" to open the 2003 Grammy Awards show at Madison Square Garden in New York City. Photo by Michael Caulfield/Wire Image.

17 Following the death of Joe Strummer, rock greats perform "London Calling," a blazing tribute to The Clash to pay off the In Memoriam segment of the 2003 show. Photo by Wire Image.

18 The Grammys tribute The Clash in 2003: Tony Kanal, Bruce Springsteen, me, Dave Grohl, Elvis Costello, and Miami Steve Van Zandt. Photo by Kevin Mazur/Wire Image.

19 Prince and Beyoncé provide one of Grammy's greatest moments with a medley of each of their hits to kick off the 2004 Grammy Show at Staples Center in Los Angeles. Photo by Michael Caulfield/Wire Image.

20 Making her first musical appearance following her breast cancer experience, Melissa Etheridge electrifies viewers, live audience, and duet partner Joss Stone with an incredible performance of Janis Joplin's "Piece of My Heart" on the 2005 Grammy show. Photo by Michael Caulfield/Wire Image.

21 Talking through the staging of the Usher/James Brown performance with Grammy winning artist Usher during rehearsals for the 2005 show at Staples Center. Photo from the author's personal collection.

22 Usher and James Brown deliver! Photo by Kevin Mazur/Wire Image.

23 A virtual Madonna meets the virtual Gorillaz in the amazing opening to the 2006 show; a mashup of "Feels Good, Inc." crossed with Madonna's "Hung Up." Even the live audience was fooled into thinking the 'real' Madonna was performing with the animated Gorillaz! Photo by Kevin Neste.

24 Kanye West is joined by duet partner Jamie Foxx for a stage-filling sendup of "Golddigger" complete with members of the USC marching band (2006). Photo by Michael Caulfield/Wire Image.

25 Pop meets Hip Hop meets Rock as Paul McCartney joins Jay Z and Linkin Park for a memorable version of McCartney's classic "Yesterday" in one of Grammy's classic mashups on the 2006 show. Photo by Kevin Mazur/Wire Image.

26 Paul McCartney and NARAS president Neil Portnow with me, during rehearsals for Paul's double appearance on the 2006 show. Photo by Kevin Mazur/Wire Image.

27 Mary J Blige joins U2 for an arena raising version of "One," to pay off the Irish band's appearance on the 2006 show where they won Album of the Year honors for "How to Dismantle an Atomic Bomb." Photo by Michael Caulfield/Wire Image.

28 With Sting and Andy Summers of The Police, onstage during the
rehearsal for their reunion, which opened the 2007 Grammy Awards.
Said Sting at the top of the show: "We are the Police, and we are back!"
They subsequently announced a world tour which set attendance records
everywhere. Photo by Kevin Mazur/Wire Image.

CHAPTER 22

The 2000 Grammy Awards

A "Smooth" Night for Carlos Santana

The first Grammy show of the twenty-first century and the first one to be done at the Staples Center in Los Angeles, was not one of my favorites. Boy bands and teen princesses dominated the charts as well as the nominations. I was to have a rocky experience with Carlos Santana's management people, Staples was not an easy place to work, and I was having one of my most difficult years with Academy president Mike Greene. Add the change in attitude that both Walter and I were to experience with returning host Rosie O'Donnell, a production period that was extremely unrewarding, and an extremely arduous show day itself, and you have the makings of a Grammy show that in many ways I'd like to forget.

In fact, while Santana's performance and sweep of the awards will probably be remembered as the highlight of the show, what may just outshine it were our first two presenters, David Duchovny (whose Grammy appearance will probably be a Jeopardy answer someday) and Jennifer Lopez, who launched her musical career when she showed up in *that dress*. My first exposure to her Grammy wardrobe was when she showed up backstage just before the show went on the air, and I found myself not looking into her eyes, which are quite beautiful. Remember, this was three years prior to the Janet Jackson Super Bowl fiasco, and although CBS did have standards-and-practices people on site, it was a different world. We went through their copy quickly due to time constraints, and as I walked away, thinking of poor David Duchovny, I remembered the classic George Gobel *Tonight Show* line as he sat in between Frank Sinatra and Dean Martin. He said, "I feel like the world is a tuxedo and I'm just a pair of brown shoes."

David and Jennifer came out to present and the audience went wild—a combination of babe shock and dude appreciation. Duchovny recovered by delivering a couple of hastily rewritten lines about her

dress, and the show was off to what might have been a great start, although in my heart I knew that the front-page picture from the show
was probably already finding its way to thousands of newspapers already. And my prediction was to prove reasonably close to the truth.

That appearance, and the subsequent furor it caused, may very well
have begun a trend in award show dress that I think we'd rather not
claim as something initiated by the Grammys. It seems that from that
moment on, female performers and presenters (but more often presenters who had no other role on the show than to show up and look
great) have tried to push the envelope a bit further every year. I would
watch other music award shows where more and more skin was shown,
reaching a point where all of a sudden the red carpet was competing
with the show for attention, not to mention the cottage industry we
created for Joan Rivers and Joan Rivers wannabes screaming "Who are
you wearing" at any pair of boobs and flash of ass that walked down
the carpet. Even in the post-Janet days, the trend continues, and there
may come a day when networks will have to put an adult rating on the
arrivals shows.

If J-Lo's coming out party was the highlight, it wasn't enough to
erase some of the more unpleasant and difficult memories of a show
that never lived up to its expectations, lean year in music or not.

It really began earlier that fall, as my company was having one of
our most successful production periods ever. We had not only done a
record number of shows, but we had produced holiday specials with
Celine Dion, Ricky Martin, and Shania Twain that all aired on CBS during the Thanksgiving weekend and were very successful in terms of both
ratings and critical acceptance.

But I was also in the second year of our *Motown Live* series with a
new production executive from Universal who had taken this lovely
little series that paid homage to the roots of R&B and tried to meld it
with hip-hop. The results were a show that lost its focus, not to mention
its core audience.

Most significant however, were the nominations themselves in
which the combined categories of Record and Album of the Year yielded
a number of songs and artists which, with a couple of notable exceptions, seemed very weak and not particularly memorable. The Record cat-

egory included Cher's "Believe" (hello?), TLC's "No Scrubs," which had a strong message but no real production values, and the Backstreet Boys "I Want It That Way," which was hooky, but banal. The other two nominees were Ricky Martin's "La Vida Loca," which was a popular smash but was seven or eight months old, and Santana's "Smooth" which was the obvious frontrunner. The album category included repeats for Santana, the Backstreet Boys and TLC, along with the Dixie Chicks' *Fly* and Diana Krall's *When I Look In Your Eyes*.

At no time in my memory was I less excited about the nominations, and with the prevailing theory that Santana was going to sweep the awards, I had to work hard to get myself, and our team, up for the show.

The one positive in the mix, as strange as it sounds, was the challenge of doing the show at Staples. Though we had done the show at Madison Square Garden three years before, that arena was a long-lived venue used to all kinds of production situations, whereas we were really "first in" at Staples. The internal production team was a good one, but as opposed to the Garden people to whom nothing was really new no matter how challenging, everything was new at Staples. To their credit, the production people at Staples gave their all, and most of the problem solving was left to John Cossette, who worked his ass off.

The show opening had to be big, showing size and scope, and it had to rock. In short, it needed to get the attention of an audience a football field away as well as people watching thousands of miles away, and in forty different languages.

The rehearsal period seemed more difficult than most, perhaps due to the newness of Staples, but more likely due to the fact that we were dealing with one of the most difficult and intransigent groups of management people in many years. Johnny Wright, obviously at the bidding of his client, Britney Spears, kept us away from having any direct discussions with her, not allowing our ideas to surface. Simon Renshaw, the Dixie Chicks' manager, is a decent sort, but he too was overprotective of his act. And despite my long-term relationship with Carlos Santana, I wasn't able to bounce some of the things that we wanted off him, instead having to deal with one of his two managers from a distance. And though we had been responsible for some of Whitney Houston's best television performances ever, it became obvious that because of her own personal problems, we didn't have access to her.

The exception, and a notable one, was Will Smith. James Lassiter, his manager, had no problem with us working out Will's number directly with him. He encouraged it, in fact, and one of the real joys of this show was the collaborative and continuing improvement of the number as Will and I talked almost on a daily basis.

Will's performance of "Wild Wild West" seemed to fit the bill. Will had given us one of our best openings in the past with "Gettin Jiggy with It," and though "Wild Wild West" wasn't a huge hit, Will Smith is a movie star and was loved by a wide segment of our audience. With the help of 20 dancers, Sisqó (before he would break wide open with "Thong Song"), and a rockin' track, we felt good about a number that let it all out, with pyrotechnics, video projection, and just about everything else we had in our bag of tricks.

But as good an opening number as Will gave us, when Rosie appeared for her opening monologue, Walter and I both sensed trouble. Something had happened to her in the year between her appearances. She seemed to have gone from being a person who loved the music and showed that love to viewers to a host who felt she needed to score by being negative, and, to prove it, she spent the rest of the show putting down the acts. Instead of acting as a cheerleader, she seemed to be a host unhappy to be there at all. Granted, an arena with 12,000 detached souls in search of a show to watch isn't necessarily the best audience for a comic, but instead of using the venue for what it was, she seemed to be intimidated by it and never even reached the live audience, most of whom would have accepted her for the fast comebacks and accessible humor she had on her own show.

The Dixie Chicks had toured arenas before, and so they seemed very comfortable in the venue, but again, the song we agreed upon for them to perform, however rocking, was a very dark one. "Goodbye Earl" is the story of a woman who, fed up with her abusive husband, who kills him. Country music has always had its performing difficulties on the Grammys, and though Walter and I had both talked to them about doing a different song, they were insistent on "Earl," and because they had several nominations, we went along with their wishes. And as it turned out, they were right! A huge hand for the number, something totally different than anything else on the show.

And then there was the "Latin segment."

The Latin Grammys had become a reality, scheduled for September of 2000, and Mike very much wanted to promote the show by putting a medley of great Latin performances in the show. As it was with the "women's medley," all of the artists objected to being categorized as "Latin," and after much negotiation, the only way we could make it work with everyone was to kick it off with Marc Anthony, who was relegated to a smaller stage on the stage-right side of the house, separate him from Ricky Martin with a short performance by the Buena Vista Social Club, and then go to the "A" stage where Ricky was prepared to blow everything out again, this time singing "Maria," accompanied by a ring of fire, an acrobat climbing down from a drape hung from the ceiling, and dancers galore. For all its spectacle, the entire segment lacked a focus, and though it served the purpose of tipping that the Latin Grammys were to come, it didn't serve the show well.

Even one of my mainstays, Whitney Houston, failed to light up the world.

Whitney was not in the best of shape, and there had been an incident during rehearsals between Whitney and Rosie that had obviously shaken Whitney. I later learned that Whitney had cancelled an appearance on Rosie's show some months ago, and Rosie had not forgotten about it, so she used the platform of the Grammys, both in rehearsal and on the air the night of the show, to get some payback. In the fragile world in which Whitney was living at the time, I'm sure it took its toll, and what might have been a virtuoso performance of an uptempo dance number combined with one of Whitney's great power ballads turned out to be just another performance on a show that desperately needed "moments."

I had talked to the Backstreet Boys about kicking off their turn on the show with a short tribute to the male vocal groups who had gone before, and they almost got it right. I had suggested a couple of Motown things, a Boyz II Men song, and even an old doo wop piece to cover the generations and set the stage for one of their huge hits, "Show Me the

Meaning of Being Lonely." They did "Papa Was a Rolling Stone" and Boyz II Men's "I'll Make Love to You," but instead of going back, they chose a Bee Gees song, "How Deep Is Your Love," which was OK, but lacked the punch of some other things I suggested.

The show took off for a couple of minutes when Kid Rock, accompanied by his little person Joe and a couple of go-go dancers we later learned were actually porn stars—as well as pyrotechnics, motorcycles, and an exploding piano—lit up the room with another unexpected moment. I liked Bob (Kid), and his sense of drama and mild amusement with his rock persona will probably keep him around for a while.

But the fact that his performance represented our rock categories just pointed up even more the sad fact that disposable pop and teen divas had replaced rock as the dominant form of the music kids had listened to for decades. Names like Everlast, Lenny Kravitz, and Buckcherry were among the nominations in the rock categories, and although Bruce Springsteen, the Chili Peppers, and Chris Cornell were there as well, they had not had significant enough presence for us to commit to performance slots on the show. It would be a few years before rock, along with hip-hop, would return to the forefront of the music that kids cared about, and I was hoping that if nothing else, this year was the watershed, and that we would see the emergence of some great rockers in the near future. And it would happen.

My least favorite performance was coming up, and when it happened, it fulfilled my every expectation. Britney Spears had wanted to do something "special," and by the time we had combined some of our ideas and hers, it was a mish-mosh of a segment. It began with "Britney's Dream" (about one day being on the Grammys), continued with her emerging from a dancer-filled "flower," and concluded with a group of marching puppets joined together by poles in a number which must have confused even the millions of 13-year-old girls waiting for her to appear.

In retrospect, I probably should have gone with a performance from Christina Aguilera, one of the other Best New Artist nominees (along with Britney and Kid Rock). At least she could sing, as she was to prove every time out, especially when she turned in an amazing "It's a Man's World" during the James Brown tribute on the 2007 show.

Carlos Santana made another trip to the stage, thereby losing any illusion of Grammy mystery that was left, and then Mike Greene came to the stage and provided one of the highlights of the show. He brought a group of teenage musicians onstage with him to support his speech about the importance of music education, one of the major programs of the Recording Academy. It even gave me some momentary relief from the extremely unpleasant conversations Mike and I had been having over the course of the show, and took a bit of the sting out of my extreme unhappiness at that moment.

Mike then introduced Billy Joel who helmed a brief tribute to Elton John who was set at the piano with the Backstreet Boys in proximity to perform "Philadelphia Freedom." One of the sources of contention with Mike was Elton's desire to have the Boys work with him (Mike was having his own problems with Elton on a totally unrelated matter, and was fighting Elton's request) and it had been a major issue between the two of us all the way through the production period. It even reached the point of Mike's asking us to define the distance (in feet) between Elton and the Boys, and in the midst of all the production problems I was dealing with, it angered me to the point of just ignoring Mike and his pettiness. It turned out to be something that he didn't forget, despite the fact that the performance turned out to be one of the few real musical highlights of the show. Elton is always amazing, and the Boys added some very fitting harmonies to the song.

There was one shining little moment of quality performance before the final performance of the evening as Diana Krall, George Benson, and Erykah Badu joined together for a truncated performance of "I Can't Give You Anything but Love." It was a lovely palate cleanser, but to me it only seemed to point up the lack of musicality of much of the rest of the show.

By the time Santana came to the stage to perform before his obvious coronation for Album of the Year, the show was over. For all of the people who continually question whether or not we know the winners ahead of time, think about this: why in God's name would we schedule Santana at the end of the show when he had already won nearly every award he was nominated for? Why wouldn't we have put him up earlier so that his performances could follow all of his wins? Why, indeed. Because we don't and have never known the outcome of the voting until ahead of the announcement on the show itself.

I might have enjoyed this version of "Smooth" as much as the house and the home audience did (the show scored very well and kept the audience to the end, unlike some years) had I not been battling Santana's management for the entire production period. His managers, goaded by Clive Davis who was anxious to promote the new single, a song called "Maria," which featured a couple of other performers, had been in a continual argument with us over the total time that Santana would be permitted to perform as well as the material performed. "Smooth" is a great track, due in part to the strong vocals of Matchbox Twenty front man Rob Thomas, and it had been the biggest single of the year. That's what we wanted, but they wanted to do a three-song medley, and they requested time enough to do it. It was not going to happen, and though Carlos and I have a relationship that goes back to an early *Soundstage* in the '70s, it came down to four or five days before the show before we had negotiated the time and the material. It was unpleasant, difficult, and I'm certain it cost me an upcoming Santana special, which they had been talking to me about doing prior to all of these machinations. But my first commitment always has been, and remains, to making a great Grammy show every year, and I know that over the years, I've pissed off as many or more people as I've made happy.

But beyond the usual drama of the small issues I was dealing with, and deal with every year on the Grammys, the overriding issue for me was what I felt was a decided lack of respect for me by Mike. Instead of accepting the plaudits and congratulations of the show afterward, I retired to my office at Staples, sat with my head in my lap for a while, and decided that this would be my last Grammy show. The thrill of crafting a show that had purpose, vision, and quality was not worth the personal torture I had endured that year, and equally, I felt that the show we put on that year contained less of those qualities. It would take several months and a certain amount of convincing for me to muster up the desire to even talk to Mike, and then some time after that to realize that more than anything else in my professional life, the Grammys are the show that I love. And will continue to do them until I either can't or aren't asked to.

Whatever pain and torture I had been through during the production period itself was more than made up for, however, by the strong ratings the show posted. We pulled a 17.3 rating with a 27 share, the highest rating since 1993, good enough once again to win the February sweeps period for CBS. And believe me, good ratings can go a long way to stop the bleeding, just the way bad ones can drag you right down to the basement when you think you've done a great show. Of course, the ideal is a good show with a good rating, but I've been around long enough to know that those two elements don't always play in the same playground.

CHAPTER 23

The 2001 Grammy Awards

Eminem, Elton, and Madonna

When we got our first look at the nominations for the 2001 Grammy Awards, I wasn't surprised to see multiple nominations for Eminem. We had trifled with hip-hop nearly every year on the Grammys since the late '80s, sticking to safe choices like The Fugees, Will Smith, etc., but it was clear that Eminem, this young white rapper from Detroit, had become a major influence on the music business and was a lightning rod for millions of kids worldwide.

The conversations with the Academy were numerous and varied. Since we had never really made a commitment to giving rap its due in the past, were we making a mistake elevating a white rapper to prominence when it was basically a black musical experience? Was the charged content of violence against women, guns, homophobia, and so on something we should celebrate on the Grammys?

To Mike's credit, as the head of the Academy, he had the most to lose if we made the wrong decision. Since his arrival, he was no stranger to controversy, both professionally and personally, and this was not going to make him any more friends, internally or outside the Academy. The special interest groups would be gunning for him, the Trustees he had brought into the twenty-first century kicking and screaming could go either way, and certainly there was the risk of the entire Grammy experience being overshadowed by the controversial appearance of Eminem.

Mike made it easy. The voters and the Nominating Committee had made their choice by giving Eminem four nominations—the impact of his presence and his music was impossible to ignore, and we were going to invite him to perform.

It all started for me with a series of phone calls to Jimmy Iovine, the president of Interscope Records. In a meeting on a cold day in December, Jimmy, publicist Lori Earl, Eminem's publicist Dennis Dennehy, and I talked about whether Eminem would perform, how we would set up the staging, and what we could do to create the maximum impact from the performance. Jimmy expressed the importance of bringing Dr. Dre into the mix as soon as possible, a task that was more difficult than it seemed. It would be nearly seven weeks before we could sit with Dre and go through the number.

On the day the nominations were announced, I followed up with Jimmy and we put the process in motion. I wanted to preserve the starkness of the song, keep the most important visual of the video, the car going over the bridge killing "Stan" and his wife, and allow the audience to concentrate on the words to the song. To do that, I suggested a bare stage with only a bed and bare lightbulb to cover the three Stan verses, then switching to a desk at which Eminem would perform his letter to the already deceased Stan. Everybody loved it.

A couple of weeks later, with controversy already building about even having Eminem on the show, the stunner took place. Doug Morris called me with the thought of having Elton John appear with Eminem. Elton had already heaped praise on the rapper for artistic accomplishment, just as he has consistently done over the years in recognizing young talent and not, as some performers in his position have done, knocking the new music.

The next morning, while I was in a meeting at Universal on another project, Doug broke into our teleconference and announced that Elton had confirmed, and it was set. I warned the small group in the room in L.A. and those in New York that the key to this was keeping it quiet until the public really started focusing on the Grammys, which is usually the last two weeks prior to the show. We all agreed that no one would know, and I even held back from talking about it in the production company, save with a few key people.

The weeks went along, we moved toward production, we met with Dre, had very limited conversation with the Eminem side, and headed into the last two weeks before the show with our "secret" intact.

The first break came in a New York paper story that hinted at Elton's involvement and credited some woman from *Interview* magazine, who claimed she was the person who suggested it to Elton. I was furious, but we denied it all, and in reality, it was still enough in flux at that time to do so legitimately. Then later the same week, a *New York Daily News* reporter posted it, and this time, it got picked up everywhere, and we were put in a position where we had to announce the Eminem performance, hoping we could still hold the Elton announcement until the week before the show. But the *L.A. Times's* Bob Hilburn got to someone at Interscope to confirm and then called Elton who, thinking it was out, confirmed it to Hilburn. Ten days before the show, the story broke on the front page of the *Times*, and we had nothing left but to send out our release to follow up. We had kept it quiet as long as we could, and—though 20,000 people had died in an Indian earthquake, an American submarine had crashed into a Japanese fishing boat, and the Israeli/Palestinian peace talks were crashing—the press jumped on the Elton and Eminem story and ran with it.

On the day the story broke, although we still didn't have a host for the show, I sat in my office thinking about how the segment should be set up. I had already put the Eminem performance at the end of the show, knowing early on that this was big news and would hold the audience to the end, but also considering what might happen either onstage or in the house if we put it earlier in the show. There needed to be some addressing of the performance, both in Mike's annual appearance as well as in the introduction of the segment. I sat at the computer and the words just flowed, even without picturing who was going to speak them:

> *In the middle fifties, the emergence of Elvis Presley was met with America's first reaction to rock 'n'roll—civilizations would fall, kids would be corrupted, and our lives would never be the same. In the sixties disc jockeys everywhere called for the burning of Beatles albums to stop us from going to hell in a hand basket. And in the seventies, after hearing "Anarchy in the UK," the doomsayers said we were already over the brink. Of course in those days, artists weren't singing about violence against women or gay bashing, but you also couldn't pick up a newspaper, turn on a television set, or walk into a theater and see running wounds, mass killings, or "reality shows" that portrayed every aspect of violence in living color and Dolby Surround Sound, either. The very same media, I might add, who are condemning music's latest rebel.*

> *Tonight a young white rapper from Detroit who has taken his influences from the black experience of the streets, performs on the Grammys. His appearance here reflects his four Grammy nominations, and in particular, the artistry of a song called "Stan," which is more an indictment of the system that created him than it is a song about violence.*
>
> *Ladies and gentlemen, with the kind assistance of one of rock's venerable and most beloved artists, here is Eminem!"*

I was proud of those words and hoped they would survive the scrutiny of the TV committee, not to mention fit whoever it was that would deliver them.

Almost immediately after I finished writing, the phone rang. It was Bono, calling from Ireland to discuss some of the production details of U2's performance on the show. We had had a previous discussion about keeping the look stripped down and very anti-television, and I had called him the previous day to let him know that Bob Dickinson and I had worked out a great look for him. We shifted to the topic of Eminem's performance, and Bono told me that he had spent some time with the rapper, who at the time was in England doing shows. His take was very similar to mine, with us agreeing that many of the things that Eminem expounded were distasteful, but that his analysis was very interesting artistically.

Bono's feeling was that with the film medium, for example, Martin Scorsese could make an ultra-violent film with Robert DeNiro, like *Taxi Driver*, and the public was able to separate the artist from the story. His comment was that in almost every medium the audience could discriminate between the two, but that in the specific field of rap the public lumped the artist in with his art.

I said that my problem was not so much with the ability of an artist to express himself and find the freedom to do so, but that the motivation of the record companies was solely based on the profit motive, and that that was the difference here. Granted, in every art form there is the disparity between the artist's reason for being and the corporate structure that "gets it out there," but in this case, there seemed to be more of a responsibility about the target audience in question. I told him that being in the music world for as many years as I had, I was around at the end of the first generation of rock, and that I was able to witness the pure love that people like John Hammond, Ahmet Ertegun, Jerry Wexler, and others had for the music.

I reminisced about a Columbia Records marketing campaign in the 1970s that led with "the man can't stop our music," a reference to the establishment putting out the creative fires. Hypocrisy at its height I felt then, and still do to this day.

On Monday, when I returned to the office, there were a whole new set of circumstances to deal with, and along with the Eminem performance there were 13 other acts to deal with, not to mention the legion of production people all of whom had various questions about how we were going to pull off this show. People in the know understand that this three-hour live experience is easily the hardest three hours of live television, Oscars included, and the shame of it all is that the show, while nominated, has never been awarded an Emmy as "Music, Variety Special." Many of our support people have won, for lighting, audio, and so on, but the voters have always failed to recognize the show for its true leadership (a fact that is never lost on the other music award shows who seem to copy what we've done on an annual basis).

Among my Monday problems were the growing complexities of two performances in particular, Madonna and a segment I was putting together with Moby, Blue Man Group and Jill Scott.

I had gone to see the Blue Man show in Las Vegas a few weeks prior, loved what I saw, and thought that it was a perfect fit with Moby. Since I loved "Natural Blues" the nominated Moby track, it wasn't a reach to think about (Best New Artist–nominated) Jill Scott to do the Vera Hall part (on the record Vera Hall was a sample that Moby had lifted from an old blues record—she had died years ago). I knew this number had the potential of being a standout number in the show, Eminem aside, and I was committed to putting our full resources into fulfilling that vision. The Blue Man people, though extremely cooperative, were very insistent on using their people, a situation that comes up all the time with first timers. It takes time to build trust. It needed to be dealt with, and after several phone calls, we were all on the same track, and I couldn't wait for the rehearsal tape they were doing to arrive in L.A. so that I could take a look at it. I wasn't to be disappointed.

Madonna was another situation entirely. We had already had a rough but ultimately great experience with her two years prior, but it was clear that whatever we were going to do, it was going to be "Madonna's way." Added to the equation was the addition of Jamie King, the choreographer/stager who had helped make Ricky Martin the big score two years ago.

We had had a great deal to do with raising King's profile (and his price), but I knew it wasn't going to be the easiest of times. We had already had several meetings and conversations where he took my thoughts less than seriously—somewhat understandable since Madonna was paying his fee, but I did feel he owed it to us to help make it work all ways.

Every act wants to be the big score on the show, and I never minimize that feeling when I'm working with them. In my mind, I had already ranked the performances in terms of "water cooler" appeal, and had high hopes for nearly every act on the show, including a classical segment which would feature the French pianist Marc Andre Hamelin racing through two-and-a-half minutes of Chopin, and the jazz performances, which had similar potential because of the pairing of Take Six and Nnenna Freelon doing the Nat King Cole classic, "Straighten Up and Fly Right."

The Eminem/Elton story continued to build up as rehearsal and show day approached, but it was important to all of us not to let any one aspect of the show overwhelm us. First and foremost, there was the problem of being less than two weeks away and not having a host. It's become a very difficult situation with a show like the Grammys, or any major award show for that matter. Personalities have very little to gain, and a lot to lose, by saying yes to hosting these types of shows. They can go out and score and still be ripped by the press, or as happens, they can go out and tank and really get destroyed. Add to that the reality of a 14,000-seat arena, and it's one of the most intimidating gigs around.

Whoopi Goldberg said yes, and then days later, due to a medical problem, bowed out. We spent nearly two weeks trying to make it work with Bette Midler, only to fail at the last minute due to her shooting schedule. We went to a couple of other untouchables—Tom Hanks and

John Travolta—and it was obvious that we were in trouble. Early on, the production company had been very supportive of Jon Stewart, who had worked with us as a presenter on several award shows in the past, and who Harriet and I had gotten to know when he was down in Miami doing an HBO standup show while we were doing Gloria Estefan's HBO special. He was glib, edgy, smart, and funny. What further attributes were needed? Name value, and in the eyes of the Academy, though he was a strong name, he wasn't "star quality."

But we were so close to the show that star quality was secondary to someone who could go out there and be funny. I called Jon's manager (it's strictly forbidden to call the act directly, even if you know them), and got a very quick no about ten days out. I wasn't ready for a no, so I called James Dickson, Jon's agent. James really went to bat for us, and set up a call with Jon so that I could have an opportunity to talk to him about the show and why it was a good move for him. We talked, and though Jon was rightfully concerned not only about the prep time but also the awesome task ahead, he agreed. Preempting his obvious question, I opened the conversation with, "Just so you know, you're not the last name on the list; we still have Merv, Mike Douglas, and Morton Downey, Jr., who haven't returned our calls."

He laughed, we talked further, and with a great deal of courage and guts, Jon joined us as the host for the show. And as it turned out, he was not only great at it, but as he said, the fact that he had less time to worry about it probably made it even easier.

On the Saturday before the show, one day before our rehearsals were to begin at Staples, Walter and I made our way around to a couple of the offsite rehearsals that were taking place around the city. Our first stop was out in the Valley where Moby, Blue Man Group, and Jill Scott were getting together for the first real run-through of their number. They were ready for us when we walked in, and we knew from the minute it started it would be one of the big scores of the night. A couple of adjustments, a few staging suggestions, and there was no reason for us to hang around. We took our notes and moved on to the Madonna rehearsal, which was happening on the other end of town in Culver City.

Obviously, we had concerns based upon how difficult our previous experience with her people had been three years earlier. We knew the number would be terrific—she's a hard worker, a pro, and committed to making it work. And, to our delight, "Music" lent itself to an opening number much better than "Ray of Light," which had opened that previous Grammy show.

It was even better than we expected. A 30-foot pimpmobile, dancers galore doing provocative moves, confetti cannons, big screens tracing Madonna's career on video, and best of all, a woman who lights up the screen each time out. And Jamie King, the choreographer/stager, had put together a great ensemble to make it all work.

The rehearsals began on Sunday, February 18, and the two-stage concept that we had come up with for the show proved to be the thing that took the lion's share of the pressure out of the picture, and allowed us to stay on schedule for the next three days, not to mention show day. From morning until night on Sunday, Monday, and Tuesday, 14 acts rolled across the stage, worked out the kinks in each number, and cooperated with us in blocking for cameras, a two-hour experience for each act. And it all seemed to be working out in the house.

Behind the scenes, we were still booking presenters and locking the final pieces of the show. There were the usual dramas: presenters who refused to appear together, those who wanted their copy changed, and the ever-present threat of disruption from the gay community, which was up in arms not only over Eminem's performance but also about Elton's participation in it.

We try to keep our rehearsals closed, but a place like Staples makes it almost impossible. Ushers continuously walk the hall checking credentials, but so many people are directly involved on the production side that we know we can't cover it all. And on Tuesday, when Eminem and Elton came over for their rehearsal, something happened that almost gave away the surprise of their performance.

Walter and I walked them through the staging for the number, suggested a couple of things that they might do during it, and we started rehearsing the song. It opened with an empty stage followed by Eminem coming out to a bed, sitting and rapping, after which he and Elton went back and forth between verses and choruses until the last verse, when the bed turned around and became the desk at which Eminem finally wrote his letter back to his obsessed fan, Stan.

It was stark, it was emotional, and it depended on keeping a distance between Elton and Eminem for the whole of the song, so that, on cue, the two of them could meet centerstage at the end for a joint bow.

As they began the rehearsal, it was plain to see that this was going to be one of those moments that people would be struck by, and the emptiness of the Staples Center took on an almost eerie silence as the vocals and Elton's piano on top of the prerecorded track boomed through the empty arena. Midway into the rehearsal, a stage manager came running up to me at our production table and whispered to me that an L.A. radio station was carrying the rehearsal live on their air at that moment. We quickly cut off the feed to the house, leaving the truck feed and the monitors to the stage on, but it was out, and there was nothing we could do. Cell phones have become the great equalizer here, and it was obvious that someone somewhere in the arena was feeding our signal via cell phone to the radio station. Security took out looking everywhere as we continued to rehearse, and fortunately, there weren't any more of those incidents.

Show day finally arrived, and with a smooth dress rehearsal save a few missed technical cues, we readied ourselves for what was potentially the most controversial Grammys in years, and a show that had the capability of becoming the best show we had ever done.

Madonna's opening performance was amazing, and the usually too-hip-for-the-room industry audience that filled much of the house actually showed some signs of life, rewarding the Material Girl's hard work with thunderous applause.

Destiny's Child took us over the half hour with an eye-popping medley of "Independent Woman" performed in front of a newly built video wall of footage from the *Charlie's Angels* video, and then they moved to our second stage to perform "Say My Name" in front of the giant head that was first seen with a series of morphed faces of the girls, followed by the twelve Rumanian acrobats moving beautifully on the various levels. All of the sets however were bested by the startling, sexy performance by all three girls, dressed in less than anyone else on that stage that night, and the particularly dazzling beauty of Beyoncé Knowles. They followed their performance by winning the second of their two Grammys of the night for the Best R&B Performance by a Duo or Group.

Paul Simon did his job and gave us a great version of "You're the One," aided, I suspect, by my last words to him before he kicked it off. Walking onstage as he was plugging in, I walked up to him and told him that he was about to give the Grammys its first truly lyrical moment, and that was why I had put him there. I knew he wasn't feeling good about the night (he wound up losing in the Album of the Year category), and I wanted him to really score with the performance, which as he knew is what people always find memorable about the Grammys.

Following Paul's performance, we gave out the first Rap award of the night, for Best Rap Album, and though no one was surprised to learn that Eminem was the winner assuring everyone waiting for the upcoming duet with Elton that he was really there. And he was quite gracious in his acceptance speech, a tipoff to what was to come later.

Because we faced our toughest competition in years, I knew that the crossover at the nine o'clock hour was our toughest spot in terms of keeping the audience and bringing over those people who were channel surfing at the time. ABC's *Millionaire* was ending; NBC was about to kick off its highly rated two-hour block of *West Wing* (one of *my favorite* shows) followed by *Law and Order*; ABC had two highly rated shows, *Drew Carey* and *Spin City*; and Fox's *Temptation Island* had become one of the strongest shows of the new season, as exploitative as it was. While it's often difficult for us to do more than one big performance in one act (between commercials), I purposely planned to have Faith Hill perform just ahead of nine o'clock, and follow that performance with what I knew would be one of the strongest performances of the show, U2's "Beautiful Day." I had been pursuing U2 for the Grammys for years, and although I had worked with them on other shows, and Bono had presented on the show a couple of times (including the infamous Sinatra incident), this would mark the band's first full performance on the show.

Jon came out to pad for a minute while we changed the audio board over for U2, and then the boys came out and gave us one of the great Grammy performances ever, rocking "Beautiful Day" as never before. Afterward, Bono told me he had never felt better about a performance on an award show—you could see it in the entire band's faces and Bono's body language as he played the whole house for all it was worth. The harsh lighting, which we had been warned about by his crew (they kept saying to stay away from it because these guys were "old" and couldn't take the light), only added to the emotional impact of the performance, and Bono's trip into the audience for the middle eight of the song was electric. It got the first standing ovation of the night, and it didn't hurt that they followed it up by winning a Grammy for Best Rock Performance by a Duo or Group.

As we headed into the second hour, we changed the pace dramatically with the most intimate performance of the night, a duet between perennial Grammy favorite Sheryl Crow and Best New Artist nominee Shelby Lynne. The performance was the payoff of a two-week struggle between Walter and me, an extremely cooperative Sheryl (she would be the first to admit that this is not always the case), and a recalcitrant Shelby, who viewed this as Sheryl's number in which she was playing a backup role. It wasn't true, but as we examined Shelby's career, not to mention the tragic incidents in her life which included being witness to the murder/suicide of both parents) we tried to be sensitive to a very difficult situation. It didn't help that after several conference calls where Walter and I tried to calm Shelby down, and after negotiations back and forth, Shelby showed up over an hour late for their only on-stage rehearsal—and was definitely less than sober when she arrived. It didn't matter musically however, and the emotionally charged situation seemed almost to propel the performance to a new high, although I think it's safe to say that those two girls shouldn't be invited to the same dinner party . . . at least not for awhile.

Because every Grammy show has a jazz (or a classical) performance, we always look for something that will be artistically relevant but also accessible to a broad audience. It's not always easy, but this year the performance jumped out at us. Nnenna Freelon had recorded the Nat King Cole chestnut, "Straighten Up and Fly Right" with Take Six, and even on CD, the track was striking. We booked them early, and as it turned out, doing the number live was even more of a treat, and captured an additional standing ovation from the house, which was now fully into the show, jaded as they were.

It was then time for one of my favorites of the night, one of those performances that the audience, both at home and in the house, had no clue as to what to expect. Jon introduced Moby, Blue Man Group, and Jill Scott as "a Benetton ad on steroids" and what happened next knocked the show on its collective ear for the next four minutes. Jill's remarkable voice, combined with the haunting "Natural Blues" from Moby's album, and layered with the outrageous visuals and music of Blue Man Group's three lead Blue Men and a rockin' band took the show to its highest level yet, resulting in another standing ovation. It fulfilled everything I was hoping for and more, and anyone leaving ABC at around 9:30 (the only "opening") couldn't possibly flip past the Grammys after seeing what was happening on that stage: huge video eyes moving back and forth, streamers spewing out into the audience, and an outrageous vocal performance by Jill.

Just before ten o'clock we put Macy Gray up on stage to do "I Try," one of my favorite songs of the year, and one of the two songs I felt had the best chance to win Record of the Year. Macy's performance, aided by pink wigs, out-there outfits, and a casual yet intense vocal that belied the laissez-faire attitude ascribed to the song's writer/performer, proved to be one more in a series of changes of pace, and a huge crowd pleaser. As Macy stood backstage with U2, I had a hunch that one of them would be coming forward to collect the Record trophy. Joni Mitchell and Carlos Santana read the nominees, and when U2's name was read, even though I would have been happy with either of them, I felt a special sense of fulfillment due to their amazing performance a half-hour previous. We were just about two-thirds into the show, still holding the Eminem/Elton moment in our pockets.

Christina Aguilera scored next, with an over-the-top performance kicked off by an entrance on a gold sputnik from 80 feet in the air, followed by a transcendent vocal performance of a ballad, then kicking into a balls-out dance number, both performed in Spanish. While we were doing Christina's special late in 2000, she had expressed to me that she had always dreamed of an amazing "entrance" on the Grammys, and you couldn't ask for a more spectacular one than what we did that night. Her only down moment came minutes later when Shakira (who had scored mightily on the Latin Grammys six months previous) took the honors for the Best Latin Album. But it was a major score for Christina that night, and though she had won the Best New Artist the year before, that night she would go Grammyless.

Even the classical moment worked on this show better than some others. Marc Andre Hamelin, considered one of the greatest technical pianists of our time, performed a Chopin composition arranged by Godowsky, and played more notes, and better, in two minutes and ten seconds, than most musicians play in an evening.

We were now minutes away from the home stretch, Eminem and Elton, but still to come was Mike's annual talk to the audience, a few minutes that in recent years had enticed, outraged, or bored (sometimes all three) millions of people, but always had its point. Mike likes controversy alright, and with everything that had gone on leading to this moment, he wasn't going to let it pass without making his (and the Academy's) case. He was even more verbose than usual, but his setup was right, and at the end of his talk, leading to the introduction of Eminem and Elton, the stage was set for one of the most dramatic moments in Grammy history.

I kind of expected the house to quiet down as Eminem made his way from upstage to the bed for his first verse, but I never expected all activity to stop backstage, which was usually close to chaos for the entire three hours of the show. I looked around, and nobody was moving.

Even the stagehands, who needed to get things ready for the closing of the show, had stopped in their tracks and were as still as our extras had been when they were asked to freeze in position earlier in the show for the 'N Sync number. As I suggested, Eminem stayed on the bed for nearly the entire first verse, getting up near the end as the verse went into Elton's first chorus. The piano, hidden behind some corrugated backing, turned and came into view on Elton's lines, and a rush came from the audience, and the backstage. Almost inside himself, Elton delivered the chorus as Eminem moved further downstage readying himself for the second verse, a rise in the anxiety level as Stan bemoaned the fact that his idol, Eminem, hadn't responded to his first letter. He moved out of the way to let Elton take the stage for his second chorus and then I watched his body language change as he came further downstage to deliver the "money"—Stan's side of the song, an angry harangue that ends with Stan's car, with his pregnant girlfriend in the trunk, being hurled over a bridge and into the depths of the local river. Elton's final passionate chorus wafted through a stilled arena filled with 13,000 people, as Stan's bed turned and revealed the table at which Eminem finally wrote a letter to Stan, although too late. The song ended, there was a moment of stillness, and then the arena exploded in the biggest standing ovation of the evening. It was then that Eminem and Elton both walked downstage and embraced.

It was almost anticlimactic when Stevie Wonder and Bette Midler came onstage to announce the award for Best Album. They joked back and forth for a moment, then read the nominees Beck, Radiohead, Steely Dan, Eminem, and Paul Simon. The question of the night was about to be answered.

Would the voters of the Academy pick a reasonably obscure Beck album that didn't have big sales, but featured an artist rewarded a number of times by the voters before? Would they go avant-garde and go for Radiohead, the critics' darling who had also been nominated before? Or would they fulfill the guesses of the Grammy critics who predicted that either Steely Dan or Paul Simon would be the traditional older voters' favorites? Or would the controversy engendered by Eminem spur his album to a Grammy, or conversely hurt the cause?

Steely Dan won, and although it probably displeased as many viewers as it pleased, upon reflection, it wasn't a bad choice. It pleased those critics of the Grammys who now could add the tired phrase "finally recognized but much too late" when describing the Steely Dan win and silenced those who never got the Eminem controversy or nomination in the first place.

The curtain came down on the 43rd Annual Grammy show a few minutes after eleven o'clock, but there was no question that the story of the show would continue to be replayed for a long time. We could be controversial without being exploitive, and we could be contemporary without losing our sense of history. That's the Grammys, folks.

CHAPTER 24

The 2002 Grammy Awards

Post 9/11: U2, Moulin Rouge, Mary J., and Alicia Keys

Perhaps the 2002 Grammy show could be looked at best from the position of what wasn't on as opposed to what was. To be sure, I was thrilled with the show, our third from the Staples Center in Los Angeles. But then again, this show has a way of always looking better to me than it does to, say, some of the critics, who seem to be writing the same review of the show they wrote in the '80s—even though it's nothing like it was in those days. Since this book finally gives me the opportunity to answer some of them in writing, knowing that it most likely won't be read by any of them (they're too busy covering the latest scandal in our business), here's a quote that was sent to me by a friend following the show.

We were both obviously affected (though not moved) by a rash of negativity that greeted us from the press, and were probably both looking for some positive reinforcement:

> *It is not the critic who counts; not the one who points out how the strong stumbled, or where the doer of deeds could have done better. The credit belongs to the one who is actually in the arena; whose face is marred by dust and sweat and blood; who strives valiantly; who errs and comes up short again and again; who knows great enthusiasm and great devotion; who spends him/herself in a worthy cause; who at the best knows in the end the triumph of high achievement and who, at worst, if he/she fails, at least fails while daring greatly, so that his/her place shall never be with those timid souls who know neither victory nor defeat.*

Teddy Roosevelt said that in the early 1900s, and though most of my knowledge about the Rough Rider has to do with *Arsenic and Old Lace*, his words certainly rang true to me.

It *is* about the battle, and it is about having the balls to go into it again and again, against terrific odds. I have very little if any respect for those who dare to criticize, either well or ill, if they haven't actually done it for themselves. After so many years, the reality is that no matter how Pollyannaish you may be, you know whether you've done well or not—you can tell from those around you whether or not you have a right to crow or should take an extended vacation from the business. And for me, I'm damn proud of the show we put on that stage from year to year. Of course I could look at specifics and say we missed this or that, but overall, there's no show that can touch the Grammys either in size, scope, or feel. We've put together a remarkable team of people who put in the time, the energy, the thought, and the *heart* to make this show what it has become over time.

And no critic, sitting in his living room, or more likely, stuffed in a hot press room paying no real attention to the show but trying to think how he'll get in his next question, one that has already been asked by five people before him—"Hey Alicia Keys, how does it feel to win four Grammys?"—or even more banal, "Christina Aguilera, where did you get that dress?" We may not be the brightest lights on the Christmas tree, but at least what we do is original, oftentimes stirring, and occasionally moving—and from a blank page: not something recycled and boring and often from the brain of a frustrated person who wishes he or she was doing what we do.

Although I've become reasonably inured to all of it, I often think about the hundreds of folks who work with us on the show, and the pride they take in their work, only to wake up the next morning and find some half-baked review that makes you wonder if the writer was watching the same show.

And speaking of this group, it's a perfect segue back to the show, and one of my favorite performances from the 2002 show, *Moulin Rouge*—a piece we put together with Christina Aguilera, Mya, Pink, Li'l Kim, and Missy Elliott. My joy stems as much from working with Ron Fair, who produced the record that became such a big hit, as it does from creating a visual and aural mindblower of a production number that brought our whole team together in a piece that demanded everybody's attention.

First of all, the number had already been performed at the MTV Movie Awards previously, and though it had been translated very literally, it was an exciting number. Our job was to take it the next step, and one night after I had watched the DVD of the film, it all became very clear to me.

Using footage from the film as a base, I knew we had to come up with a number downstage (close to the audience) that was as exciting as the upstage big-screen visuals. I asked Tina Landon, who has worked with us on a number of shows and also choreographs for Christina, to step in and create the choreography, which was fresh and hot. When they first came in, Christina's management was concerned about the wardrobe for the girls, which both in the film and in the MTV Movie version was about as trashy as it could be. Granted, the girls were portraying prostitutes from the movie, but they had taken some heat from fans after the MTV performance, and didn't want any more. So I suggested that we do the first part of the number with beautiful but tasteful costumes that hid what lay beneath, and then midway into the number, I wanted to create dressing screens that the girls could go behind and change into the payoff: the sexy stuff. Bob Keene went beyond my vision, putting up separate screens for the girls that would move up and down to reveal them at the top of the number, then would go up again for the costume change, and ultimately with Bobby Dickinson's backlighting, make the costume change itself exciting.

Ron's live charts were even better than the record, and with limited rehearsal time, the girls all rose to the occasion, and the number was terrific. So sensational, in fact, that during our rehearsals on Tuesday, there was a movement afoot from those who didn't know what was coming to open the show with the number. I still had U2 coming to rehearse, and I was counting on them to give the show the opening lift it needs every year to counter the normal sitting and waiting by the audience, many of whom had already been there for hours for the pre-telecast awards that are given out directly before the televised show. And this year there was even more of a reason to kick it into high gear, because the additional security meant that the 14,000 people coming to the arena needed to arrive even earlier than normal, and then go through metal detectors and wand searches.

I resisted what would have been a sensational idea for any show other than the Grammys, and held off several attempts to restructure the show and open with "Lady Marmalade." As exciting as it was, the Grammys is and always has been about the music, and this particular year, in my opinion at least, there was no better music created than the U2 CD, a feeling that would be borne out on Grammy night when they won four awards.

The Irish lads showed up for their rehearsal, and we began to put together the set that we had discussed with Bono over the previous six or seven weeks. At last year's show we had gone with a very black-and-white look, with backlighting careening around the arena and a sense of simplicity that matched the stripped-down, honest feel of the CD. This year, even though our instincts were to stay simple, we needed to come up with something different, and our two Bobs did just that: a modest plexiglass platform of equal-sized rectangular pieces that swooped up at the back to create a seamless, floating feel when placed in the midst of the black stage that surrounded it. And to make it even more striking, Bobby D. had the brilliant idea of lighting it all in red, a color usually avoided by television in the past because of the camera's inability to read it. But the newer-technology cameras were able to handle red, and we had never done anything quite so vivid. It was striking to the eye, and even more striking in the camera.

But we had a problem. It was a heavy, bulky set and one that needed the most time to set and strike of any set on the show, even the Dylan box, which we'll speak of later. Not only was the crew having trouble setting it for rehearsal, but Bobby discovered that he had very few lighting positions to put the lights which, when cycled to, gave a true red. And as they worked frantically to get everything ready for what would be the last rehearsal before the dress the next day, another problem surfaced that could have been even more disastrous than the set.

Bono and I had talked about having a choir there to join in at the end of "Walk On," and I had suggested Kirk Franklin's group. We've used Kirk a number of times, and Bono had also met and worked with him, and we both felt it was a good call. But Bono was clear that he wanted a multi-racial group and also mixed ages so that it didn't conflict with other pieces we were doing on the show that used a choir. When Kirk's group showed up for the first time for their onstage rehearsal, I knew this was not going to work to put Kirk's group onstage. There wasn't enough room.

Compounding all of this was a very precise team that works with U2 to make sure that the sound is absolutely right . . . and they're very good at it. But when the boys took the stage, there were still problems, and at first, no one seemed happy with the sound.

So with all of these factors at work, after what had been a remarkably smooth rehearsal process, right at the very end, it looked dismal. I took Bono aside and told him and the other guys not to worry about the choir. I knew the answer, and had already put some steps in motion to solve that. I went to our seat-filler person and asked him to put aside 75 young, mixed-race seat fillers and bring them to me just before show time, and I'd place them at the foot of the stage to "fill in" with the choir. I knew that would do two things: it would give us a great look at the top of the show, and it would take it away from looking like a 25-member choir singing a song from the front of the house, which was a strange idea. What I didn't know right then was that it would do one more thing: it would act as a conduit, connecting U2 and the audience, and making it easy for the jaded industry audience filling the entire front of the house to rise from their seats and join in one of the most thoughtful, but celebratory songs of the year, if not in modern music.

And it did just that. For the first time in my memory, the entire audience, not just the front, stood up en masse and cheered along through the entire opening number of the Grammys.

Sound problems were solved, Bobby knew he would be able to deal with his lighting situation, and together with U2's great production manager, Steve Iredell, our guys had solved the set problem—so U2 left happy.

Walter and I were left nearly exhausted by a rehearsal schedule which, because of the Staples basketball schedule, was exactly the same as the previous year's show, but with one major difference. The Academy and CBS, for a number of reasons, had elected to add a full half-hour to the three-hour show we were doing, but they had not given us more rehearsal time.

On the day that the nominations came out that year, we had our annual gathering with Mike and the television committee, and once again their thoughts about performances on the show jibed with ours quite a bit. We all obviously agreed on U2, "Lady Marmalade," and Alan Jackson, but because Josh Bell was only nominated in the Classical Crossover category, they weren't ready to settle for what might have been called a less-than-pure classical performance. That would come later after we had exhausted a number of other considerations, and both Walter and I lobbied hard for the Bell performance, which turned out to be a stunner.

The other unanimous choices for the show included the Billy Joel/ Tony Bennett duet of Billy's "New York State of Mind," particularly those components that reflected the state of the country after September 11; Alicia Keys, who had been music's biggest story in the preceding year and had six nominations to her credit; and a performance from the soundtrack of *O Brother, Where Art Thou?* the fine T-Bone Burnett album which had won the CMA Album of the Year Award three months earlier. Other unanimous choices were performances by the Dave Matthews Band, which had become rock music's biggest-selling live act; Bob Dylan, who I had already put on hold thinking that he would be nominated for Album of the Year; Outkast, the Atlanta-based rappers who were also nominated for Album of the Year, and were loved by critics and fans alike; and the combination of Alejandro Sanz and Destiny's Child, a number we had already put together and would have done on the Latin Grammys, the show that was to have aired on September 11. We also knew that there would be a spot for 'N Sync.

With those bookings already set within hours of the nominations, there were still several slots open, and I was pleased that there were. There are always things that come up between the nominations and the show, stories that emerge, gems that we find we overlooked in our haste to make the initial bookings, and slots we just want to leave open in hopes that something special will come along that we want to accommodate.

One of those spots, as far as I was concerned, belonged to Mary J. Blige, and another consideration needed to be India.Arie. We'd worked with Mary a lot over the years, and to be blunt, she's just the most emotionally charged singer in contemporary music, a woman who puts her heart and soul into every performance, and one of the sweetest people I've ever met. I wanted to hold a spot for her, and though some members of the committee questioned it, I felt strongly about keeping one of the spots open until we could make it happen.

Another act I felt strongly about was the rock group Train. Two songs had come out before September 11, but seemed to take on greater impact after the tragedy. One was Five For Fighting's "Superman" which is a marvelous song and featured a great performance by young John Androsik, who is destined for greater fame, and the other was "Drops of Jupiter," which is one of those songs that you remember hearing for the first time. I was driving, listening to some rock station, and I nearly had to pull over when I heard the song. I don't know if it would have had the impact on me had it not been for the events of September 11, but I suspect it would have.

Either way, this was another act we all wanted to find a spot for, but wasn't one that could be booked until closer to the show. When we did book them, we not only made them the happiest bunch of guys in the world, but also gave ourselves a reality check into the lives we lead and the kind of impact we can have on people's lives. I was there through the whole process: from the nominations where Pat Monahan, the lead singer, was present to hear his nomination read, to the rehearsal process where I watched his face as he first encountered the notorious "front row" of pictures of music superstars, on through to an amazing performance, followed by watching him from behind the camera as his name was read winning the Grammy for Best Rock Song on the show. I never forget what this is all about, but sometimes it's refreshing to look at it all through fresh eyes, and I'm not sure I'll ever see eyes wider than Pat's at that moment in his life.

And finally, from the world of pure pop, there was Nelly Furtado.

I was torn here, because we do have a mandate to present mainstream music on the show and questioned whether 'N Sync and Alicia, our two acts with the most sales, might not be enough for viewers. We had worked with Nelly on two shows in 2001, and while she was terrific on the John Lennon show in October, I felt that she did not deliver a strong performance on the Women Rock show later that month. None of us were sure about what to do with her.

As the weeks drew down to the show, we delayed making firm decisions on the last few spots. I was more committed to Mary J., however, and she became the next booking, followed by the gospel segment, which fought its way into the show due to the lack of adequate performance-oriented jazz nominations. Because Al Green was receiving a Lifetime Achievement Award from the Academy, I booked him first, and next moved Brian McKnight, someone who had never performed on the show and should have just out of pure talent reasons. Still uncertain as to what to do with India, I added her to the gospel segment, with the possibility that we might give her a full performance closer to the show date.

Nothing made me happier than calling Simon Renshaw, Mary J.'s manager, with the offer to perform. And though I knew she'd give it her all come show day, I needed a little insurance to settle a still-uncertain TV committee member who had openly questioned the booking on one of our conference calls, as well as my partner Walter, who had not really seen her as I had in the past couple of years. The dynamic of the committee is such that when the two or three most vocal members question our judgment, sometimes doubt spreads, as it almost had the day that one of them "suggested" we make sure we have Mary's video prominent during her performance for people to "really understand" what she was singing about in her hit, "No More Drama." I had a rare lapse of restraint, and didn't even let the committee member finish her sentence before interrupting with, "Mary J. could stand onstage with a bare light bulb, sing the phone book and people would understand what she's singing about."

But for insurance, when Mary J. showed up for rehearsal, tired after a day-long trip from the Midwest where she had cancelled a show to get to L.A. in time for rehearsal, I walked up to her just before the first run-through, gave her a kiss, and told her that a few people out there were doubters, and that rather than just marking her rehearsal, she was to give it her all—in order to quell the naysayers. She did just that, and the entire crew stopped what they were doing to give her a standing ovation . . . in the *rehearsal*. Sensing that I had gotten through to her, as I often do during the show, I walked up to her on show night as she was standing upstage moments before her performance, hugged her again, and said three simple words, "This one counts." Moments later, she delivered simply the best performance I've ever seen her give, and it was rewarded by another standing ovation, this time from the 14,000 people who filled the Staples Center that night.

I also had numerous conversations with Bono about an idea I had had long before the nominations came out. In fact, I had been thinking about it since September 11. We needed to respond with a segment that had some bearing on the events of that day, and had a second need to reflect the passing of George Harrison in early December. As we began to book the show, adding Alan Jackson and Tony Bennett and Billy Joel singing "New York State of Mind," we all felt that the national tragedy of the 11th was being addressed, but there was still Harrison to think about. There has always been an unwritten Academy policy, and a good one, about recognizing the deaths in our industry over the year. The reasoning is simple: where do you start and where do you stop? Anyone left out feels slighted, and we were bound to leave out someone. Beyond that, I have always felt that the reason that other award shows feature these segments is to fill some sort of a "performance" slot—but none of those shows have 17 performances fighting their way onto the show. At the gospel rehearsal, Mike and I went up to India.Arie and told her we had opened up a spot for her to do her nominated song "Video." Her jaw nearly dropped, and she quickly left Staples to round up her band and rehearse for the following day. Bob Keene put a set together of great West Indian material, and she was set. It wasn't so easy with Nelly Furta-do, who, truth be told, was getting tired of being jerked around with the vague promise that something would open up if she could be patient. Her manager, Chris Smith, and I were talking almost hourly the last five days of the show, and he was terrific about listening, but I could tell he felt I was just shining him on and wasn't going to put Nelly on. When I called to tell him that I wanted her to do a stripped-down version of "I'm Like a Bird" accompanied only by a guitar (who turned out to be the amazing Steve Vai), he tried to convince me that she needed her band. I felt that if we just did the song as it had been done on a number of other shows over the previous year, we'd lose, and she would too, so I insisted. Nelly and Steve got together later that same day, and the report from the rehearsal off-site was that it was great. And when they came in for the dress and finally the show, it was one of those moments that people remembered . . . not the same Nelly at all.

Working out the production ideas for the show is always the most creative part of doing the Grammys. Many of the production ideas, whether they involve video background, staging, or even the music breakdowns, begin with us, with the acts themselves taking them to the next level. On the 2002 show, we had the initial ideas for several of the numbers, although we truly do encourage the acts to grow them and make them their own. This is not the case on many of the other music awards show, where the record labels fund the sets, props, and so on—often bringing in their own people to execute the ideas. It's become so prevalent that even though we strongly solicit concepts from the acts, they often come to the first meeting they have with us bringing little or nothing. Unless, of course, they've been with us before and know that it's an open dialogue where we welcome their ideas and also ask that they respect and listen to ours.

Bob Dylan is an exception to the rule. Each time we've had him on the show, he assigns a creative team to come in and work with us on building something unique (thus the emergence of Soybomb on the 1998 show). This show was to be no different. Two weeks before the show, some drawings came into the office from Bob's people, showing Bob performing in a box. The drawings were intriguing, the idea equally compelling, and we quickly expressed our desire to make it happen. It was certainly different, and gave Bob a look that was like nothing else on the show. After two off-site tests of the box which showed us that the dimensions needed to be reduced to feel intimate and to have some sort of scale both inside and out, we moved on to constructing it, and it became one of the most talked-about performances on the show—due not only to the box itself but also to Bob's insistence that he be shot with only three cameras and that no swooping crane shots be used.

The performance that no one saw on the show was Michael Jackson. It was rumored that he would appear, but it never happened.

My friend Jack Sussman at CBS had done Michael's special in 2001, and it was the highest-rated music special of the year. He had developed a relationship with Michael, and both he and Les Moonves were anxious to have Michael on the show. But Michael only appears on award shows if he gets an award. And we were not about to do that.

We began the discussions with Michael's manager, Trudy Green, and let her know early that we were interested in having Michael perform, but not under the condition that we would give him an award. Through the record label, we assumed that was understood, but about ten days before the show, Trudy scheduled a meeting at our office, ostensibly, she told Tisha Fein, to discuss the creative approach to Michael's appearance. But when Trudy came to the office, it was merely to ask again about "Michael's award." I was getting more and more frustrated (and frankly, pissed off) at this lack of understanding and respect for us, so before I expressed my frustration, I got up from the conference table and walked out of the room. I'm glad that I did, or it could have gotten ugly.

Trudy stayed with Walter and Tisha and finished the meeting, but there was no way we would agree to giving him an award on the air. We did say that following his performance, we would make mention of his 30-year career and recognize his achievements. If that was enough, we offered to move ahead.

A few days later, Jack called and said that Michael wanted to meet with Walter and me at the Bel Air Hotel to talk about his performance. I spent two days putting together an absolutely riveting mega-mix of Michael's hits that could serve as the basis for his performance, and took it over to the Bel Air the following Saturday to play for him. He seemed to love it, and more-or-less told us that he was in. He gave me a home number and asked that I call him on Monday if he had not already called Jack and confirmed everything.

Three days later, still no word. And then finally, via the record label, we heard that Michael had declined. It's too bad, because for whatever Michael has become in recent days, he had a tremendous influence both on the sound and the look of pop music, and this performance would have been a virtuoso opportunity for him to receive credit for what he's done.

So, with no Michael, we locked the show, added the final presenters, and, with the rehearsals over, did our usual anxious hours-before-the-show dance, waiting to go on the air at 5 p.m. West Coast time, 8 p.m. live to the east.

The show was a big winner with the live audience. Although the ratings were down from the previous year—due in part to NBC's airing of the Winter Olympics, which meant that fewer people were watching CBS for the two weeks prior to the show—it handily won the night and clinched the February sweeps for CBS.

Lest you forget, the big winners were Alicia and U2, who split several of the major categories, and *O Brother, Where Art Thou?* which was the surprise winner for Album of the Year. As we were laying the show out, and I faced the annual dilemma of where to place the two biggest awards, Album of the Year and Record of the Year, I chose to put Album in the middle of the show, trying to second-guess the Grammy voters, and having the feeling that that soundtrack might win. If not, I had picked Dylan, and had placed the award directly after both he and *O Brother* had performed. I held Record of the Year until the end of the show because having opened with U2, I guessed that "Walk On" would be the Record of the Year, and it was.

But as usual, as far as I'm concerned—and this was borne out by the record sales increases the week following the show—the big winners were the artists who performed on the show. There were huge sales bumps for nearly every act that performed, with *O Brother*, Alicia Keys, Train, and Bob Dylan leading the way. Total sales for the week jumped over 40 percent from the previous week, and—at a time when the record business was beginning its major decline—those were spectacular numbers.

CHAPTER 25

The 2003 Grammy Awards

*Simon and Garfunkel, a Tribute to the Clash,
and a Great Night for Norah Jones*

S ome people will remember the 45th Annual Grammy Awards as the Year of Norah Jones, but for me, it will always be the Year of Neil Portnow, the veteran record executive who replaced Mike Greene, the first paid president of the Academy, after Greene was forced to resign at the insistence of the Board of Trustees. As I've said before, what Mike did to expand the reach of the Academy and bring the membership into the present is his legacy, no matter how it all ended.

Up until the time Neil arrived in late 2002, I thought I had a pretty good take on much of the Academy leadership, both those involved in and those outside the show, but I really didn't know Neil. We had said hello on various occasions, but he was clearly someone whose record and music publishing industry successes at Zomba Records made him the perfect choice to restore a sense of respect and integrity for the Academy after its highly publicized personnel problems.

And that's precisely what Neil did, and did in a hurry. In a period of three months, I was witness to an organizational turnaround that I can't imagine even the trustees believed possible. And for me, there was the beginning of a personal friendship that I hope will continue for many years.

To understand, I probably need to backtrack a bit and make the obvious comparisons between Neil and Mike. From day one, where Mike was petulant and demanding, Neil was collaborative and patient. Where Mike needed the gratification of being "in charge" (and to have his ego fed on a daily basis), Neil was content to share the credit, to seek advice, and to listen.

As you might imagine, the Grammys are a show in a constant state of flux in nearly every area, from the day the nominations are announced until the credits roll seven weeks later. And the 45th, the first Grammys to return to New York since Mike had had his tiff with Rudy Giuliani five years previous, coupled with the ever-present sense of physical jeopardy that seems to follow every show we've done since September 11, only added to the difficulty as we approached the show.

Fortunately, I was to have two important allies in this initial year of new faces at the Academy. I had developed a good working relationship with Garth Fundis, the then Academy chairman and the person most responsible for Mike's departure—a bright, thoughtful, and very humane guy. And over the past several shows, I had enjoyed working with Terry Lickona, a member of the TV committee and also a producer (*Austin City Limits*) who had become an extremely helpful liaison between the Academy and the production company when it came to show issues. Both had been around enough to know the ins and outs of the show, and though it was Neil's first barbeque, it certainly wasn't theirs, and they set out to help.

Thus began a series of numerous and varied conversations with each of them individually and collectively as we approached nominations day early in January, 2003. I felt it was my job as producer to bring all of them into the process in a very short period of time and to hopefully develop the same kind of working relationship I had with Mike, minus the intrigue.

The January nominations at Madison Square Garden were reasonably uneventful, save for the surprise of Norah Jones's eight nominations. We all suspected Bruce Springsteen, Eminem, Nelly, and the Dixie Chicks would dominate, but I was surprised to find Bruce's "The Rising" not nominated for Record of the Year and more shocked to see Nickelback's "How You Remind Me" in its place. Because it had been a good year for young artists, Norah was joined by Ashanti, John Mayer, Vanessa Carlton, and Avril Lavigne in several categories, and when we looked at the landscape, it all looked juicy and promising for the show.

As usual, I had made some preliminary "if come" bookings with artists I would talk to prior to the nominations and then confirm once I knew that they were nominated (that's the Grammy rule, to perform you must be nominated). So between the nominations and our annual

TV Committee meeting I made some quick calls to Jon Landau confirming Bruce, to Simon Renshaw to confirm the Dixie Chicks, and to Nelly's people as well. I walked into the meeting, the first of the new regime, with those three in my pocket and about 50 voicemails on my cell phone from other managers regarding their artists.

The meeting itself—and remember, this was my 24th—was one of the best in memory. Without Mike around to polarize our two respective camps, there was a much more positive attitude in the room, certainly aided by Neil's opening remarks. As in past years, the Academy people had put together their list of performers and we at the production had ours, and as usual, they were pretty close. But for the first time in many years, the X-factor of doing special segments surfaced early and was championed by Neil, Garth, and Terry.

Those special performances, often peopled by non-nominated artists who could creatively be brought into the show, had become somewhat of an afterthought in Mike's years. As I wrote earlier, Mike was much more interested in booking and performing the hottest acts, and while I am certainly mindful of their importance to the show, in recent years I was troubled by how the Grammys had come to resemble the other music award shows. It had certainly not been the case before Mike came on the scene, and though the ratings of the show were almost always good, in my heart I knew that the Grammys needed to separate themselves from the wannabes instead of trying to copy them. And most significantly, as a portent of the future, was Neil's very reassuring statement to me in a conversation as we talked about my feelings toward special segments that he had been to all the Grammy shows, and how memorable they had been to him.

Garth and Terry were also big supporters of these segments, several of which I outlined or alluded to at the nominations meeting. I had researched a number of them, taken quiet steps to find out talent availability in others, and had nothing more than one-liners for a couple more. But with Neil, Garth, and Terry's support, I was able to do what had been very difficult in previous years: to assure the committee that we didn't have to book the whole show the first day, and that time would tell the tale as to which of these segments could be delivered, which ones filled a need as the mainstay bookings came in, and which ones served to give credence to my feeling (shared by all three of my compatriots) that the Grammys needed to be the leader, not the follower.

Neil had called me while we were in Hawaii and told me of the death of Joe Strummer and after I recovered from the news, my first thought was that a tribute to Joe was not only appropriate but something that could counter the rock-lite tag that Grammys had always had. And more to the point, Strummer and the Clash were a perfect magnet to bring artists together, beginning with target number one, Bruce Springsteen. Remember, the year before I had Bruce, Bono, and Mary J. ready to go before Mike stopped it from happening.

The Clash segment made the initial cut, as did several other thoughts I had including a lacing of the show, our 45th, with the 45 greatest Grammy moments of the past, a way to integrate the New York Philharmonic (honorees of a Trustee's Award this year); a rock group (Coldplay); a divas segment (which would have brought together Aretha Franklin, Mariah Carey, Beyoncé, and Mary J. Blige, none of whom had major nominations); a tribute to Capitol Records (which was a disguised attempt to get Paul McCartney, Brian Wilson, and Les Paul on the stage together—it wasn't to work); and a tribute to the Bee Gees (who had never performed on the show even though they were multi-Grammy winners and beloved by audiences from 12 to 60).

We also found ourselves in the middle of a major discussion about an In Memoriam segment, which had been mandated by the Grammy Board of Trustees the previous summer. I had been quite vocal about not doing this segment, primarily because no matter how we did it, it would take the place of having one more performance on the show, and believe it or not, even with three-and-a-half hours of show to fill, every year we would kick ourselves for not including some performance or other that couldn't be booked due to time constraints. But now, it was law, and we were on our way to doing it, and trying to make it something distinctive and right for our show.

It was during these conversations that I said, in retrospect somewhat prophetically that rather than an In Memoriam segment we should honor performers like the Bee Gees and Johnny Cash while they were still alive. I had no idea that in just five days, Bee Gee Maurice Gibb, a friend and a great guy, would pass away in Miami.

Almost as an afterthought, I mentioned the possibility of one other segment I wanted to pursue. Looking at my notes from that day that I distributed to the group, I now see the parenthetical statement that followed the names, "Good luck with this one." It referenced the fact that Paul Simon and Art Garfunkel would be receiving a Lifetime Achievement Award and maybe we should invite them to sing "Bridge Over Troubled Water" or "Sound of Silence." New York City, world conditions, major Grammy winners, all rolled into one. At the meeting it was met with more discussion than I thought possible, but the bottom line was that it, too, made the cut to "look into."

So the landscape was laid out for us. We headed back home from New York with confirmed bookings for Bruce (even though I expected some flack from Jon about Bruce's non-appearance in the Record of the Year category); Nelly; Norah Jones; the Dixie Chicks; and Ashanti (booked in the car on the way to the airport). I had a mandate to explore the Clash, the Bee Gees, and a segment that would pair Coldplay with the New York Philharmonic. In the wings were Eminem, Avril, and a potential segment that might pair Vanessa Carlton with John Mayer. I was also thinking about Faith Hill, No Doubt, and a more significant rock presence for a show that was seven weeks away.

Back in Los Angeles, the process began, or continued as it were. John, Walter, and I called in Bob Dickinson and Bob Keene to let them know that we had our first bookings and wanted to discuss some ideas for supporting the acts scenically. We made some initial calls to bring some of the acts and their management in to meet with us while they were in town for the American Music Awards. And as opposed to other years, I hesitated doing what I had always done upon embarkation—sitting down and doing a rough sequencing of the show just to take a look at the palette. But this year, because we were embracing the special segment concept, I wanted to wait until the show took a path that might be different from previous years.

And it certainly did.

The weekly conference calls took place as they always had. Because we had over half the show booked before we started, the pressure was lessened to fill the remaining slots, and I had time to work on several of the special segments, knowing that not all of them would make the show. I did my layout of the 45 Greatest Grammy Moments (it wasn't difficult to get to 45, rather it was more difficult getting it down *to* 45), moved ahead with some production ideas for some of the acts, and even explored a few additional concepts that I wanted as insurance if the things on our plate didn't pan out. And in between, I fielded the dozens of calls each day from managers, labels and publicists pitching the myriad artists who to that point hadn't been asked to participate. That's an annual adventure and once you realize that every call comes from someone who sincerely thinks his/her act belongs on the show and will do and say anything and everything they can to get them there, it's as much a dance as you'll let it be.

You listen, you give them the time, you try and be sympathetic, but there always comes a time when it's decision time. And whether you delay it or get to the point early, it's never easy to say no. It's always about relationships, sometimes about artists you'd really like to have but can't book, or in some cases, performers who just don't get there and probably never will.

My first disappointment didn't take long to surface. Elsewhere on these pages you've read about the relationship I have with Bono, and—with his being named Person of the Year for the annual Musicares dinner—I knew it was a lock for him to participate in the Joe Strummer segment, which Bruce had already confirmed through Jon Landau. So it was painful when I spoke with Paul McGuinness, U2's manager, who told me that Bono had a longstanding commitment for his wife in Dublin on show day, and that he'd be leaving directly after Musicares on Friday night. And as disappointed as I was, Paul told me that Bono felt just as bad. He loved Strummer and the Clash. But this one wasn't to change, and I moved on.

The other area that wasn't looking good was a critical booking: the show needed Eminem. He was nominated in a number of categories and was very much on everyone's radar with the opening of the movie *8 Mile.*

There was only one problem; he didn't want to do it.

Once again, I enlisted Jimmy Iovine and Dennis Dennehy, my Interscope folks, to help, but it wasn't looking good. Even though two years earlier Eminem's appearance with Elton John had been the highlight of the show, the fact that the Grammy for Album of the Year had gone to Steely Dan was a major burn for him, and he had a bad taste in his mouth, not about the show but the awards structure. We were in for trouble, and we knew it.

Jimmy continued to work on Eminem, and show day grew closer and closer. But we knew then and there this was not going to be an easy one, and once again, the patience of the committee and Neil would be tested. Fortunately they remained patient.

༄

About three weeks out from the show, Tom Ridge and the Office of Homeland Security raised the Terrorist Alert to Orange—extreme danger. And the President made it obvious that it wouldn't be long before we were at war with Iraq. Obviously, our first thoughts dealt with our sense of responsibility for the safety of our staff, our performers, and our 11,000 guests. It was the second show that we had done since September 11 and those thoughts had come to mind. And while you might assume it would get easier to think through, in fact, it only gets harder. I sat with John Cossette and we discussed alternate plans for the show, and what steps had been put into motion already to secure the venue. An extensive security plan had been designed dealing with all possible scenarios, but reading through that was small consolation; it only brought up more questions.

And then it came clear to us: prepare for whatever comes, and wait to see what the reaction of our booked acts was. After all, two of the Dixie Chicks had just delivered babies, Faith Hill had three little ones, Bruce has three as well, and surely, if they're concerned, they'll let me know, and probably soon. At that point, there wasn't any reason to make a decision, just to keep a pulse on what was going on in the big world, and in our little world as well.

Neil and I continued to move ahead with our numerous daily conversations, and with the show itself taking shape, I was able to spend a bit more time on coming to some closure on the special segments, which still included Coldplay with the New York Philharmonic (technically a nomination but labeled a special segment), the 45 moments (which was losing momentum principally because it would take at least nine minutes of airtime), a reassessment of the Bee Gees tribute (with an available 'N Sync to do a medley), the continuing Divas segment, the Clash tribute, and one or two other possibilities.

But then a conversation occurred that had me rethinking much of the above, and as is the history of the Grammys, changed the course of the show.

I had put a call into Paul Simon just to see if there was any possibility he'd consider singing with Art Garfunkel, knowing the strained relationship between the two of them and the fact that they hadn't spoken in over ten years. I got a call from Vaughan Hazell, Paul's assistant, that Paul was moving to a new home, but that Vaughan would get to him soon and get back to me. I hadn't heard anything, and assuming that Paul might even be upset that I'd even suggest such a thing, considering our friendship. I had pretty much given up.

So imagine my surprise when Jeff Kramer, Paul's manager, called and told me that in fact there was interest on Paul's part, he knew there would be from Artie, and that Paul was coming out to L.A. for the Golden Globes and could we have dinner with Paul to talk about it?

We did, and Paul, who doesn't make quick decisions, made it clear to me that he was more than interested and would take steps to contact Artie to see if the two of them could get together and talk about performing on the show.

The obvious musical choice was "Sound of Silence" for all the reasons outlined above, and the only problem seemed to be matching their schedules for a meeting.

As it turned out, with the show nearly full (two slots remained open, one for Eminem and the other for this wild card) and only a couple of weeks to go, their meeting kept being postponed until the only likely date would be five days before the show, with no promises.

I let Neil, Garth, and Terry know what the reality was, and that though I had been given assurances by Kramer and Artie's manager, John Scher, that this was "going to happen," it is not the smartest thing to do to wait until the day before our rehearsals started in New York to get a final answer. But we all agreed that this one was worth it, and held our collective breath until that Wednesday and I got the call from Paul's brother Eddie, who was at the meeting, that in fact, they were going to do it. He put Paul on the phone, I thanked him and assured him that we'd do our part to make it great, and then laid it on him that not only did we want them to open the show, but that we wanted to put them out in the house to perform. There was a palpable silence, yes, the true sound of silence, and then Paul said that he understood and we'd make it work. We had them, and it was to be one of the truly memorable Grammy show openings ever.

And then in came Eminem. Debates over position in the show, further questions over how this might affect an Academy Award performance (which never happened), the ultimate question of how we could make this an amazing moment followed, and others took place in a very fast-track environment, but reason prevailed and he was in the show as well.

And if those couple of days weren't heady enough, the Clash tribute firmed up amazingly. The show was still teetering on the brink of rock-lite, but I knew that if we could add the right personnel to the already committed Bruce Springsteen, we could satisfy that area as well. So, after David Bowie considered joining but didn't, and Elvis Costello came in, and I added Steve Van Zandt to the mix, there was really only one other perfect possibility, and Dave Grohl, a huge Clash fan, excitedly agreed to come in. I even had discussions with Mick Jones and Paul Simenon about joining the group, but the word kept coming back that they just weren't ready to perform, and I obviously needed to respect that. But now it had a great lineup, "London Calling" was the song, and we had scheduled the rehearsal for Saturday before Bruce and the E Street Band rehearsed at the Garden.

To complete the show, we made room for a Sheryl Crow/Kid Rock duet to add a touch more rock, and we were off to New York for the final week.

You'll note that nowhere in this chapter have I referred to one of the true staples of award shows, the host factor. And there's a reason for that.

Of course we made our usual efforts to book the usual suspects, but after Billy Crystal, Ellen DeGeneres, Chris Rock, and a couple of other logical performers passed, the thought occurred to me that rather than get someone of lesser name value and host ability, we should consider bringing New York musical and other icons to fill the host role (since we were coming back to New York for the first time in five years and we had wanted to honor the city in an appropriate manner) but not call them "host." So in the midst of everything else, we set out to book a group of New Yorkers who fit the bill and, by the time we were finished, we delivered a great list of people who not only made the word "host" almost outdated, but gave the show a fresh feel. The real bonus was that in any of these shows you need to service the host, often creating on-camera appearances that are extraneous, and this time out we didn't need to do any of that. Instead our "New York hosts" ranged from Tony Bennett, Queen Latifah, and Harvey Fierstein to Ed Bradley, Mayor Michael Bloomberg, and Willem Dafoe.

Rehearsals were as good as rehearsals ever are, although by the time Nelly finished emasculating the concept we had for him it had lost the bite and originality I had intended for it, and we were all disappointed in Ashanti—a booking that needed to be there because she had enjoyed such a big year—who was clearly outclassed by most of the other acts.

On the other hand, there were those rare rehearsal standing ovations for several of the acts including Coldplay and the New York Philharmonic, the Clash, 'N Sync's tribute to the Bee Gees, and of course an intense rehearsal version of "The Rising" by Bruce and the band.

And then came the Simon and Garfunkel rehearsal. That two-hour block on Thursday, four days before the show, was one of the most harrowing couple of hours of my professional life, and there were several times in the midst of it that I thought we were going to lose this one.

Not only were Paul and Art trying to mend ten years of strained feelings onstage, trying to make the "in the house" concept work for me, but they were also actually trying to make it work musically, together, after years of working separately.

After the first hour, I knew we were in trouble. None of us gave up hope, but I felt it was best to break the rehearsal, let them go back to their dressing rooms and work a bit more together, and hope for the best. I also told them that where they performed was much less important than the performance itself, and that I was more than willing to give up the "house" and put them back onstage than watch this thing go away. A few minutes later, both managers came to me and told me that they wanted to try the house once more and if it didn't work, we'd move to the stage, where we had more control over the monitors and the mix.

They returned to the house, ran the number twice, gave me the thumbs up, and one more classic Grammy moment was in our bag. On Saturday night, after the final rehearsal, I sat in the office I shared with Walter, Pierre, and writer and pal David Wild and ran back the show in my mind. A few disappointments: no Bono, my failure to find a place for the 45 moments, and not enough time to make it work for Johnny Cash. But on the plus side was perhaps the most balanced Grammy show in years, some remarkable once-in-a-lifetime pairings, and a show flow that couldn't have been better. Even with the awful chest cold and cough that had reached epidemic proportions in our office (me included), I hadn't felt better about the upcoming show in many years. At 7:57 p.m. on Sunday, February 23, Paul and Artie were ushered to an eight-foot-round platform in the house in the dark (their appearance had obviously leaked in the last two days, but it was still a shocked audience that greeted them), and two minutes later (after a slightly awkward introduction by Dustin Hoffman, whose history with Paul and Artie went back to *The Graduate*) those memorable four bars of guitar ushered in the 45th Annual Grammy Awards.

The performance was electric—excuse me, acoustic—brilliant, and it sent a signal to 11,000 people in the Garden and millions more at home to stay with us, this was going to be a special night.

And it was.

Dustin came out again and introduced No Doubt, who rocked through a medley of "Hella Good" and "Underneath It All," counterpointing the remarkable resonance of "Sound of Silence" and we were off to the races.

Norah Jones gave a poignant reading of "Don't Know Why" and then won the first of her five Grammys that night.

Faith Hill followed with an uneven but intermittently powerful version of "Cry" in a dress so abbreviated that we wondered about the wisdom of putting her on a raised platform.

Vanessa Carlton did "A Thousand Miles" better than I had ever seen it before, accompanied by a string section led by my friend Ron Fair, and John Mayer followed it with a solo acoustic version of "Your Body Is a

Wonderland," and then James Taylor ambled onstage and brought the house down with "Sweet Baby James," followed by a seemingly touching Mayer win as John and James stood next to each other backstage and John was congratulated by James.

The Chicks scored with "Landslide" and scored again immediately after by winning the Country Album Grammy.

The New York Philharmonic did a short version of "Mambo" from *West Side Story*, a nod to New York, Leonard Bernstein, and the cross-culturalization of music, and then we whisked Coldplay onstage for "Politick," which received a standing ovation.

The second hour continued with Avril's "Sk8er Boi," and Nelly, and then Bruce and the band brought everybody back into the show with a stirring performance of "The Rising." We presented Song of the Year immediately following Bruce's performance, and as we like to do in the show, positioned it because I at least felt that it would be Bruce's award. But it was not to be, and young Jesse Harris, whose father and I had done TV shows together in the early '80s, was honored for Norah Jones's "Don't Know Why."

Ashanti did the best she could with "Dreams," our weakest performance of the night, but the one that Irv Gotti insisted on doing, and Ed Bradley of *60 Minutes* came out to introduce 'N Sync to pay tribute to the Bee Gees. Standing offstage I had one of several flashbacks I would have that night connected to artists with whom we had a history. In this case, as I watched 'N Sync nail the three-song medley, I thought back first to the several shows we'd done with them over the past several years and how they had grown both as performers and as individuals. They're really terrific guys, and the CBS special we had done with them in the Bahamas a year previous to this appearance had been a great deal of fun.

Then my mind wandered back 29 years to a small Chicago television studio where I had worked with the Bee Gees for the first time, and my times since with Barry, Maurice and Robin. They had been very responsible for my success in television, asking for me to do two specials, the *Music for UNICEF* show (the first ever to be done from the floor of the General Assembly of the UN) and then, a year later, their own NBC special, both of which took place at the height of their popularity. We had stayed in touch, and over the years I had carried the burden of not properly giving payback with an appearance on the Grammys, knowing how important it was to all three of them, but particularly to Mo. Now they were on the show, but Mo wasn't there with them.

Even though I had spoken to Barry by phone several times over the past weeks, I hadn't had a chance to see them in their dressing room, and the appearance of Barry and Robin coming to the stage brought tears to my eyes. Tears of joy and sadness mixed, but the overall effect was one of warmth, and as they left the stage after giving their speeches, I walked up to them and we embraced. It took me a moment to recover, and then, as television demands, it was on with the show.

Eminem, who had brought The Roots along for a rocking performance of "Lose Yourself" was next, and perhaps the title was too appropriate as he lost the Record of the Year Award to Norah. My next conversation with Jimmy Iovine was not going to be an easy one.

Then it was time for Neil's speech, several drafts of which I had contributed to. It was critical in this first year after Mike Greene to send a message both to the industry and to the public that a change had occurred, that humanity had returned to a wounded Academy, and that everything was alright. Of equal importance, in a period when the music industry was going through some pretty tough times, this needed to be a clarion call that we would survive, even prevail. And Neil expressed it wonderfully, never pointing his finger in the faces of the audience as Mike had done so often, never chiding, but presenting a message that was absolutely uplifting. After the requisite two-and-a-half minutes (setting a modern-day record for brevity), Neil led into our "In Memoriam" segment, a meaningful listing of music industry individuals who had passed away in the previous year. And then, as if on cue to bring it all back home, as Joe Strummer's visage appeared on the two huge screens onstage, I asked Bruce to kick off the first four bars of "London Calling"—the appropriate coda to the segment with a message that though fame is ephemeral, great music outlasts its creators. Nothing said it better than the blazing guitars and intense vocals to drive home a message.

In a way it was the end of one era, but more important, the beginning of another. The return to a broader set of performances, the ability of the Academy to return to its leadership role in the industry by recognizing the past as well as the future, and most significantly, a show that was truly all about the music, had served us well. The ratings were up, the next day showed, the reviews were better than they had been in years, and once again, people were saying it was "the best show ever." Only this time, rather than the mixed feelings I had about everyone forgetting about some of the great things we'd done in the past, I too felt that way.

And then it hit me, as it always does at some point in the process: How were we going to top this one? But this time the anxiety subsided as I said to myself 24 years into the game, Don't worry, we always do.

CHAPTER 26

The 2004 Grammy Awards

Prince, Beyoncé, and the Ghost of Janet Jackson's
Super Bowl Performance

As I've said elsewhere, every Grammy show starts with a blank piece of paper, and the first thing that goes on the page is the list of nominees, our palette for the upcoming show. As we approached the 2004 event, with the success of the previous show and segments like the Clash tribute, the Simon and Garfunkel opening, the Bee Gees tribute, and other highlights, we were filled with conflicting feelings. On the positive side, we knew, as with every year, that we had to top ourselves once more, that being the best fire-starter there is. On the negative side, there was a shared feeling, even before the nominations came out, that 2003 was not a banner year for music, either in terms of CD sales or breakthrough acts that would find performance slots on the show.

It wasn't difficult to recognize that our 25-year history of creating "Grammy moments," a concept that had fallen out of favor during the Mike Greene years, was warmly embraced by the new president, Neil Portnow, and the newly revised and streamlined Academy Television Committee, with whom we work very closely. This year I was committed to making every performance a Grammy moment, and by the early fall while speculating on the nominations, I had come up with a few thoughts that would jumpstart the show in the right direction. But even I was surprised by the confluence of events that would shake up the 46th show and create the scenario that would not only give us our best-received show in years, but allow for a creative playground that would set a high-water mark for future shows.

And much of it hinged on a couple of circumstances that no one could have even imagined taking place four or five months prior to the show.

For as long as I've done the Grammys, the show had aired in the last week of February, a month before the Oscars, and a month after the

Super Bowl. Tucked into that time period, though the American Music Awards show was usually held within a couple of weeks of the show, the Grammys were definitely considered the prime late February event, and benefited from this protected position. All that changed in 2004 when ABC announced that it was moving the Oscars into the last week of February. In order to keep our distance from the only other major award show that we felt crossed over in terms of viewers, we moved the Grammys into early February, just a week after the Super Bowl.

That move, and the subsequent events that surrounded the show after the most controversial and highly debated Super Bowl halftime show in history, created the platform for one of the most unusual, potentially disruptive, and, at the end of the day, satisfying shows we've ever done. And though, as the Brits say, "it was alright on the night," the course taken by the show as a result of the move is a fascinating study in both the best and the worst in people—not to mention the effect of music and popular culture on all of us and our audience.

First, the good news, and this too, was affected by the move of the show to early February.

One night in August, as I was sitting at home listening to some music, I happened to put on the first Beatles album, *Meet the Beatles . . .* no reason, just wanted to hear it again. But two minutes hadn't gone by before I jumped out of my chair, ran to the computer to double-check the new Grammy date, and jumped on the phone, seemingly waking my friend and CBS executive Jack Sussman.

"Jack, you're not going to believe this. This year's Grammy show is forty years to the month, the day, the hour, and the network of the Beatles' first Ed Sullivan appearance. Is this fucking amazing or not?"

I guess it's not fair to ask someone startled out of a deep sleep to grasp the full meaning of something that at that moment was electrifying to you, so I gave Jack a minute to regroup, which he did and became as excited as I was.

In the next ten minutes, we had laid out a plan not only for a true celebration on the Grammy show itself, but also a subsequent special which would air on CBS on the following Sunday, the date of the Beatles' second Sullivan appearance. The muse had arrived, the spark plug that every producer needs to set the stage for creative thinking. Everything that followed would be amplified by the knowledge that once again, we had something in our hands that nobody else would have, or be able to take advantage of. The combination of the power of the Grammys, its institutional ability to foresee and recognize great events, combined with the nearly karmic coincidence of stars aligning in our favor, was really the catalyst for the 2004 show.

Of course, I had visions of a Beatles reunion of sorts, a plan that would be dashed in future days by the reluctance of Paul McCartney and Ringo Starr to come to the show in person. But all of those things lay ahead.

The second special, which would have been done for the Academy as well, was never to be, a missed opportunity, but for the next five months, we would weave and bob through the front offices and back streets of Apple Corps, Ltd., its helpful head Neil Aspinall, and the living ex-Beatles and Beatle widows as we moved toward two spots on the show that would pay homage not only to the Sullivan appearances but to the cultural revolution they initiated on February 9, 1964.

But since the process was not to be fully evolved for months, it's probably better to leave that to its timeline and return to the next important date in our Grammy decision-making journey, the nominations themselves, which were announced on December 3, a full month earlier than in the past.

In retrospect, the nominations actually turned out to be a better group than we had anticipated. Though logic prevailed in multiple nods for Beyoncé, Outkast, Justin Timberlake, and Evanescence, all of whom had big sales years, the major categories were peppered with interesting (and performance-friendly) acts like the Black Eyed Peas and the White Stripes, as well as strong recognition for two acts whose presence might be felt at the Grammys even though they wouldn't be able to perform, Luther Vandross (still recovering from a major stroke) and Warren Zevon (who had passed away from cancer late in 2003). Both of those acts were already on my radar to be recognized by some sort of tribute performance, and both turned out to be extremely dramatic moments in the show.

The post-nomination meeting was a very collaborative one. There was a true understanding by both the production company and the committee about listening to each other's ideas, and by the end of the meeting, we had agreed on a majority of the bookings for the show, with the proviso that I inject each year into the process that we don't have to fill the show on nomination day, but rather should build blocks, revisit, and then find the balance.

Back in the office after the meeting, I quickly made calls to my friend Mathew Knowles about Beyoncé, to Johnny Wright about Justin Timberlake, to Irving Azoff regarding Christina Aguilera and the Eagles, to Dan Miller about the White Stripes, and to Marty Erlichman about Barbra Streisand, all of whom had been nominated. I also called Blue Williams about Outkast, and Carisse Henry about Madonna. Finally, since the committee and the production company were in agreement about doing something for Luther Vandross and Warren Zevon, I set into motion segments that would honor both of them on the show.

That, coupled with the Beatles segment we had planned, and my preliminary thoughts about the eventual funk segment, gave us the layout for about two-thirds of the show, with the remaining bookings to come from other things we had discussed in the meeting.

By the end of the day, Beyoncé, Justin, Christina, the White Stripes, and Outkast were confirmed in principle, pending creative discussions. Irving had agreed to try and finalize the Eagles, and Marty was talking to Barbra.

Not a bad first day, but the early burst of booking success was to be tempered by the inevitable malaise that rears its ugly head every year in Hollywood and New York after the first of December. It's called MIA— missing in action. Even voicemails seem to go on vacation after Thanksgiving, and, as deception is a tenet of the entertainment industry, the traditional return to work after New Year's Day stretches itself out to the second week in January. Forget the fantasy, the fact of the matter is that for all intents and purposes, our Grammy show, additional bookings, early stages of meetings and production ideas were put on hold until well after January 1. Not a good thing with a show less than five weeks away.

There was some progress (or retrogression, actually): the Eagles fell out because Glenn Frey wanted to play in the AT&T Pro Am, which was the same weekend as the Grammys (in truth, if I had a game like

Glenn's, I'd probably have done the same thing), and after much conversation, Barbra Streisand decided to go to Cabo San Lucas and sing Happy Birthday to John Travolta rather than promoting her nominated Movie Song CD on the Grammy Awards. Go figure. And while we continued to talk to Madonna's people, she would ultimately decline a performance but agree to introduce Sting, who had introduced her to her husband, Guy Ritchie.

Early January came sooner than expected, and we were back in action, trying to pack seven weeks of production and booking into four. While we were frantically setting up meetings with each and every act on the show to discuss ideas, we were looking at the status of the show and trying to decide how to proceed.

The Funk segment was shaping up. I had gone to see a little-known Christian rock band, Robert Randolph and the Family Band, fallen in love with their sound and their presence, and added them to the already committed Earth, Wind & Fire. I went back and forth on the closer for the segment, knowing that George Clinton and the P-Funk gang would be incredible onstage but indecisive about two other possibilities which represented funk at its best. To host the piece, Tisha firmed up Samuel Jackson who was the only person I had ever considered for it and hoped that the copy that David Wild and I wrote would entice him into it. It did.

And then there was Outkast, whose song "The Way You Move" had given me the idea for the segment in the first place—Earth, Wind & Fire–like as it was. I had already committed to doing "Hey Ya," the most ubiquitous song of the year, which was nominated for Record of the Year, and was heavily favored to take the prize (it didn't).

The Outkast CD was actually a double CD, one recorded and produced by Andre 3000 of "Hey Ya" fame and the other by Big Boi. I had met with Andre 3000 and agreed upon a performance that would meld a Native American theme with a marching band, and set the whole thing on a planet "far, far away." The Native American idea was Andre's, the marching band mine, and the space theme mutual—and as crazy as it sounded, it was exactly the right concept for the song I had already decided in my head would close the show.

But Big Boi, the other Outkast principal, was another story. He was convinced that by participating in the funk medley, he was getting less play on the show than Andre, and no matter how I tried to convince him that in fact by being a part of the funk medley, he'd equal if not surpass the other Outkast performance, he wasn't buying it. My negotiations with label head L.A. Reid, I thought, had moved us past this impasse, but one day I picked up the trades to see that Reid was gone, and I was back at square one. We went to the wall, and in the end Big Boi agreed to participate, a decision he went out of his way to thank me for at the end of the day. The segment was to become one of the real highlights of the show and demonstrated, as I had hoped it would, the through-line of one of music's most exciting genres. People are still talking about this amazing 12 minutes of Grammy music that truly showed the family of music at its best.

But there was still one more major Grammy moment to come, and though in hindsight it may seem to have been the most logical and perfect of all, it was actually years in gestation.

I had first met Prince on the 1984 Grammys, when he came and performed "Baby I'm a Star." Our paths had crossed several times since, and at least once or twice a year we would talk on the phone, or I'd go see him and talk about television, music, and some larger questions of life. I don't say this often, but he's a musical genius, one of the true visionaries I've been fortunate enough to meet over the years, and hands down, the best guitar player I've ever seen on a stage. He's also quirky, sometimes distant, and often reluctant to allow you to talk to him about what you really want to talk about . . . until he's ready.

Mathew Knowles and I had talked about Beyoncé's performance months before the nominations came out. I was insistent that with all of the television exposure she had gotten, we needed to do something totally different on the Grammys. When he pinned me, without having totally thinking it through, I knee jerked and said, "I want to see her rock." His eyes lit up, he got it, and we set out to find the right person for Beyoncé to rock with.

He called me one day and informed me that Prince had called the office a couple of times wanting to hook up with Beyoncé . . . musically.

They had met once, and hit it off, and agreed to work together sometime in the future. I said to Mathew, The future is now.

I called Prince—thinking hard about how I'd approach this, knowing that it's always better if it's *his* idea. I presented a couple of side conversations as to how we both saw the performance, and we agreed that we'd try and work it out. I can still remember hanging up the phone and letting out an uncharacteristic scream. I felt this was going to happen, and I knew it was going to be historic.

One of Prince's few conditions in doing it was that he and Beyoncé open the show, and since I was agonizing over what to put at the top of the show, it was the easiest yes I ever gave.

It wasn't three days later that a track arrived with the heavy warning that this was not to be played for anyone, and when I put it on the CD player and listened to those five minutes, I let out my second scream of the week. It was unbelievable, a blending of Prince hits with more than an obligatory nod to Beyoncé's "Crazy in Love" (nominated for Record of the Year). Best of all, for an artist never known to be predictable and one who shunned doing his hits for years, it opened with the most slamming intro to "Purple Rain" I could imagine and just rocked from there. It was amazing, and nearly afraid to jinx it by defying Prince's edict, I called Mathew and played it for him over the phone, to equal glee on the other end of the phone.

There was just one problem: Beyoncé couldn't understand why, with all of her nominations and acclaim, she was being asked to perform with another artist when she had certainly earned her own spot, and wanted to do a dream version of "Dangerously in Love," her favorite song on her solo album. Mathew called me after talking to her and told me I was responsible for the first fight he and his daughter ever had, and it didn't look like she would do it.

As fate would have it, Beyoncé and her mother, Tina, were in L.A. for a photo shoot, and I insisted that I go over that night to talk to her about it. I showed up, waited an hour, spent some quality time with Tina (whom I love), and finally sat down with Beyoncé to try and convince her that this was a moment that almost never comes in an artist's life. I probably oversold it, and as sweet as she is, I wasn't winning until I asked her about her ideas for "Dangerously in Love" and said that I wanted to think about doing both numbers in the show, an absolutely forbidden thing in the Mike Greene era.

There was no way that I was going to lose this, however, and the next day we put all of our efforts into coming up with a way that would take her basic idea, which was fine, and make sure that it wouldn't be totally overshadowed by the duet. I wanted to protect her. I felt an obligation to her that went back to the first of many times we had worked together and I'd seen what a talent she (and at that time her group-mates Kelli and Michelle) were, and are.

I called Mathew and told him we'd do both numbers and that in fact, she deserved both of the spots on the show.

An hour or so later, Beyoncé called me, thanked me, and we were off to the races, and arguably to the best opening number we've ever done on the show.

For the remaining open performance slots in the show, two others were already committed, at least in principle: the In Memoriam slot, which the Television Committee had mandated the previous year and turned out to be one of the real highlights of the telecast after we put together the Clash tribute; and, the slot I was holding for the Luther Vandross tribute, still pending due to the question of whether or not Luther would be well enough to travel to Los Angeles to be acknowledged by the audience.

There was no question in my mind that we couldn't out-rock "London Calling," the revolutionary anthem that was such a dramatic counterpoint coda to last year's In Memoriam segment. My only recourse was to go 180 degrees in the other direction and find an emotional touch point that would resonate with viewers in a totally different way from the Clash song.

From the beginning, I had wanted to take the Warren Zevon song, "Keep Me in Your Heart," and cast it with Warren's friends who had participated on his last CD, which he had recorded, literally, with his last dying breaths. The song was a deeply touching and emotional goodbye from a man who was able to eloquently express himself in music and lyrics. With the help of Jorge Calderon, Warren's producer and friend, we tightened up the song to reveal its essence, and then asked Emmylou Harris, Jackson Browne, Billy Bob Thornton, Timothy B. Shmit, and

Warren's children to appear in a simple setting to perform the choruses, with the exception of the last line of the song, which had Warren's voice in the clear. On show night, that last line rang out in Staples Center with every bit of heartfelt emotion that the last chord of "London Calling" had the year before.

The Luther segment remained in limbo until two weeks before the show, when the committee, sensing my concern that Luther's attendance was looking dim, decided to proceed with the segment, Luther or no Luther. It turned out to be a wise decision, as I booked Alicia Keys to perform a remarkable "Lutherized" version of one of Luther's first crossover hits, "A House Is Not a Home," followed by a touching yet restrained version of "Dance with My Father," performed by Celine Dion (whose father had passed away earlier in the year) accompanied by Richard Marx, the co-writer with Luther of the song. Though both segments were separated by more than an hour-and-a-half, the strength of these two deeply felt performances added tremendously to the show. And when we finally knew that Luther was not going to be able to fulfill or our dream of coming to the Grammys, we scrambled to get a taped thank-you which was delivered to me again with the proviso that I show it to no one until after I had given the family my thoughts about it. When Clive Davis's representative walked it into our office and we closed the door to take a look, it was amazing. Having worked with Luther for years before his stroke and having heard the stories about his condition, I was surprised to see that he looked remarkably well, and you can imagine my face when at the end of it he delivered two vocal lines from "The Power of Love."

The next morning, I called Carmen Romano, Luther's manager and the person who had told me that the family was reluctant to let us use the tape, and told him that if we didn't play it on the show, we would be doing a tremendous disservice to Luther. He called me back shortly to say that the family had approved our using the speech, and when it played at the end of the segment, Luther, watching at home in New Jersey, was able to see the loving standing ovation he received from the 12,000 fans at the Staples Center for the show.

And the Beatles tribute that catalyzed just about everything that was to be part of the show that year? I still had the spot for it, but with the non-participation of Paul and Ringo, I wasn't sure it would come off. After all, you just can't "cover" a Beatles song. I actually put a grid together, mixing and matching available and desired artists that covered a lot of bases, but it still didn't feel right to me, so I refrained from pushing it on the conference calls. Then one night, less than two weeks away from the show, as clouds clear to reveal the sun, I saw it. Sting was already coming and an English bass player would be good. Vince Gill's a helluva guitar player and had a voice, though not similar to John's, in the same register. Dave Matthews wanted to participate on the show and though not left handed, felt right for the McCartney part. And multi-nominated Pharrell Williams of the Neptunes would bring a generational freshness to the three veterans. The song: obvious . . . "I Saw Her Standing There," one of the six songs performed by the Fab Four on Sullivan, and the only song that could both be done with a nod to the Beatles and wouldn't be compared to their version. I made the calls, booked it, and laid out the easiest stage plot of the show. How could we go wrong setting the four of them up exactly the way the Beatles performed in every live appearance they ever made?

On the page, the show was now complete. The weekly conference calls, in which I played both cheerleader and realist, had taken a radical turn from the Mike Greene years, which had often found Mike interrupting me mid-sentence to take issue with one thing or another. Now there existed a sense of trust, support, and even jocularity that was based in the foundation that together we had developed a show that we all felt could be truly unique and true to the root belief that the Grammys were the only true place left on television where it was "about the music," a mantra we had mutually developed and that had always stayed with us when thinking about the show.

And at the same time, within the production company, the spirit of the show had an equivalent effect on all of us. I had developed a closer rapport with John Cossette, who has capably and nearly always without complaint dealt with the myriad technical problems that if ever let go could take us down. Walter Miller saw the special nature of this show early and rose to the occasion, digging into the music in general and the complexities of the funk segment in particular, and created a great shooting pattern for the new set design for the entire show. And our design team of Brian Stonestreet and Steve Bass, who Johnny and I had put together to carry on the work of Bob Keene, our longtime designer who had passed away the previous year, weren't thrown by the incredible demands we put on them to make the new set they had designed work for us. I can't remember a year when it felt as much like a team effort both inside and out, and it was all because even with the shortened production period, we knew we had the potential of a great show on our hands, and no one was going to let that get away from us.

Nevertheless, our goodwill was to be severely tested just seven days before we went on the air, during the Super Bowl halftime show, which also happened to belong to our home network, CBS.

The show was produced by MTV—we had actually been asked by the NFL to bid for the show based on the very successful NFL kickoff show we had produced the year before in Times Square. But because of the proximity to the Grammy date, there was no way we could even consider doing it, so it went to MTV.

I don't believe I have to go into detail: it was the "breast seen round the world" and though the breast was only the "tip" of the iceberg, the rest of the 12 minutes, filled as it was with crotch-grabbing rappers and American flag-draped rockers hawking their sponsorship deals, did more to set back music on television, and in some eyes the ability of television to control itself, than any other event in TV history.

And because we were a music show, and we were next up after the fiasco, it was to impact our show in a way that, given other circumstances, could have brought down the whole show.

Rather than rehash the whole week of hell, suffice to say that the show, the Academy, and television in general came under incredible pressure and scrutiny because of the Janet/Justin affair. That week, the most intense week of the year for most of us who are involved in the show, became a series of conference calls, rumor and innuendo, speculation, and an added layer of tension that might have been fatal had it not been for the leadership at the Academy, and specifically Neil Portnow. Talk about a baptism of fire!

Both Janet and Justin had been confirmed for the Grammys, Justin to perform and Janet to host the Luther Vandross segment. In our attempts to avoid a rush to judgment, we had initially decided not to react but to move ahead and do the show which was already on its way to the stage, and had about as much to do with the halftime show as Vanilla Ice has to do with Beethoven's Fifth. We were proud of what we had put together to that moment, and didn't want to be swayed from our course.

The Janet situation however changed when we considered the sensitivity of the Luther Vandross segment. We went as far as to discuss Janet's participation with her management, but found no resolution as to whether she would beg off or whether we even wanted her off the show. In fact, as the week wore on, the resolution was played out in the press when we learned from the media that "Janet wasn't coming to the Grammys."

Justin was another story. His multiple nominations, coupled with what we felt would be a great performance, and overlaid with speculation that questioned whether or not he was a part of planning the wardrobe malfunction or had merely been duped into doing something that Janet had asked him to do, left us with conflicted feelings. We ultimately decided to continue with his performance on the show. In conversations with his management, we were continually informed that in fact he had not been a part of the planning and had been told that there was another article of clothing that was to have been revealed once he pulled off the outer covering.

Daily conference calls between the Academy, the network, the principals, and other interested parties working on our behalf helped us steady our course, and though the issue didn't resolve until show day and we were "on" with Justin and "off" with Janet, we pressed ahead and made it through our dress rehearsal in fine style.

But we still faced the issue of what might happen on the live show where some as yet unknown Grammy winner could take the stage and use the platform to comment, to get some extra press, or just to express their feelings about something that really had nothing to do with what the Grammys are all about. To counter that, we accepted the CBS decision to put a delay on the show, although we felt that a five-minute delay was overkill. It was not a precedent, as the show had been on a delay in years past, and only in recent years had we gone "live/live."

As stated before, at the base of it all was our belief that the show we were doing that night at the Staples Center that would be seen around the world would, by execution, counter so much of the bad press that both the music industry and the television industry had received in the days since the Super Bowl show.

If there was a better example of the flip side of the previous Sunday than Prince and Beyoncé lighting up the stage in the first five minutes of the show, I don't know what it would be; if there was a better example of the power of music to heal than the Luther segment or the Warren Zevon segment, I haven't found it; and if there was a better example of the family of music coming together to share all the things that music can do to light up our lives, make us happy, and allow us to celebrate diversity, pride, and accomplishment than nearly every performance on our three stages that night, I'd like you to show it to me.

Outkast rightfully took home the Album of the Year Grammy, Record of the Year went to a surprised Coldplay (whose Chris Martin stopped me backstage immediately after getting the Grammy and said that if it weren't for their performance on the show the previous year they wouldn't be standing there that night), Luther and Richard Marx's "Dance with My Father" deservedly won Song of the Year, and Eva-nescence walked away with Best New Artist. Other awards went to No Doubt, the Foo Fighters, Justin Timberlake, and Christina Aguilera. Yes, most of them performed also, extending the "you perform, you win" philosophy, but if you want to play that game, then you have to look at the converse, which is that if in fact popularity is a factor, then that's a great deal of our booking philosophy as well.

If the show was a critical and creative success, then it was also a major score for the artists and record labels who benefit from the awards and performances. In fact, two weeks after the show, the entire industry was abuzz when *Soundscan* announced that the previous week had been the biggest CD sales week since they began charting sales in 1991. Nearly every artist who performed on the show showed sales increases of anywhere from 50 to 400 percent, with the biggest incremental jumps for Outkast, the Black Eyed Peas, Warren Zevon, and Luther Vandross. Robert Randolph, our personal pick for an act we wanted to benefit from the exposure, came back on the charts after a long absence, as did several other acts whose CDs were basically over. It was satisfying for us because it once again proved the power of the show.

And if there's a coda to the whole affair, it's that my car CD player, which fed me nothing but Grammy-nominated performances for the three weeks prior to the show, still serves up "Dance With My Father" on a regular basis, and I get a lump in my throat thinking about my dad, who passed away some 18 years ago. That's what music does to us, and for us. You can't say that about much else.

CHAPTER 27

The 2005 Grammy Awards

"The Best Grammy Show Ever!"—Bono

As my partner Walter Miller and I sat in the Staples Center production office that we shared, in between the dress rehearsal and the live show, my mind drifted back over the 25 years of these rare moments of peace and quiet that preceded the countdown to the live three-and-a-half-hour show we were about to begin. I remembered moments that were nowhere near as calm as this particular moment, times when I would spend the final minutes before the show cutting dialogue here and there or rushing to an act's dressing room to assuage an unhappy artist; one year when I stood outside waiting for Stevie Wonder's limo to fight its way through traffic so that he would be onstage to open the show, another when my father was watching the show from a Fort Lauderdale hospital, and still another, the year that Pierre had sent me packing, when I watched the show from home, a pretty miserable experience.

Walter looked over at me, sensed my pensive mood, and in the way only Walter can, said, "Hey pal, we'd better go and get this thing on the stage," breaking the mood and bringing me back to reality. At 79, Walter was still full of what his generation had called piss and vinegar, but only those of us who knew him well knew what a soft underbelly hid behind that gruff exterior. He could still lash out with the best of them, but it was always understood that, as with his contemporary, Don Rickles, there would be some ultimate apology at some point, no matter how true or how late. This year, however, there hadn't been any of those "Walter moments," and I actually found myself missing a bit of the bite. But I knew that once again, for the 25th time or so, I was grateful that I was walking into this behemoth, certainly the biggest show on television in any year, with him at my side.

The story of the 2005 show is so big, I'm not really sure where to begin. So let's start with a short statement of facts. Whereas critics and fans alike heralded the show as the best ever, we also suffered the lowest rating for the show since 1995, ten years previous. How those things relate and how we got there is a truly fascinating chapter in Grammy show history.

After the 2004 show, which was, to date, our most Grammy-moment-laden show, and which found the ratings up 24 percent from the previous year, we knew we were in for a challenge, both in terms of how to top ourselves creatively (our yearly goal), and also how to match the ratings—which benefited from the high level of interest created by the Super Bowl debacle the week before. I think we've learned over the years that these two goals are not mutually exclusive, and that in fact, when we do a truly memorable show, it's because commercialism and creativity work in tandem. But because both are often the product of the nominations, until those nominations come out in early December, the page is blank. This time, however, I had some thoughts in mind that I felt would work whatever the nominations.

The first was the challenge to come up with something that rivaled or surpassed the funk segment we had done on the last show, which scored big with audiences and critics alike. That segment crossed a number of age groups, combining the heat of Outkast, the freshness of Robert Randolph, and the classic material and love that fans had for Earth, Wind & Fire and George Clinton. So, one night after a bad pizza in Australia where we were shooting an Eagles special for NBC, I woke up with an urge to vomit—and an idea.

Simply, I wanted to target a few of the country nominees and pair them up with some classic artists from the southern rock period of the '70s, bands like Lynyrd Skynyrd, the Allman Brothers, the Marshall Tucker Band, and Elvin Bishop. Those songs, and those bands, were so memorable and had become such anthems that it seemed right to do as a special segment on the Grammys in 2005, about 30 years after they had appeared. And when the nominations came out and I saw the expected nominations for Tim McGraw, Toby Keith, Keith Urban and the multi-category recognition for Gretchen Wilson, it all began to take shape.

I made sure the classic acts were available first, and in a few days had the present Skynyrd group, with Gary Rossington, Allen Collins, and Johnny Van Zant, as well as my old friends going back to my *Soundstage* days, Elvin Bishop and Dickie Betts of the Allmans, on hold, ready to go. Then I went to Tim McGraw and Keith Urban, who both said yes, and after some prodding and the usual protestations about why she wouldn't have her own slot, Gretchen joined up as well. Only Toby Keith turned down our invitation, a decision I hoped he'd regret once he saw the segment.

With that piece in hand, I turned to the other tent-pole piece that I felt could work, even before the nominations came out. We had set the bar incredibly high with our past several opening numbers on the show, particularly with Prince and Beyoncé in 2004, Simon and Garfunkel in 2003, and U2 in 2002.

The Prince/Beyoncé number and Simon and Garfunkel had nothing to do with the nominations (other than Beyoncé's multi-nominated categories), so I started thinking early about something that would have that kind of power for this year. I couldn't find anything at first—until I flashed on an idea that might not have the individual impact of a single artist, but would in fact be a change-up and bring several artists together musically. I figured that the Black Eyed Peas would get nominated for "Let's Get It Started," a hot song with a great hook that would definitely provide the base for an opening number but probably wouldn't work as a standalone performance. But the idea of building a group number around it was set in my mind as we met on the day the nominations were announced, and though I didn't bring it up at the first meeting, I definitely felt we could find something that could be a killer number.

Nominations day was reasonably predictable, and found Usher, Alicia Keys, Kanye West, the Ray Charles *Duets* CD, and Green Day dominating the major categories. Only the inclusion of Los Lonely Boys was a surprise to me. The Song of the Year category saw the emergence of Tim McGraw and John Mayer to major categories, and the nominations of Gretchen Wilson, Maroon5, and newcomer Joss Stone in the Best New Artist category put them on our radar as artists we wanted to include. That core list became the chessboard for the year's show, and with a mutually desirable palette of artists from both the Academy Television Committee and our production team, we finished our lunch and headed back to the office to make the first round of calls.

That first day, with calls out to Kanye, Alicia, U2, Tim McGraw, and Green Day, the spine of the show was falling into place, and from that day on, it would be about building on that foundation and taking the show to places that it hadn't gone before. And factoring in a series of both expected and unpredictable opportunities that would result in some truly incredible moments six weeks later in the process.

The first of those opportunities began to take shape as I looked at the nominations and realized just how perfectly certain major 2004 hit CDs fit with "Let's Get It Started." Without even listening, I knew that Maroon5's "This Love" would blend with the Peas song, and that the hook of my favorite new band this year, Franz Ferdinand ("Take Me Out") was in perfect time with "Let's Get It Started" as well. I also felt that Record of the Year nominees Los Lonely Boys (whom we had featured with Carlos Santana on the Latin Grammys the previous September) and their track "Heaven" would find a place. And there it was, an opening number like we had never done before, in fact, a number that no one had ever done, putting together four extremely familiar songs (to our audience) that would bring four very different genres of pop music together in one great stage-filling moment. It seemed incredibly *right*.

Right, that is, to me, and to the Peas and friend and producer Ron Fair, who on previous pages you've met as a musical collaborator and in my eyes a visionary. Will (of the Peas) got it, Ron got it, and for the moment, we were the only three. I met resistance from each of the other three bands' management, and it was only with a great deal of coaxing and implied threats ("We'd really love to have you on the Grammys but . . .") that we reached the point where they all agreed to work out the jam at a rehearsal we would hold offsite a few days before the show. Even with the help of a demo that Ron, Will, and I put together to send around, they still didn't get it, but we had enough faith in the idea not to abandon any part of it. In the back of my mind, I had a safety net that if necessary I could back off to the point where instead of all playing together, which was my hope, I could weave them in separately after they had each played, and it would still work—albeit nowhere near as well as if it became a true mash up.

After reading about 24 previous shows, I'd imagine you've all become co-producers, so you're probably thinking, well, it looks like about 40 minutes of show so far, where are the other two hours plus?

In no particular order, here's how it went—conversations began with Tim McGraw about doing the duet he had done with Nelly, "Over and Over." Frankly, it was a lightweight track, but it was racing up the charts, and though the thought of combining a country star with a hip-hop star had its attractiveness, I just wasn't feeling it. I had halfheartedly listened to Tim's "Live Like You Were Dyin," but really hadn't listened to it with an eye toward putting it on the show. And then, one night as I was driving home with a CD filled with musical possibilities for the show, the track came on as I was passing an accident on the 405 Freeway, and it took on a whole new meaning. It was powerful, it was Tim at his vocal best, and it had an incredible build musically that was perfect for television. As fast as I could, I backed off the Tim/Nelly idea and pushed the TV committee for a solo slot, which would wind up being a perfect choice for the show. And since Tim was already confirmed for the southern rock piece, it was something that Tim's people were very happy to hear about and do.

We had done a number of shows with Alicia over the past couple of years, and each experience was more of a joy than the previous one. I'd watched her develop and grew to appreciate her wide-ranging musical knowledge as well as her chops, and knew we had an opportunity to do something special with her that went beyond the hit record. And don't get me wrong, I loved "If I Ain't Got You," a throwback to some of the great, dripping R&B standards of the '60s and '70s but as up-to-date as today's newspaper. But it wasn't enough for me, and I wanted to find something that would give Alicia an even greater moment on the show. We talked back and forth, but it wasn't until after we had done the Ray Charles special (for CBS) and I had worked with Jamie Foxx, that the idea hit me of how wonderful the two of them would be together, and that to do a Ray Charles song was not only appropriate, but could also be musically rich.

From the core group, it was only Usher that I didn't confirm early, and for a very good reason. He'd been everywhere—on all the other award shows, on one TV special after another—and each time out, it was exactly the same Usher we saw, and I believed that the audience, Usher fans included, were tired of seeing the same old thing. So I purposely slowed the process with his mother, Jonetta, while I started thinking about what we could do with his appearance that would be startling, exciting, and, most of all, have some added value that would make it a true Grammy moment. It would take a while, finalizing itself less than two weeks out from show day.

Walter and I had a good meeting with Kanye West during the L.A. floods of early January, and together we hammered out an idea that took the foundation of "Jesus Walks," his Record of the Year nomination, and built it into a great gospel piece that worked in Mavis Staples (the Staple Singers were to receive a Lifetime Achievement Award on the show) and added one of my favorite nominated gospel acts, the Blind Boys of Alabama. As we got closer, and Kanye's protégé, John Legend flew up the charts, I put him with Mavis in a brief but authentic version of "I'll Take You There" to kick off the performance, and with a process that was reasonably time-consuming and occasionally frustrating, we moved toward one more Grammy moment.

Green Day was an easy and mutually satisfying booking and although I try and keep my personal favorites out of it, I was thrilled that "American Idiot" would find a place on the Grammys. It was a great track, they were good to deal with in the process, and it turned into a fiery live performance, less about posing and more about rock 'n'roll fireworks.

It was all going well. With the exception of Usher, a work in progress, the multi-nominated artists were in, and they were all doing something that had value and worth, so it was time to start looking for things that would take some of those performances even higher and to invent some other segments that hopefully reflected the nominations but went beyond them. I was energized, feeling good that we already had a number of Grammy moments in our pocket. Although I can't remember exactly when the light bulb went on, I started to think about doing a Grammy show where *every* performance was a Grammy moment, and from that time on, that thought never left my mind.

And just then, with a certain irony that has often connected the Grammys to the real world, the tsunami struck Asia and for the first couple of days, who to book and who to invite to present, and how to produce these acts took a back seat as we watched thousands of lives washed away in a single moment. As the death toll rose, and the impact on the world at large began to be felt, it became apparent to us that we needed to do something to respond.

Neil and I had already been talking about some way of recognizing artists for the charitable work they do all the time, particularly in time of need. And this seemed to be an appropriate time to use the reach of the television show both to acknowledge our artists and at the same time to help raise funds for the victims of the tragic events in Asia. I thought that "Across the Universe," the Lennon-McCartney song would be a perfect song to perform on the show, so I put a call in to Yoko, who within a day had instructed the publishers, Sony/ATV, to grant us a free license to perform the song on the show with proceeds to go to charity.

And at the same time it struck me that we could have a huge impact if somehow tied in the Internet in such a way that viewers could download the song via computer with the proceeds going to Tsunami Relief. I began discussions with a major Internet provider, and the Academy already had a partnership in place with iTunes, and within days, we had put this thing on its feet, and I felt ready to go out and book it.

Of course, I went to U2 first to be the backing band, but while Bono immediately agreed to be a part of it, the band wasn't able to participate fully because of a full rehearsal schedule for their upcoming tour. My next thought was Velvet Revolver, the blending of Slash, Matt, and Gibby from Guns N' Roses with Scott Weiland from Stone Temple Pilots. Scott had performed on our John Lennon show a few years earlier, and was a huge Lennon fan, as was Slash, and they signed on quickly and easily. For the next couple of weeks, as they toured in Asia, Slash and I talked through the arrangement and I began thinking about the right talent to invite to take part in the performance.

It was reasonably simple: Bono had already said yes, and Stevie Wonder responded immediately. Norah Jones wasn't a part of the show yet, and I wanted her to be, so we asked her. When Steven Tyler heard about it, he called us and said he'd love to do it, so we added him. And I went to Alicia Keys, Tim McGraw, and Billie Joe Armstrong (Green Day) and added them right away as well. I thought Brian Wilson, who was being honored at Musicares, would be a great addition to these voices, and he agreed as well.

So, by this point in the project, the show was going to rock—U2, Green Day, and our opening number would see to that. And it was going to have a strong R&B hip-hop presence thanks to Kanye, Alicia, and the Peas, and it would have heart, thanks to the emotional presence of Tim McGraw's "Live Like You Were Dyin" (a song he wrote about his father, Tug) and our tsunami segment. And nearly all of the above had potential to become true Grammy moments.

It would be the final three weeks that would really make the difference in the show—because we had the patience not to fill the show earlier, a few possibilities arose that turned out to be the frosting on the cake.

In November, when I first heard about Melissa Etheridge's diagnosis with breast cancer, I had written her a note of support, ending with the few words, "We'll see you in February." We both knew what that meant, and though I didn't speak with her then, her manager, Bill Leopold, called me and told me how much those five words meant to her. I began checking with Bill after the first of the year to see how she was doing, and when Bill and I both felt that it wouldn't push her too hard, we asked her to do the show, and Bill called me to tell me she'd be there. And I had the perfect offer for her.

Janis Joplin was one of 12 artists receiving Lifetime Achievement Awards from the Academy this year, and Joss Stone was nominated in a few categories, among them Best New Artist. What better way to bring Melissa back than by asking her to perform something by Janis, her musical idol, and to perform with the young (17) Joss, tying together three generations of special artists.

But as perfect as it sounded to me, it didn't sound that way to Joss's manager. We had had our differences in the past when he represented my friend Bonnie Raitt. One year he rushed past a crowd of people in the production office and virtually pushed me against a wall, screaming, "If you ever call my fucking artist without calling me first, I'll kill you." My response to his public intimidation made a bad situation even worse as I said to him, "Maybe you'd better tell that to your artist, who called me." Though I had worked with him for years after that, it was never the same, and though I continued to work with Bonnie on shows, I almost never talked to him again. Here we were again, and he was dead set against Joss working with another artist and not doing her own song.

So, because I had no choice, called Steve Greenberg, president of the small independent S-Curve Records, for whom Joss recorded. Steve saw it immediately and, right after our conversation, took Joss to a CD store where they bought a couple of Janis's CDs. She took my recommendation about doing "Cry Baby" on her own, which would then be followed by Melissa coming out, and doing part of "Piece of My Heart," after which Joss and Melissa would duet on this classic of American rock music. It would turn out to be perhaps the highest moment of the night, and not just due to the emotional pull of Melissa's return, but largely due to its musicality and dynamic.

Then Tommy Mottola called from out the blue and offered us something that I had never even considered, primarily because though I try and review all of the possible nominated material, I had totally missed this one. On Marc Anthony's CD (his client and our friend) was a duet with Jennifer Lopez, and Tommy was offering us the first-ever live duet by Marc and Jen. Too good to pass up, and though it became an on-again off-again booking that didn't settle until three or four days before the show, I knew it could be truly magical.

But Usher was still a question mark, and even though I had led his mother Jonetta to believe that he was confirmed, in my own mind I had serious doubts about even putting him on the show. Sure, he was multi-nominated, and the biggest-selling artist of 2004, but frankly I felt we had seen all he had to give, and I was dead against doing just another Usher performance "just like the other ones." I had daily conversations with Jonetta and Barry Lather, Usher's "creative" advisor, and though they had come to me with a couple of basic ideas, I wasn't happy and kept pushing some other agendas, including one that had Usher performing with someone else. My first choice was Sly Stone; nobody had seen Sly in years, and he fit musically and choreographically with Usher. But repeated phone calls resulted in nothing, and it was only then that I pulled out my trump card, one that I knew would be great but wouldn't be easy: my old friend from a bunch of shows over the years, James Brown.

After checking in with "Mr. Brown" to make sure he'd do this, I made the Usher booking, insisting to Jonetta that this happen, and initiated an inordinate number of daily calls to move them toward the production concept that I wanted. I had already told them that we didn't want a bunch of dancers around Usher for this number, and as it turned out, there was only one section with dancers. The other three sections had Usher on his own at the beginning, which I had insisted on, followed by a verse/chorus where he came out into the house to a platform in an aisle where he would dance with one girl, and then of course the finale with J.B. For all of that, I was happy to give up the one group dance section, knowing that we'd have a number that was totally different than any previous Usher appearance, and would probably turn out to be his best television appearance ever—and which, at the end of the day, even exceeded my hopes.

Even our weekly conference calls with the Academy Television Committee were more fun and faster than they had been in earlier years. Within the production company, as complex as this show was shaping up to be, everybody was not only into it, but pumped about the possibilities. And my numerous daily conversations with both Neil and Terry Lickona, the co-chairmen of the TV committee, were joyful, tempered only with the occasional peaks and valleys that accompany any show of this scope and size. Everyone saw the potential of this show, and where it was headed creatively, and the best news of all was that there were still a couple of cherries to be added on top. The first of those came within a week or so of the show itself.

My conversations with Alicia were all moving in the right direction, but neither of us felt that we had quite found the magic. She's so bright, and intuitive about herself, and we both felt that ultimately if we didn't find the key, a performance of "If I Ain't Got You," would be terrific. But neither of us were ready to give up, and about a week out, I got a call from Clive Davis's office asking me if I could find a place for Jamie Foxx, already nominated for an Oscar and already having won a bunch of awards for *Ray* and a couple of his television projects.

We had done the Ray Charles special for CBS in November when the film came out, and I had enjoyed working with Jamie. The show had been emotional, soared musically, and with the nominations the *Genius Loves Company* CD had received, I was looking for a way to feature Ray on the show, but to do it in a different way. I didn't find anything on the CD other than the Bonnie Raitt duet that I wanted to do on the Grammys, and I had already decided that would be a wonderful way to end our In Memoriam segment.

So when the call from Clive came, I immediately thought about teaming Jamie with Alicia on a Ray Charles song and make it a "surprise" appearance after she finished a shortened version of "If I Ain't Got You." Because of Jamie's filming schedule, it became an on-again, off-again booking, but patience will out and the performance of "Georgia on My Mind" that found its way to the stage on Sunday night was truly magical and riveting—a proper send off to "The Genius."

I've left out some of the trials and tribulations that occur on a daily basis with this show—dialogues with unhappy managers, songs that came in too long when we need to make them TV-friendly, impossible rehearsal schedules, and so on, but a week out we hit one wall that nearly derailed the balance of the show and certainly took the wind out of my sails for a while.

First came a call from Lori Earl, the former Interscope publicist who was now working independently with U2, telling me that she had spoken with Bono, who asked her to call and tell me that they would not be able to perform "Vertigo," an uptempo track that would have energy and drive, because he had a serious back problem that put him flat on his back. And since that was the only nominated track from the CD (released after the nomination period), he was asking if he could do "Sometimes You Can't Make It on Your Own," a song he had written in tribute to his father but that wasn't nominated. Our policy is that we don't do material that could be nominated in the following year, and though we've broken that policy once or twice (Celine doing "My Heart Will Go On" after the Streisand duet fell through due to Barbra's illness), it wasn't something taken lightly by the Academy, or us.

Of course we all wanted U2 on the show, but there were other circumstances at play that made this a difficult decision. Difficult, that is, until Bono called me at the office the next day and I could sense the pain he was in and how important it was for them to be at the Grammys. Neil and I discussed it and mutually decided to let them do the song, a decision that on show night turned out to be the right one, as this highly charged love song to his father became one of the standout performances of the show.

Then, just as I thought we had put the show to bed, U2 included, I got a call from Kathy Kane, Bonnie Raitt's manager, (I had booked Bonnie to do the In Memoriam segment with Billy Preston) telling me that Bonnie's dad, the great Broadway singer, John Raitt, who had been ill for a while, had taken a turn for the worse and might not make it until the night of the Grammy show. Bonnie had asked her to call me and let me know, and that she (Bonnie) wasn't sure what she'd do if the worst happened. I told her that Bonnie should deal with her father and not worry about the Grammys, that we would come up with some alternative, and that her father was her first priority.

But Bonnie was determined to come to the rehearsal two days before the show, which she left her father's bedside to make, so we made her rehearsal with us as brief as possible so that she'd be able to get back to him as quickly as possible. When she arrived, I could see that she was not focused on any of this. But Bonnie's a trouper, and we made it through and released her, telling her that we'd roll with whatever happened.

We were set, though not without some trials ahead, and with the addition of Queen Latifah, as host as well as performer on the show, we headed into rehearsals feeling great about the show—its range, its emotional pace, and some truly soaring musical moments.

We have a policy that before any of the multi-artist performances, duets, and special segments hit the stage, we attend offsite rehearsals and make sure that they're what we expect and because we lay out many of these segments musically in advance, we have a vision for them that in the best of circumstances sets the standard for a home run before they even walk into the venue. We needed to see the southern rock piece, the tsunami piece, and of course, the opening number which featured five groups working together.

Rehearsals were to begin on the Thursday before the show, and we had scheduled southern rock with Lynyrd Skynyrd as the core band for

Wednesday night at our rehearsal site. I had laid out the four songs and the vocal parts, opening with Gretchen and Johnny Van Zant doing "Freebird," Elvin Bishop and Keith Urban doing "Fooled Around and Fell in Love," Tim McGraw joining Dickie Betts for "Ramblin Man," and then everyone joining in for the anthem "Sweet Home Alabama."

The Skynyrd boys were there and after a few conference calls to talk it down, had put together a great arrangement. It was fun to meet these guys—no pretense, just happy to be there to play and sounding absolutely tight. Elvin came in and the 20 years since we had seen each other melted away in an instant. Gretchen Wilson came in on time and was ready to go. Keith Urban, whose plane was late, stopped to eat and was late, and Dickie Betts walked in, appropriately accompanied by a six-pack, which only seemed to add to his playing prowess as he unassumingly stepped to the front to deliver one of the most incredible blazing guitar solos I'd ever experienced the first time through a piece. The blind and the deaf would have known that this ten-minute segment of the show would be amazing.

The rehearsal for the opening number, which took place the next night, after our on-stage rehearsals, didn't start out quite as well. I had had resistance from everyone but the Peas about everybody playing together, and I had told them all to wait until they all got in a room together before they came to any conclusions. And to their credit, by the time I got out to the rehearsal in the Valley, after the long day Walter had on camera at Staples, all the acts were jamming together, although not getting any closer to my opening mash-up part. I made a reasonably passionate and adult case for what I wanted to do, and then, beginning with Maroon5, I brought them individually over to the Peas' musical director, Prince, and Will-i-am, and laid out their parts for the jam. I knew the meter of all the songs would fit, and it was simply a case of walking through it with them to find their parts. Maroon5 got it right away, and though Franz Ferdinand was at first resistant, they got it and I saw the smiles appear on their faces as they heard the hook from "Take Me Out" fit into the hook of "Let's Get It Started." And Los Lonely Boys was an easy fit, and within an hour of getting there, the mash-up part of the number was on its feet, and everybody now saw what we had been talking about for weeks.

At the Friday rehearsal, Bonnie walked in, I could see from her face that it wasn't my old Bonnie, and we took extra care with her and Billy Preston, there to rehearse her simple verse and instrumental portion of "Do I Ever Cross Your Mind." I could see that behind those eyes as she sang those words, she was thinking not only of her idol Ray Charles, but of the sick man at home with whom for years she had sung "People Will Say We're in Love." We talked a bit about her dad, and then Walter came out and told stories of the many shows he had done in the '50s and '60s in New York when John had been a huge Broadway star. It was comforting to Bonnie, and before she left I told her once again that our thoughts were with her, and if either her father passed away or if she just didn't feel like she could perform, we'd be fine. We'd known each other for 30 years, and on my part, I knew the depth of her feelings about the important things in life.

⌒

Show day came and I reflected on just how good the production period had been this time out. Relations were good not only between the Academy television committee and our production team, but also within our production team itself. This show would be Pierre's final show as executive producer, and though the way the show functioned would not change much in terms of responsibility and job function, just the fact that John and I had shared that title made for a much more comfortable situation between us and elsewhere within our dysfunctional little family. But now it was a much more level playing field, and it just made for a much better, balanced relationship throughout the show. And of course, that seemed to carry over to the Academy/production company relationship as well, which had become so much better during Neil's three years at the helm.

When I walked out onstage to see a half-empty house 15 minutes before air, I had my usual panic attack wondering if we were going to kick this show off to an audience still scurrying to their seats—a number that featured a Los Lonely Boys performance out in the house at that. But then it was time to talk to the audience, one of the tasks I least enjoy, but in this case, I had a few things I really wanted to get across to them. First and foremost, more than any other year, I wanted them to know it was OK to get up off their butts and get into the show, to forget about the cameras and the five-minute commercials, and to believe that they were at one of the greatest live concert events they would ever see. And though they responded half-heartedly at first, I hoped that they would soon see that tonight was something special, and respond in kind.

As Walter counted the seconds down to air, Neil, Jack Sussman, Terry Lickona, Garry Hood (our unflappable head stage manager), Claudine Little (Neil's assistant), and I stood in our compact cave under the stage position through which all of the show flowed, looked at each other once, and watched our monitors and listened as the Peas' Fergie hit the first, soaring notes of "Let's Get It Started" and the 47th Annual Grammy Awards were on the air. And for the next three-and-a-half hours, one performance after another scored with our live audience, and I'd never seen one-eighth of a day go by faster or with more incredible moments.

The opening number slammed, one band after another, and the mash-up section at the end melded like it never had in rehearsal. For this night anyway, relative chart positions and "my band is better than your band" melted away, and East L.A. met Mexico while Jewish lead singers harmonized with Scotsmen.

And then out came the Queen, Alicia Keys, royally bedecked and ready to rule her loyal subjects on a musical journey through rock, country, R&B, hip-hop and a honeycomb of musical combinations and solo performances. She scored big with the house, and from watching the monitors, I knew she was scoring at home. After all, she brought with her a hip-hop background, an Oscar nomination for playing a jazz age chanteuse, and street smarts that were perfect for the show. She delivered the copy that David Wild and I had written for her without a single change, a rarity with talent these days.

When Jamie Foxx appeared onstage, the place went up, an overdue recognition for almost 20 years of hard work and dedication in television, film, and music, but the acclaim was nothing compared to what met Jamie and Alicia as they glided through a brilliant Ray Chew chart of "Georgia on My Mind" in our first tribute to Ray Charles. Staples Center might one day have a more vocal crowd, but the Lakers would have to come back from a 30-point deficit to equal the emotion onstage and in the house that moment. Another commercial, and then on to the night's third performance, U2. During his Saturday rehearsal, during the break in between takes, Bono had talked to the crew and assorted members of the audience, and told them how he had come to write the song about his father. I went up to him onstage and asked him if he would condense those thoughts and set up the song with those words on the night of the show, and he thought it was a great idea. Tonight, his eloquence exceeded the norm, and focused both the live audience and viewers at home on the lyric, which was at once a love song to his father, and an appreciation of fathers and sons that is universal.

We were now ready to cross the nine o'clock hour, and we had labored long and hard to find the right combination of artists and performances that might help us keep viewers from using their remotes and going over to *Desperate Housewives*. We launched into Marc and Jennifer, set in a gorgeous New York apartment look, and staged simply but beautifully for the two of them to work in. Personally, I thought the performance was perfect, Marc killing vocally and Jennifer, not known as a great singer, delivering one of her strongest vocal performances ever. Critics took out after the number like crazy, calling it a scene from a Mexican soap opera, but as I searched the Internet following the show, fans loved seeing the two of them together and being brought into the classic feel of the performance. But then again, the two of them, and Jen in particular, were easy targets, and I felt bad that they were singled out.

We had crossed nine o'clock and now Matthew McConnaughey, a southern boy at heart, echoed the words of Lynyrd Skynyrd's Ronnie Van Zant, "What song do you want to hear?" launching the Gretchen Wilson/Johnny Van Zant mantra of "Freebird." We were off, and we knew that as strong as our funk segment last year had been, we were going to top it this year.

For one moment in time, we were all rednecks, including, according to my friend Ron Basile, entire rows of African Americans. Standing ovation number three.

Green Day slammed through "American Idiot" replete with network audio dropouts so that words like "motherfucker" and "faggot" didn't go home to viewers who probably heard worse from their kids, or their parents for that matter, on a daily basis. But the FCC was watching, and by the way, so were we. Our philosophy is never to censor our musical guests, and in fact, the Academy has been proactive for years in the area of artist rights and free speech, but self-censorship is one thing and network guidelines are another. We try to respect both, and have been pretty successful at that over the years of the show.

I realize that nearly every segment I've written about up until now has been in glowing terms, so you might want to bring your own memories into play about them, but there's no doubt that the next performance joins that pantheon of Grammy moments that will live forever.

After some appropriate words about Janis Joplin from another Lifetime Achievement award winner, Kris Kristofferson, the waifish, barefoot, 17-year-old named Joss Stone came onstage and kicked into high gear with a version of "Cry Baby" that could bring tears to your eyes. It was a Grammy debut to remember, but unfortunately for Joss (and not my intention), what was to come would probably make everyone forget that there was anyone else onstage when Melissa was introduced by Joss. A few pounds heavier, and bald, but in one moment, Melissa Etheridge made it OK for millions of women to celebrate their loss of hair, to walk into a chemotherapy or radiation session with courage, and to say, "Fuck cancer, I'm going to make it." It was a moment in time, three minutes and thirty seconds of exultation and exhilaration, a congregation led by a preacher more fiery and more brimstone-laden than the minister who had just been onstage with Kanye West, and with enough emotion and triumph that it made the entire watching world jump up and shout and cry at the same time. How many times in your life can you feel that way?

John Mayer and a somewhat stunned Lisa Marie Presley joined together to announce U2's name as winner of the Best Rock Duo or Group award, and the band, with a hobbling Bono, came to the stage. Bono delivered the line of the night, most memorable to those of us who toil in the world of Grammy shows, saying that this was the "best Grammy show . . . ever," and making my offer of $50 for the line seem low (only kidding). As always, they were gracious, deserving, and appropriate winners, acknowledging Green Day, making mention of Franz Ferdinand, and playing down their place on the All-Time Great List—somewhere very close to the top.

And so it was tsunami time. I went to the stage-right stage position, and watched as Steven Tyler, Stevie Wonder, Bono, Alicia, and all the other artists made their way into position like horses at the starting gate, just a little bit ragged, and then I ran offstage to the bunker to see what this thing would look and sound like.

And here's what I saw: it was ragged, it was raw, it was real. The artists got into this performance just as they had on their solo perfor-mances—they weren't delivering lines, they were singing with their hands outstretched, trying to coax, cajole, and convince viewers to get on line afterward and put up a pittance to help people in need. They didn't hit all the right notes, but they hit the high note—the note that said once again that differences between their backgrounds, their music, and their relative status in the music world didn't matter. They became one voice, united in song, and the right song at that.

At the end, the audience once again rose en masse, not so much in tribute to any single great virtuoso rendering of a song, but reminding all of us that we are human, and we are one as well. Job well done, mis-sion accomplished, and still left unsaid was the fact that our folks were there this time when called upon, and we would be ready to do it again, when asked.

But we still weren't done; and coming back after that touching mo-ment wasn't a hard call for me. It had to be Usher, but not the Usher that people had seen over and over on the passel of shows that preceded the Grammys. No, not by a long shot, because this was an Usher with renewed passion, thanks in no small part to the pushing I had done for weeks with him, his mother, and Barry Lather. No, this was an Usher who showed us new moves, new steps, who took his show out to the house on a platform barely big enough for himself and one hot dancer whose movements intertwined with the kid so that at one point you couldn't tell there were two people out there. No, this was an Usher who almost flew back to the stage where he seemingly couldn't wait to play second fiddle to his source of soul, the great James Brown, who appeared in a puff of smoke, resplendent on the second level of the set, and pranced his way down the steps to engage his young protégé and melt away about 40 years in the doing.

And it was electric. Maybe it wasn't the James Brown of the Apollo in 1954, but it was a pretty good imitation. As opposed to rehearsal, their eyes never left each other as they ESPed one another and made an internet connection worthy of broadband, challenging at one moment and dancing in sequence the next, the father taking the challenge of the son, the son paying homage by interpreting with ease the steps that Mr. Brown had patented some 50 years ago. If it was history, as many have said, it wasn't ancient history, it was a new chapter to add to the incredible history of soul music, and it was live, vivid, and engrossing to watch for nearly two minutes.

An easy standing ovation, and one of the biggest of the night. Was it for Usher? Was it for James Brown? Was it for the Grammys? Who knows, who cares, and who can tell, but it crowded the memory banks of a nearly dazed audience who had already seen so much to remember.

In Memoriam turned from recognition of over 40 music industry performers, composers, and musicians into one last love song for Ray Charles, aided by the unique pairing of Bonnie Raitt and Billy Preston.

Now we were almost home. The Ray Charles duets CD won both Record of the Year ("Here We Go Again" with Ray and Norah Jones) and Album of the Year, for *Genius Loves Company*; and Ray's longtime manager Joe Adams spoke appropriately and lovingly of the man he had led to the stage and whose career he had managed for more than 50 years. U2 won the right categories, Green Day scored big, my friends the Peas took home their first of many Grammys to come, Maroon5 upset Kanye to win Best New Artist, but graciously acknowledged him in their acceptance speech, and pretty much everybody who should have won did.

Usher didn't sweep, maybe due to a bit of backlash, but the Grammys did their part to extend that career with a defining moment that I have yet to hear thanks about from the mother/manager. Neither Usher nor his mother, both of whom I truly believe think what we did for him that night. I'm sure they believe they don't need to call, that they did this all by themselves, and that we were just there to serve. Well, we serve alright, but we also learn by experience, and in this case, experience will serve us well for the next time. And unless Usher or Jonetta ever read this, or someone reads it to them, I doubt they'll ever know how close they came to not being a part of the Grammy show, or having Usher be anointed "the Godson of Soul" by the Godfather himself.

As the credits rolled, the long walk back to the production office was made a bit longer by having to traverse dozens of stagehands already in process of moving scenery and lights to the loading dock so that they would get home before dawn. I took a look around and in an instant saw this glorious Cinderella coach turn back into the pumpkin—namely a hockey arena where nearly a thousand people had spent months working in tandem to create an evening's entertainment for millions of people at home and about 10,000 live attendees.

When I reached the office, already filled with milling staffers and guests, I saw a sea of happy, proud faces, all having shared in this mutual experience and all having contributed in some way to its success. Christine Bradley, Walter's associate director, and one of our key partners in the direction of the show, had done a great job of feeding Walter the shots they had laid out together over a week of breaking down the music, and of calling the myriad cues for staging, videotape playback, and others that a great quarterback has to be aware of during a live show. Ron Basile, always my right hand, had already packed me up, and I hesitated asking him about the dozens of things he had handled during the show that he knew should be kept away from me during that concentrated period. And there was Pierre, basking in the glow of his final show, content to share the credit and happily surrounded by his wife Mary and her brood. It was a wonderful thing to see.

∽

Melissa Etheridge called me two days later and made the glow of success about the show itself pale in comparison. I won't be specific, but typical of Melissa, she expressed what a life-changing moment this had been for her, but more importantly for all women going through what she has been dealing with. She thanked me, we reminisced about

20-some years, and she mentioned my note to her in November as being something "very important" to her.

And then I received a letter from Bill Leopold, Melissa's manager, with the following note that he had gotten from a friend of his, whose wife is a breast cancer survivor who had seen the show

> and then they say "welcome back, Melissa Etheridge." Because you know, she's been going through breast cancer treatment. And here she comes . . . And she's . . . bald . . . as an egg. And not that she shouldn't be, but who does that? And there's more, if you know what to look for, as some of us do, though we perhaps wish we did not know from first hand experience, you can tell she's painted on her missing eyebrows, and she's wearing false eyelashes, and she's got heavy foundation on to hide the blotchy skin, and there's probably fifteen more pounds of Melissa than there normally is, it's all those too-familiar chemo side effects, and you know what? She looks fan-fucking-tastic, partly because she can hire pros to make her look like herself, but mostly because she's flat out, unabashedly out, balls out, clutching life by the throat. And WAILS "Another Piece of My Heart" like her life was not on the line, but right back in her hands, and my own heart jumped into my throat because not a fan, but for that moment, it's one of my fantasies come to life, it's what I wish I could have done, jumped on stage at the worst moment and beat it down with a Stratocaster and a voice. And she stood there in her joy, brave enough not just to be bald, but appear next to a 90-pound teenager with hair down to her waist, and who was more beautiful? How was life celebrated more, by the promise in youth, or the victory in no sur-render? And if it made me feel good, three years plus—oh, it's three years plus, by the way, and last time I only made it two years and eleven months, so that has to count for something—down the road, what must it have meant to women going through it right now, with their own missing eyebrows and their own muted voice? St. Melissa, all hail.

One last note: the tsunami segment, the first time a television performance has been directly connected to a fund-raising effort, was an incredible success. It had tens of thousands of downloads, spent weeks as the No. 1 download on iTunes, and has been hailed as a breakthrough moment in both television and music.

The 2005 Grammys. In the book. Now, as I've said in previous chapters, the same thought begins rolling around in the minds of all of us, just as it does every year when the euphoria ends and reason returns.

The mantra: What do we do next year?

CHAPTER 28

The 2006 Grammy Awards

Sir Paul, Sly Stone, Madonna, and Gorillaz

Two things have changed over the past year, which have most certainly influenced my perspective on the show, and even more on my life. The first, the lesser of the two, is that I'm actually writing this on the patio of the La Quinta, California, desert home that my wife Harriet and I bought a couple of years ago. This is the first post-Grammy rest and relaxation visit we've ever taken.

The second change is that this is my first Grammy show since the quadruple bypass operation that I had in October 2005.

Yes, that's what I said—a "four bagger" as bypass patients call it. It was quite an experience, a journey that began on a Sunday morning in October with a trip to the emergency room for shortness of breath, shoulder pain, and an EKG that was met with silence by a slew of emergency room nurses—saying far more to me than any conversation I ever had with, say, Michael Jackson. It continued on Monday with an angiogram with similar raised eyebrows. One day later, I found myself on the operating table for four hours of open-heart surgery.

Forgive me if I digress for a moment or two and reflect on the capacity of the human body to heal and, more to the point, how this year's show actually contributed to my overall healing process. And perhaps, at least to some of those around me, how past shows and my this-can't-happen-to-me lifestyle all contributed to me being flat on my back in the surgical suite at Tarzana Hospital on October 12, 2005.

I will confess that though the thought of the Grammys flashed before my eyes while lying in my hospital room the night before surgery, my most immediate thoughts were much more directed toward getting through the next morning as opposed to what I was going to do with the Black Eyed Peas four months later.

Not that my immediate thoughts had *nothing* to do with work. In fact, we were supposed to leave the morning after I entered the hospital for the Bahamas to do a Patti LaBelle special for UPN, and that was to be followed two weeks later by a Johnny Cash special for CBS to coincide with the premiere of *I Walk the Line*, the Cash biopic that would go on to win a raft of awards in the coming months. Two shows, and instead of my being there, I had a 7:00 a.m. appointment with Dr. Gharavi, the heart surgeon who probably couldn't hum either a Johnny Cash or Patti LaBelle song to save his life . . . but then again, my hopes were that he was there to save mine.

Because I am already feeling guilty about getting off topic here, let me condense the following couple of months into a few succinct paragraphs. The surgery was successful, I was up and walking the following day, and I was sent home within a week of the operation. I threw away the cigarettes I had smoked for 35 years, got on an exercise program that I still find distasteful but necessary, and within a month was back on the phone beginning to line up talent for the Grammys in anticipation of the nominations, which were two months almost to the day from my operation. And so I don't have to continue using it as an excuse, with all of the normal pressure of a show like the Grammys, much of which will be delineated as this chapter unfolds, I felt as good or better than many of the previous shows with all the incumbent *chazzerai* (Yiddish for "bullshit") that is part of the joy of this show.

One last thought, however, and for whatever it's worth to you, dear reader: I can't pinpoint the moment, but there was one point at which I basically surrendered to the process. If you've read this far, you probably can't help but notice that like most people who work at this level I like to be in control. In fact, for the most part, we have to be in control. And guess what, when your life's on the line and your very being is in the hands of a practiced surgeon and a host of support people—anesthesiologists, cardiologists, nursing staff, and the like—there is just no way you're going to be in control, and the sooner you put yourself into their care and understand that if you are to get through this it will be on their terms and not yours, the better off you'll be. If you're anything like me, this may not seem an easy give, but I promise you, when that moment arrived for me, it was the easiest thing I have ever done. And the feeling of release knowing that I had done it was in itself an incredible feeling. And though I can't prove it, I have a very strong sense that I am here today precisely because I did surrender.

There is a qualifier for the above, however. Though I abdicated my role as ruler of my destiny, my wife Harriet was there to act as ombudsman, best friend, medical advisor, and creative consultant (in my business there always has to be a creative consultant). Hourly, daily, and weekly, she was at my side, in communication and watchful of my medical care. There is no question that she deserves nearly as much credit as my doctors for getting me through it all. It's a whole lot easier to concentrate on getting well when the person you've shared that life with for nearly 40 years is on patrol for you, is your biggest confidence builder, and is also the constant reminder that you need to do more for yourself to heal. And that's what she did, and continues to do.

⌒

Oh yes, the Grammys.

There were the obvious, or at least seemingly obvious choices for this year's show: Mariah Carey, the comeback story of the year and holder of eight nominations including Record and Album of the Year; and Kanye West with an equal number of nominations, the person of record of some pretty outspoken and (some would say) outlandish press quotes, and an impressive CD that not only advanced his creativity from *The College Dropout* significantly but also contained the year's most ubiquitous track, "Gold Digger" with guest star Jamie Foxx.

The third member of this triumvirate of eight-times, nominated artists was the young R&B singer with a very old soul, John Legend, whose "Ordinary People" hearkened back to the great R&B tracks of the '60s and '70s and whose career is under the tutelage of the previously mentioned Kanye.

And while those three bookings seemed very obvious, the fact is that Mariah had appeared on a number of other award shows, and in my opinion, walked through most of them, dressed or undressed, and in my opinion, was nowhere near what Mariah was capable of. I was determined that this would not happen on our show, and committed to the point that I had this very discussion not only with her two managers, Benny Medina and Michael Richardson, and the head of her record label L.A. Reid, but in a gentler but honest manner, with Mariah herself. Over the years we had worked together a number of times, and had reached the point where we didn't have to hide our feelings and where she understood that what I was saying to her was genuine and coming from the right place.

And, said the producer, she listened. And so, following an evening in New York the night before the nominations were to come out where she was honored by the New York chapter of the Academy (which included a great performance of one of the songs from her CD, "Fly Like a Bird," performed by gospel great Karen Clark-Sheard), we agreed that while Mariah needed to do part of "We Belong Together" which had been performed on other shows, for the Grammys it would be "Fly Like a Bird" that would be the keystone piece. After the show, I received the following lovely e-mail from Mariah:

> *Dear Ken . . . I really appreciate everything YOU did to help make that performance so right for me. The comment that everybody made to me was that they really loved "fly like a bird" and as you know that was YOUR idea and I tried to talk you out of it!!!!*
>
> *Thank you for caring enough about me to want that moment to feel so special—you're a wonderful person.*
>
> Love and God Bless, MC.

At the same New York event that honored Mariah, I made another conditional offer to perform on the show, this one to Jay-Z to perform "Numb/Encore," the track that he had done with Linkin Park and performed first on an MTV mash-up show and followed by a performance at Live8, the Geldof/Bono epochal rock event of the previous summer. We had done the Philadelphia show, which paled in name value to the London show the same day, but certainly had the edge in having an urban face, a rather important factor for a fund-raiser whose intent was to get the G8 to forgive the world debt to African nations. Bono had asked me to do the show and though there were already a number of cooks in the kitchen, I was happy to do it and was told throughout the process that we were there to clean up what was on its way to being a mess. I was very proud of what we did not only in terms of a great show, but because of the incredible job of interfacing with AOL we did, while the folks at MTV suffered with a poorly conceived and embarrassing version on their networks.

I had already been in touch with the Linkin Park guys who wanted to do this performance with Jay, but I could tell from my conversation with him that night in New York and subsequent conversations that by no means was this a slam dunk, and it was killing me. The Live8 performance was one of the most dynamic expressions of the melding of rock and hip-hop I had ever seen, and it needed to be seen on the world stage of the Grammys. How it finally got there is one of the more interesting Grammy stories of this year and is interconnected with another artist, in this case, Sir Paul McCartney.

Paul had done the Grammys once in my tenure, appearing but not performing at a previous show that honored him with a Lifetime Achievement Award. In fact, the issue of his performing or not was at the root of that show which found us putting a piano onstage, as we were told by Paul's then manager, "just in case Paul felt like sitting down and doing something." Yeah, right. It was embarrassing but had set into motion a series of yearly letters and then e-mails back and forth between Paul and myself that evolved into a rather pleasant personal correspondence that, while pleasurable, never led to his actually coming to perform on the show—not until this year, that is.

His most recent CD *Chaos and Creation in the Backyard* was nominated for several Grammys including Album of the Year, but we had actually begun conversations about his coming to perform before the nominations came out, in anticipation of some pretty significant recognition. All during the Christmas holidays, spent for me in the desert but trying very much to advance the bookings and production of the show, we had gone back and forth with Paul's people, in this case a rather lovely bunch of Brits including Barrie Marshall and Robbie Montgomery, and a very helpful publicist, Paul Freundlich, all of whom wanted to see Paul on the Grammy Awards. Early in the process, thinking it might help to bring him here if I offered him something in addition to his nominated performance, I mentioned the idea of pairing him with Fats Domino, one of Paul's idols. In light of Katrina, I felt that it would be very touching, not to mention fitting. Paul loved the idea and I set about trying to deliver Fats, only to be met with a reality check that Fats was traumatized after Katrina and wasn't leaving the house he had fled to after the hurricane. Though I thought I had made clear to Paul's people that I would try to get Fats only after they said they liked the idea, I think they told Paul that I already had him, and when I couldn't deliver I was concerned that we would lose credibility.

Shortly after the New Year, Paul accepted our invitation to perform and I once again e-mailed him with a lovely letter thanking him and telling him how much we looked forward to his appearance. In his response came the message that he was still interested in doing something in addition to performing his own number, and that I could keep looking. Little did I know that shortly would come an opportunity that would turn into one of the most significant Grammy moments ever.

As I said before, I was having trouble locking Jay-Z, and as we moved closer and closer to the show, I was concerned that I would have to look elsewhere for something to replace it, and the fact of the matter was, nothing really could. It was unique and neither Rob McDermott, Linkin Park's manager, nor I were ready to give up on it, even though he knew that if it didn't happen, there was no booking for LP. And we just couldn't get a confirmation out of Jay.

Finally, the reason for Jay's reluctance surfaced. In his mind, having done the duet for MTV and on Live8 was enough, and unless we came up with something that changed it up, he didn't want to repeat himself. I could respect him for that, but tried to tell him that neither of those venues was the Grammys, and that if in fact he wanted to back away from being a performer and concentrate on running a record company (his other reason), there was no better place to put it all away than on the biggest music show of all, the Grammys. But it was to no avail, and it looked bleak until one day Rob and I were talking and I told him about a couple of the other bookings on the show and that maybe we ought to try and tempt him with one of those . . . and that one was McCartney. After all, Paul had told me that he was looking for something else to do on the show, and what better idea than to come out onstage with one of today's coolest rock bands and the most respected name in hip-hop culture?

Within a day, Brad Delson put together a brilliant scratch track that took "Numb/Encore" and wove it with "Yesterday," one of pop music's greatest anthems. And then off it went to Sir Paul, who, according to Barrie, would be in the office in a few days and would listen to it then . . . and all the while, my clock was ticking. We were now within two weeks from show day, a very late date to be thinking about replacing a major piece in the show.

Then it happened. Paul loved the idea, loved the track, and wanted to do it. We put him on the phone with the Linkin Park guys first and they had a great conversation. Then it was Jay-Z and another great call . . . it was a done deal. Or was it? My litmus test is always to tell the act that we're ready to announce their appearance and if that's cool, then I know we're cool, and when I brought that up to Jay-Z's manager, he hemmed and hawed and said, "let's wait til tomorrow, we need to figure out a few things."

And then John Meneilly, Jay's manager and Jay disappeared into the ether . . . for a full day.

I called both with no return calls. Rob McDermott called to no avail. No one could understand it, but it didn't make a difference. It was over. I set out booking the replacement act.

One last call to Jay-Z resulted in a promise to call me back, but I wasn't holding my breath . . . until the phone rang on Friday, 12 days before the show, and there was Jay on the line. We talked, me trying to convince him how historic this would be, how important this would be toward uniting cultures and generations, and I could feel him weakening after his opening statement of why he wasn't going to do it. I think he was just about to say yes when he put me on hold, came back a minute later and said that Sir Paul was on the other line and he'd call me back. We had told Paul what was happening, and to his credit, he had put himself on the line to make this happen. Minutes later, Jay called back and put me on notice: "I'm going to do this . . . you told me this would be historic . . . it really better be ι . . see you in L.A."

Historic is in the mind of the beholder, but if you saw it on February 8, 2006, I hope you agree that it was, but there is no denying it was very, very cool.

All the while we were agonizing over the Linkin Park/Jay-Z situation, the larger issue was how we were going to handle the Rock categories on the show. Our audience is very rock friendly and there were a number of great rock nominations this year, everything from U2, Cold-play, Springsteen, and the Foo Fighters to System of a Down, Nine Inch Nails, and others. From the beginning, I felt that we needed to have U2, Coldplay, and Bruce—not just because they had strong appeal to our core CBS audience, but also because they are great live performers who can't miss. Of course I felt the show needed to be current as well, and even though the Linkin Park thing dragged on, in my mind it was going to happen and cover us with that need for the show.

Bruce was easy. "Devils and Dust" cried out for simplicity. U2 was nearly as simple, but for different reasons. After last year's "Sometimes You Can't Make It on Your Own," it was time for U2 to rock, and "Vertigo" was the obvious choice. But during a conversation we had in December to talk about the Grammys I mentioned that I had heard the track he had done with Mary J. Blige, a version of "One" that was as close to going to church as this Dublin band could get with the world's most authentic R&B/soul and hip-hop woman. Not that "Vertigo" on its own wouldn't have been a great performance, but in line with our continuing desire to create great moments on the show, I suggested that "One" was, hands down, destined to become one of those moments if they were up for it.

I had gone to see Coldplay earlier in the year to scope out which of the numbers from the new album, *X&Y*, worked best live. Coldplay is another band whose records, well made as they are, don't come up to their live presence. I've watched them develop over the past few years from a band based on pure musicianship to a band that can rock with the best of them, and at the show it was pretty clear that "Talk" was one of the numbers that resonated with the kids in the crowd. So "Talk" it was, and we were happy, the band was happy, and Andy Slater, the president of Capitol, was happy.

Of course there's no argument that these three bands, as popular and as great as they are, don't cover the spectrum of rock music, and it's always a dilemma with the show, not just in this category but in R&B, country, and even hip-hop where we don't really cover the bases. I was particularly disappointed not to find a place for the Foo Fighters and also for the White Stripes, both of whom had made great CDs this year, and both of whom deserved to be on the show. Beyond that, there's no question that Nine Inch Nails and System of a Down had also pushed the envelope this year and in fact *Mezmerize* was one of my favorite CDs of the year. But it was just a fact of life that with everything else we "had" to do on this year's show, we just weren't going to be able to go that far out with our rock choices.

There was one act, however, that while certainly not fitting easily into our traditional booking strategy, couldn't be ignored, and in fact, I was entranced by Gorillaz, and when we opened our nominations packet in December and I saw that it was nominated for Record of the Year I knew it was something I wanted to do on the show.

The idea of presenting a "virtual" band on the Grammys was one of the most exciting and innovative opportunities ever, and I was determined to figure out a way to make it work for our show. And that led me to a lovely group of Brits, all of whom immediately saw the value of the Grammys for a group that had taken most of the rest of the world by storm—remaining relatively unknown in America in spite of their huge radio hit. We started talking, they told me about an effect that they had done once before on a live show that sounded both incredibly complex but worth the risk, and we skipped off on a journey that would not only lead us to a great opening number, but would also give us a reason to book one of music's most appealing pop stars.

Madonna's people called shortly after I had booked Gorillaz to say that they were interested in doing the Grammys. In a conversation with Neil, Liz Rosenberg had mentioned Madonna's interest with a reference to the new CD, which was not nominated, and something about John Travolta and *Saturday Night Fever*. As you know by now, having an artist on who is not nominated is difficult, and only rarely do we do it, and when we do it, we frame it as a special segment. As far as the *Saturday Night Fever* idea was concerned, it didn't feel right to me, but I knew that her hit single "Hung Up" had a very similar hook to "Feels Good" by Gorillaz—so similar that when I went home that night and played the two tracks against each other, I knew there was a great fit between the two songs, and that I might be able to come up with something totally new and different: a pop star with a virtual band!

Before I went back to them with this idea, however, I spoke to Gorillaz' management, and as I figured, they got it right away. There were a great many worse things for a band of animated figures than to appear on the biggest music show of the year with one of the world's biggest female stars.

Then on to Madonna management, and as I thought the minute I made this marriage, they knew this was right. For Madonna, who stays on the cutting edge, wanting to reinvent herself on a regular basis, how much better could anything be? And from the first phone call where we put her folks, the Gorillaz' management and creative team, and our guys together it was destined to be something very special for all of us.

In particular, our scenic team of Brian Stonestreet, Steve Bass, and Bob Dickinson took the lead, spending hour upon hour on the phone and on e-mails back and forth across the pond to see that this was going to happen, and would work for television. Johnny and Tzvi went the distance here to make sure it would work, adding sufficient rehearsal time to work out any kinks—critical as it was to be our opening number.

With two Nashville representatives on our TV committee and a Texan who considers himself countrified, there are always spirited discussions when it comes to country, and this year was no exception.

In the end, though many of us very much liked the idea of Gretchen Wilson singing a duet with Merle Haggard, who was receiving a Trustees' Award this year, Keith Urban also got the nod. Keith had done a great job for us last year in the southern rock segment we did, and more important, he was the country music story of the year, as far as male artists went.

Keith is managed by Gary Borman, who also manages Faith Hill. In one of my first conversations with Gary about Keith he lobbed a soft offer that Faith might very well be interested in doing something with Keith on the show, and we asked Gary to check it out on Faith's side. He came back with a very positive response from Faith, and we were on. It was only after I booked it that I realized that we had unintentionally put into motion one of those *People Magazine/Entertainment Tonight* tabloid situations that always have less to do with the show and more with exploiting the show. In this case, here we were musically separating country music's first couple, Tim McGraw and Faith Hill, and pairing her up with Nicole Kidman's newest boyfriend, Keith. What photo ops lay ahead one could only speculate.

While we're on the subject—a slight digression. From the mid '80s when the specter of Michael Jackson just being in the audience at the Grammys would overshadow this remarkable three-hours-plus of performances in the press, we have been careful about turning the Grammys into the same kind of sideshow many of the other music awards shows, and some of the other award shows in general, have become. In fact, we have been very watchful of maintaining the cachet of the Grammys as non-exploitational (except in rare cases where the party who felt they were being self-serving were in fact serving our own selves—if that makes any sense). We may have been the only awards show this particular year to say no to Paris Hilton, Nicole Richie, and a couple of other 15-minute personalities, all offering themselves to us as presenters.

In fact, on the same day Britney was all over the headlines for failing to seat-belt her baby, I received the following letter from her, an offer to present on the show:

> *Dear Ken . . . I am writing to let you know I would love to be a presenter at this year's Grammy Awards. I know it is very short notice and you probably have all the presenters lined up already, but I wanted to write to you personally in hopes that you might be able to find a place for me in the show. As you know, I recently had a baby and I am so excited about this upcoming year and getting started on a new album . . .*

I turned it down. I was actually tempted to respond with a note that asked how she would prioritize the new album vs. the new baby, but then I realized that I had a better thing to say to her:

> *Dear Britney . . . thanks so much for your offer to present on this year's Grammy show. I would have responded earlier but I kept thinking back a few years to the one year we did invite you to the Grammys and heard from your manager that no one was to speak to you, and if there was anything we wanted, we should talk to him and he would then communicate with you. I think we ought to keep the relationship the way it was then.*

But what purpose would an e-mail like that serve? None, but to give me another good anecdote for this book.

Back to this year . . .

We were running out of performance slots and there were still things that needed to be put in the show. One of those was the tribute to Sly and the Family Stone that I had wanted to do for years. Even with the intervention of Jerry Goldstein, Sly's longtime manager (at times nearly as loopy as Sly himself), I could never get Sly's attention.

Until this year, that is.

Jerry had put together a tribute CD that was terrific. A great list of contemporary artists had taken some of Sly's classic tracks and built their own stylings on top creating a whole new genre of tribute album that was neither fish nor fowl (no duets because no Sly), but actually better. So, with that as a base, I contacted Jerry, told him that this was the year, and that we would do it only if we had Sly come out and appear with these artists, ending by reuniting with the Family Stone band.

Jerry went to Sly, who got it right away, I presume. I say "presume" because during this entire process, from the laying out of the medley musically, to putting together a scratch track with the help of Ron Fair, to booking it exactly the way I wanted to book it, through Sly's phantom rehearsal two nights before the show, I never had one conversation with Sly until the night of the show itself when I walked up to his blonde-Mohawked self and introduced myself, to hollow response.

But that's not what this is about. And with John Legend, Joss Stone, and Van Hunt ready to do "Family Affair," Maroon5 set to do "Everyday People" (eventually adding Ciara), will.i.am ready to do "Dance to the Music," Devin Lima (managed by, guess who, Jerry Goldstein) doing "If You Want Me to Stay" and ultimately teamed up with Fantasia, and Steven Tyler and Joe Perry on hand to set up Sly's entrance, we had the makings of another iconic segment in the manner of the southern rock piece and the funk segment of the past two years. That is, of course, if we could count on Sly to deliver.

And why should we have any doubt? After all, no one had seen him since 1993, he had missed more gigs over the years than he had made, and in the dictionary, next to the words "self destruct" are two words: Sly Stone. What, me worry?

It's either a tribute to our faith in the artists we work with or our love of gambling that we would risk anywhere between four and ten minutes of priceless network airtime, not to mention the credibility of the Academy, on a series of unlikely appearances: an opening number that paired Madonna with a bunch of animated rock stars, and—the ultimate challenge—a tribute to an icon whose music has had a profound influence on at least two successive generations but who was almost a guaranteed no-show.

And it wasn't as if there weren't clues to be followed along the way. Even though I knew Jerry Goldstein to be a little crazy but also crazy smart, as we progressed from the idea to the reality, I watched the rules change. First of all, what was going to be a two-week rehearsal with Sly working with the Family Stone band melted down to a week, then five days, and then three days. Then a couple of potential meetings with Sly were changed and then cancelled, all the while Jerry telling me just how incredibly excited Sly was to be a part of this.

Then came rehearsal and the first few passes with all of the talent—save Sly. I will say this, the Family Stone band sounded great, and Nile Rodgers put the whole number on its feet and shepherded a very difficult situation, doing it with grace and love for the music and the process. And then just as we were about to wrap rehearsal, in came Sly in one of the most bizarre entrances I've ever seen at one of my shows: In a three-quarter-length parka with the hood covering his entire face, motorcycle boots up to his knees, and a huge bandage covering his left hand. Bandage? Gee, Jerry must have forgotten to mention the BANDAGE!!!! I left my producer's table and quickly found Goldstein who professed total ignorance of my lack of information, and brushed it off by saying, "I thought I told you he had a little motorcycle accident . . . THREE WEEKS AGO!"

Sly rehearsed the song twice, and the next thing I knew, and only because Garry Hood, our head stage manager, has good eyes, Sly exited the arena without a word. The stage had been set, and from that moment on, nobody, Jerry Goldstein included, knew whether or not we were going to see Sly Stone two nights later when the show hit the air to millions of viewers worldwide.

However, the mere idea of a possible Sly Stone sighting was enough to excite the music press everywhere, and if there was any specific story that fascinated that constituency, it was the return, real or not, of Sylvester Stewart, better known as Sly Stone.

There was still a major X factor to come in this show, however. We were less than two weeks out, Linkin Park and Jay-Z had come in with the added historic bonus of Paul McCartney performing with them, most of the special segments and duets were coming through to my relative satisfaction, and even the wildest card of all, Sly Stone, had the insurance of a stage full of extremely talented people to pick up the slack should he decide to spend Grammy night at Barney's Beanery. But as I looked it all over, we were not quite where we needed to be in the youth department, and there actually was a simple fix, simple logic of course, but not quite so simple in my own mind.

To their respective credit, several members of the television committee as well as Neil himself were very vocally supportive of booking Kelly Clarkson. Additionally, I was being lobbied fast and furiously by her manager, Jeff Kwatinetz, but less than aggressively by her record label. Although I had gone to see her live and was impressed with her vocal range and, to an extent, with her emotional range, I will confess to a major bias about *American Idol* and all that it represents, or more accurately what it doesn't represent. To me, it's not a music show. With its procession of Whitney and Mariah wannabes, it promotes imitation and prevents unique talented young artists from finding forums for their music. In other words, there are only a certain number of spots out there, and if they're taken by mimics as opposed to artists with something original to say, that's not good.

To be frank, I was so blinded by these feelings that I failed to recognize that in fact there just might be something special in a few of these artists that I would never find because I didn't want to look there. And it took some time for me to admit that I was wrong about Kelly. And by the time I did figure it out, it was almost too late to correct it.

After a few failed attempts with Kwatinetz in which I tried to pair Kelly up with a couple of other promising nominees in segments that I know would have worked, I finally yielded, and we confirmed her appearance to perform "Because of You" on the show, not our first choice, but a big power ballad in which I felt she could score with the house and at home. But because this was the last booking in the show, we were really up against it production-wise, and we wanted to make sure that we could support this number correctly.

It took a while, but no more than four days before rehearsals began we finalized Kelly's appearance, her staging, and our approach to the number. Her idea of having some child musicians blended with my idea of introducing Kelly by playing a four- or five-year-old clip I had found of her talking about how her dream was to be on the Grammys. Her reticence about moving at all onstage was tempered by Kwatinetz seeing that our plan to move her away from the kids to centerstage where she could own the stage was the right idea, and helped me sell it to her.

As I usually do about ten days out, even though I do cheat and start sketching out a rundown weeks earlier, I allowed myself to take a good look at the particular Grammy show, weigh it against other shows we had done, weigh it against some of the other award shows on television this past year, and weigh it against my own particular standards, which, I have been told by any number of people we work with, range from unattainable to impossible. I'm kind of proud of that.

And what I found was pleasing. We had more than covered most of the bases. Not everything, but then again, we never do. But there was rock in all its glory, there was urban music and R&B. There was country. There was youth, and there was tradition. There were duets and there were great solo numbers. And looking at this tapestry that we had woven from what had only been raw silk three months ago, it all looked pretty good.

But not perfect.

And that's when New Orleans came back into the picture, and that's when Wilson Pickett chose to pass away, although if given some options, he might not have chosen that date.

New Orleans first. You know my love for this great city and in particular my being consumed with making sure that every generation understands that without New Orleans, there would be a much different musical history in America. A bold statement perhaps, but just think of music without Louis Armstrong, the Neville Brothers, Professor Longhair, Allen Toussaint, Huey Piano Smith, and the list goes on and on.

We've done some amazing shows celebrating this culture over the years, the most recent taking place two nights after the Emmy Awards show, when my staff went from the Emmy party to the airport, got on a plane, flew to New York, and did this giant show in Madison Square Garden that brought the likes of Toussaint, Irma Thomas, the Neville Brothers and the Meters, the Dirty Dozen Brass Band, Clarence "Frogman" Henry, and many others together with Jimmy Buffett, Simon and Garfunkel, Bette Midler, and John Fogerty in a fundraiser for the victims of Hurricane Katrina. It was an incredible evening, not only musically, but in giving upwards of 75 New Orleans musicians who had lost everything their first appearance before an audience, and in this case, an audience of cheering, floor-stomping New Yorkers who were there to celebrate the culture that they too loved and didn't want to see die.

That was the New Orleans I wanted to celebrate on the Grammys. *Celebrate* . . . not like the dirge-like, staged TV benefit a few weeks after the hurricane that might as well have put an aboveground headstone in the middle of the set and buried the city in it. No, not like that, but a show that started with the Rebirth Brass Band walking through the aisles of the Garden in a traditional New Orleans jazz funeral and grew to an epic retreat through the house five-and-a-half hours later with a second-line celebration to literally "beat the band" . . . that's the New Orleans this show needed to proclaim . . . that it would take more than the country's most devastating hurricane ever to kill the spirit and the culture of this city.

But until just about a week before the Grammys, even though I had privately put together a few different ways to approach a New Orleans piece on the show, I did nothing about it other than to keep bringing it up on the weekly conference calls. And then I realized why I hadn't acted on it—in fact, because New Orleans had such meaning for me, I couldn't face the disappointment if I had laid something out that I fell in love with and then because of time we weren't able to do it on the show. And this year, because of all of the circumstances that surrounded the show, the lack of production time, the lateness of locking certain elements, the Jay-Z factor, my normal "let's go for it" attitude needed to be tempered somewhat. But now the blanks were all filled in and if we were very careful about it, we could eke out five minutes at the end of a jam-packed Grammy show to do something that probably should have been there at the beginning.

It came together in a few quickly answered phone calls, particularly when the idea of coupling it with a remembrance of Wilson Pickett, the southern soul man who had died a few days prior, was added.

To me, Allen Toussaint is a god, a gentle man, and a gentleman. He is *the* writer who took the tradition of the second line rhythm of New Orleans and popularized it through songs almost always done by others, even though Allen has one of God's angelic voices.

And because my New Orleans starts at the piano and people like James Booker, Professor Longhair, and Huey Smith are the Holy Trinity, it needed to be about Allen and one of his anthems, the incredibly appropriate "Yes We Can Can," a bayou classic familiar to at least a portion of our viewers. Adding Dr. John on B-3 was just the right thing to do, and then asking New Orleans' own Irma Thomas to join this Holy Trinity gave the piece the authenticity it demanded. My friend Elvis Costello jumped in to help put it together, Edge was there from the beginning, and I knew that Bonnie Raitt and Yolanda Adams would be a part of it.

It might have been, as we say, "soup already" (maybe gumbo?), but then I added one more layer that made sense to me, if at first it seemed a bit strange to others. To honor Wilson Pickett, a son of the south (isn't that term usually reserved for white guys) and the man who took "the Midnight Hour" to prime time, I asked Bruce and Sam Moore to join the already gathered New Orleans delegation to bring the show home.

And now it really was soup, and the little offsite rehearsal we did the day before the show, the only chance I had to get everybody together in one place, provided a series of memorable moments that I only wish we could bottle.

Rehearsals actually went better than usual; perhaps it was God's way of making up for a miserable pre-production period fraught with over-involved managers, either an imagined or very real shortage of time to get an impossibly long list of things done by the time we hit Staples Center, and a purposely dragged out presenter process, slowed so that unlike in some years we didn't turn around three days before the show and wonder why we had booked some of the people we had booked. Not this year.

There's no question that the most complex aspect of both the pre-production and rehearsal period, not to discount the show itself, was the Madonna/Gorillaz opening number, and it's a tribute to all three entities—our production team, Madonna's people, and mostly an incredible group of Brits involved with Gorillaz—that it came off as well as it did. And while so much of it was theoretical until we actually put it on its feet at Staples (adding a half day of rehearsal to an already jammed schedule), when we ran it for the first time in front of civilians after a full night of shaking it down, it was almost jaw-dropping to be sitting there watching this virtual band enter and exit the stage, do their trademarked anti-rock-and-roll rock and roll moves, be joined by De La Soul for two verses of "Feels Good," and then up from beneath the stage appears Madonna who performs in and among them, struts around behind Murdock and in front of Noodle, and then exits the stage, only to reappear on a second stage to do the rest of "Hung Up."

Except for one thing; the "real" Madonna never appeared on that stage with those characters. To this day, friends who were live there in the house as well as those who saw it on television can't believe that it was a virtual Madonna, filmed in England in late December, who performed with Gorillaz!

In our bunker under the stage where Neil, his assistant Claudine, CBS Vice President Jack Sussman, lead stage manager Garry Hood, the accountants and the Grammy trophy girls all hang out, it was a happy and crowded group that stood around several monitors (standard definition and high definition) a bank of telephones (for me to the video truck, teleprompter and announcer; for Jack Sussman to network control in New York), and assorted vegetable trays and water, all trenched in for the three-and-a-half-hour siege which we witnessed from below the stage. And then we were off, the tease that I had designed to let people know that more Grammy moments were on their way this year, leading into our animated Gorillaz/Madonna performance, and hopefully enticing millions of viewers not to even think about changing channels. The Gorillaz/Madonna piece drew cheers from the house, and I imagined people at home saying to themselves, "Well, I've never seen anything like this on the Grammys before, this is going to be a cool show."

Alicia Keys and Stevie Wonder kicked off the rest of the show welcoming people to the Grammys, and saluting Coretta Scott King (who had passed away the previous week) with a little piece of "Higher Ground," and then into the first award which was promptly snatched by underdog Kelly Clarkson over Mariah Carey, Gwen Stefani, Bonnie Raitt, and Sheryl Crow. I was glad I had booked her, and even happier when as the "kid" she rushed the stage, got all caught up in what she wanted to say, and started bawling on camera. We *love* those moments!!!!.

The U2 solo performance of "Vertigo" was followed by Mary J. Blige coming out to join them on "One." This was the first litmus test of our live Grammy audience. Notoriously slow to get off their feet, the first ten rows so wrapped up in their own nominations, if not nominees themselves, the executives too busy looking around to see who's looking at them—it often pains me when we put such amazing moments onstage and this industry crowd sits there without getting into the music and the artist. This was my first "money back" standing ovation, and if it didn't come, I knew we were in big trouble with this house. As innovative and different as the opening number was, I didn't think it would get a standing ovation; it was too early in the game. Both of them did. Coldplay might have gotten one, but we moved on to commercial so quickly that the house didn't have a chance to respond, and though isolated pockets in the house stood up for young John Legend, it wasn't a unanimous move. But after Mary J. and the band, aided by an inspired Bono who was ready to go toe to toe with Mary, lit up the room with "One," there was the ovation. It was an amazing moment and made the near sweep that the band was to achieve over the course of the night a lot more understandable to those partisans of other acts. There could be no denying that this is a great rock 'n' roll band.

Rap Album could only have gone to Kanye, who came to the stage with a rather gimmicky acceptance speech idea that didn't quite score the way he hoped it would. So he moved through some perfunctory thank yous and tipped the house that the real reason he was here would be clear later when he would perform.

I thought I had a horse race going into the Rock Album category, what with the Stones, Coldplay, Foo Fighters, and Neil Young up against U2, but it was a harbinger of the rest of the night when Gwen Stefani and

Billie Joe Armstrong yelled out U2 to the 13,000 folks at Staples, and the band bounded up onstage to deliver a great acceptance speech.

When Ellen DeGeneres walked out at the top of the next act and said only, "The next performer needs no introduction" and walked off, you could feel the excitement in the house as we raised our closedown wall and there was Paul McCartney launching into "Fine Line," not a song like "Lady Madonna" that you've heard most of your life, but a song that set all kinds of memories in motion thinking about just how much of our collective lives have been spent accompanied by the music of McCartney and his mates. And then he topped it off by jumping into "Helter Skelter," a Beatles classic that I had seen him do on the most recent tour and had suggested as the perfect "flip side" for his first-ever and, for all I knew, his last-ever Grammy appearance. I escaped from our bunker under the stage just long enough to head to the side of the stage where I could watch this guy, perhaps the last of the legendary performers of my lifetime with whom I hadn't worked, deliver a blazing version of the song that has so many meanings to so many different generations. The crowd rewarded him with the second full standing ovation of the night, not knowing that he'd be back again in about an hour's time to collect one more standing O, this time shared with Jay-Z and Linkin Park.

Keith Urban and Faith Hill did extremely well in a house not particularly receptive to country artists, and then Jay-Z and Linkin Park were awarded a Grammy for Rap/Sung Collaboration, the category they would perform about a half-hour later. I had purposely put that category there because I was hopeful of a win for them, setting up the performance, but I could have been sorely disappointed if they hadn't won and then had to go out and perform after losing. Those are the breaks, and I knew that it wasn't about the award in this case but about the performance.

And then came Sly. Or as they used to advertise the show *Beatlemania*, "an incredible simulation." All of my Sly tributors, including Joss Stone, John Legend, Fantasia, Maroon5, will.i.am, Steven Tyler, and Joe Perry did a great job setting up the segment, although there would be mixed reviews about each of them following the show. But to me the love and respect came through, and the Slyster couldn't have asked for

a better tee up. Then out he came, Mohawk and all. For all of one minute and thirty seconds, the man no one had seen for 16 years was on
national television, being seen by millions. As the original Family Stone
Band, minus one or two players, ramped up into "I Want to Take You
Higher," Sly, who may have had enough of all of this, or maybe not, I'll
never know, waved to the crowd and left the stage, leaving the finish of
the song to the all-star aggregation out there, some of them as puzzled as
the people in the house were, and others just still having a great time.

I've got mixed feelings now that it's over—I think I was let down,
over-promised and under-delivered by Jerry Goldstein, but it wasn't as if
he were trying to sell me something. I pursued this, I wanted it to happen, and if it fell short of a great Grammy performance, at least we got
Sly onstage and, whether he chose to take advantage of the moment for
himself or not, we had done what we said we would do.

It's not the first time I've taken a chance on an artist on this or other
shows, and again it goes back to my faith in these folks to deliver for
whatever reason. My only regret is that all the effort that we put into
this could have re-launched his career or at least have ended with a huge
standing ovation in recognition of what he had done to revolutionize
music, much as we had done with Prince a few years ago and, to a lesser
extent, for Earth, Wind & Fire.

And if you were one of those people who were disappointed that
you didn't see the Sly Stone of the '70s, hopefully you kept your faith in
the Grammys and stayed around to see what proved to be the biggest
moment of the show and certainly one of the best-kept surprises we had
ever been able to keep.

Jay-Z and Linkin Park's performance was great—"Numb/Encore"
was every bit as exciting as it had been when they had done it for me on
Live8 in Philadelphia over July 4, but then the music blended into "Yesterday" and out came Paul McCartney to make this a true triumvirate of
our contemporary musical history and genre. Paul singing with LP lead
singer Chester Bennington and augmented by Jay-Z dropping in incredible rap riffs throughout was one of those mesmerizing moments you
just never forget. I don't believe there was anyone left sitting in Staples.

From the stage-filling presence of Linkin Park, Jay-Z, and Paul Mc-
Cartney to a solitary Bruce Springsteen with guitar performing "Devils

and Dust" to a hushed Staples audience, that's also what the Grammys are all about. And Bruce, framed by two screens that were locked on a close-up of that face for most of the number, delivered with the intensity and drama that he always brings with him—it was a guaranteed show stopper, whether flying across the stage with the E Street Band doing "Rosalita" or just looking you straight in the eye and reaching way down into your heart when he sang "Philadelphia" on the show years ago. That's Bruce, and no matter how many times you see him, you continually see something new there.

In less than an hour we had gone from Keith Urban and Faith Hill to a Sly Stone tribute to Linkin Park with Jay-Z and Paul McCartney to Bruce Springsteen, and now we were about to blow the place open with Kanye and Jamie Foxx doing "Gold Digger" complete with the Florida A&M Marching Band and dancers.

And break it open they did. Starting in the house, Kanye and Jamie led the respective parts of the band onstage and into formation while driving "Gold Digger" to heights it had never been taken before, followed by sorority steppers taking it to the street and then finishing it off with "Top of the World Ma," West going into another anthem from the *Late Registration* CD, "Touch the Sky."

Would it be rewarded with the next award, Record of the Year? No, that honor would go to another marching band, U2, that marched to the stage for the third time on the show to pick up the Grammy for "Vertigo," and to deliver another intelligent thank-you speech, counter to the long-standing rock band tradition of incoherent mumbling.

Almost home, and after one more win for U2 for Album of the Year, presented by past Album and Record of the Year winners James Taylor and Bonnie Raitt, Neil Portnow took the stage to share some thoughts about music's role in helping the victims of Hurricane Katrina. In my opinion it was the most successful of the three speeches he's given, primarily because he kept it to one simple thought, traded the stock Academy message for something from the heart, and then got us into a closing number that many have said could have played earlier in the show, our New Orleans/ Wilson Pickett salute. And while certain numbers of attendees, nominees in particular, had left the building, a resounding majority of the audience, many of whom would later tell me this was the fastest-moving award show they had ever been to, stayed in their seats to witness this final expression of artists representing a cross section of our musical experience once again sharing a stage for the purpose of saying something through their music. To see the likes of Allen Toussaint, Dr. John, Irma Thomas, and Sam Moore—all of whom had influenced so many of today's vital artists—onstage with Bonnie Raitt, Bruce Springsteen, Edge, and Elvis Costello was a moment all its own—a mirror of what I had seen earlier that evening in the faces of the Linkin Park/Jay-Z number.

And then it was over. For the first time that I can remember, I didn't do my usual tour to thank our crew folks and the talent who were still there at the end. I just wanted to have a couple of quiet moments to reflect on all that had happened in the four months to the day of my coronary bypass surgery. To think how far I had come over that time, but more to think about what so many others had done to make me healthy and bring me to this day.

So I went back to the office that for years I had shared with Walter and Pierre, and for the past two years had shared with John, and broke into tears, letting my emotions take me to a seldom visited place. Then it was time to go to the parties.

Quint Davis, our friend from New Orleans, and Terry Lickona, the chairman of the Academy, joined us for the first leg of our party crawl and we were the object of a lot of back slapping and congratulations, much appreciated and nearly always said in earnest, but still with the rosy glow of the show still in their thoughts. I'm much more impressed with people's reactions the next day or from people who weren't there but watched it on television. The press has never been particularly kind to the Grammys. As I've said before, we're an easy target, but for some reason, this year the number of positive stories far outweighed the negatives, and that added to my personal pleasure.

Somewhere along the way, in the limo between parties, Paul McGuinness, U2's manager, tracked me down on my cell and said that they were disappointed not to have seen me after the show. I immediately regretted my decision not to have done the dressing room tour, but I was very happy when he asked if I would join the band and their principal management staff people at a lunch the next day at a Hollywood restaurant. Gladly, I said, and the following afternoon, after a meeting that my friend Jack Sussman had scheduled for a few hours after the Grammys about another show (thank you Jack), was treated to an afternoon of Irish appreciation with the attendant wine, whiskey, and words worthy of melody. I returned the plaudits in kind, praising the band for never losing their thirst for winning. I said that what impressed me most was watching the band each time they won an award and came down through the tunnel into my bunker acting as if they were 19-year-old kids winning their first talent show in Dublin. It was that enthusiasm that separates a good rock 'n' roll band from a great rock 'n' roll band— they've never lost the thrill of what they do.

The fallout from the show was incredibly positive, as opposed to the ratings, which dropped for the second year in a row. All kinds of excuses were made, the primary one being that the move away from *Desperate Housewives* on Sunday night was a good one, but being put smack up against *American Idol*, which soundly beat us the first hour, was a death wish. And though I might have been comforted somewhat knowing that we won the second and third hour and still wound up in the top ten shows of the week, it's not fun to lose, and we had lost. So millions of fans who love music passed up U2 and Mary J., John Legend, Madonna, and Coldplay to see a bunch of kids looking for their 45 seconds of fame, most of whom, most likely, would not pass this way again.

But then I step back and look at the other side, and what we did do, and I look at the editorial in the *New Orleans Times-Picayune* the following Monday, which said in part:

> The most beautiful sound at the 48th Annual Grammys didn't come from a singer or musicians but from Neil Portnow, president of the Academy, who offered support for hurricane stricken New Orleans. The Awards program . . . ended with an emotional musical tribute to New Orleans and a plea by Mr. Portnow to show support by visiting during Mardi Gras and Jazzfest: "Let's join in giving something back to this singular city that has given so much to our world and keep the music playing forever."

And this e-mail from Bonnie Raitt: "I LOVED the show . . . love what magic you spin out of thin air every time. Year after year, more incredible than any one guy or team could come up with . . . ."

So into the books goes number 48 and soon it would be time to start thinking about 49, and if all goes well and the world stays sane, maybe we'll all make it to number 50 together. I'd certainly like that.

Postscript: a week or so later I was at my regular appointment with Marc Ehrich, my cardiologist, the first since he and his wife had come to the show. It was his first time at the Grammys, and his "gee whiz" reaction to the show was as refreshing to me as I knew it would be. Every time I talk to someone who's never been there before, I'm reminded of what an amazing experience it is and how important it is never to take it for granted. While he was giving me his observations of the show, he told me that at one point, a couple of hours in, his wife said, "Are you seriously telling me that Ken Ehrlich produced this whole show just four months after his surgery?" and that after a short pause, Marc turned to his wife and said, "No, he's producing this show because he had the surgery four months ago." Of all the words in this book, those may be the truest of all.

CHAPTER 29

The 2007 Grammy Awards

The Police Get Back Together;
The Dixie Chicks, Still Not Ready to Make Nice

Trust me, the 49th Annual Grammy Awards show didn't start out to be a politically charged show that meant to send a message to the Bush Administration, but by the time we played the Dixie Chicks off for the fourth time on the air and said good night, perhaps the Academy membership had more in mind for this show than just a whopping good time, some truly great Grammy moments, and a 22 percent increase in viewers over the previous year.

It's probably best to begin with the story of the Chicks, starting with that fateful London concert in 2004 where lead singer Natalie Maines expressed her shame at being from the same state as George Bush. The reaction and subsequent two-and-a-half years for the Chicks have been well documented, but until you sat down and talked to the women and their manager, Simon Renshaw, you couldn't really understand just how devastating this period was. Shunned by country radio, who were primarily responsible for their success, and compounded by the lack of recognition by the Country Music Association, who ignored the Chicks' *Taking the Long Way* CD totally, the girls found themselves characterized as pariahs who had forsaken their core audience in "the Red States," the stereotypical country music crowd.

It was a rough couple of years; concert tours were cancelled or moved to smaller venues. CD sales were slim compared to the three previous offerings, and even the press, which usually loves a good controversy, seemed to grow tired of this story even when the girls came out and tried to explain that their remarks were not as politically charged as they were philosophically motivated by the fact that each of them had recently become mothers.

In the fall of 2006, the Country Music Association rewarded the CD with no nominations at all, this for a group that had been CMA darlings in the past. And maybe that, without negating the brilliance of an album that contained a collection of songs that were broader and more compelling than any previous Chicks album, was partially responsible for across-the-board nominations from the girls when the Grammy nominations were announced at the press conference on December 7.

Joining the Chicks with the most nominations that was a particularly musical palette of offerings that ranged from Mary J. Blige (who led the nominations with eight); newcomer Corinne Bailey Rae, who cornered noms for Record of the Year, Best New Artist, and Song of the Year; Gnarls Barkley, whose *St. Elsewhere* got a nod for Album with the quirky "Crazy," nominated for Record; Justin Timberlake; the Red Hot Chili Peppers; and John Mayer, all of whom scored in one or more of the major categories. It was the first time in several years where I didn't see a name that I wouldn't consider a strong contender for a major performance slot.

As in the past, the post-nominations television committee meeting was a reasonably agreeable affair, with a majority of the performance slot discussions universally embraced. Some obvious choices were easy: Mary J., the Chicks, the Chili Peppers; Gnarls Barkley; and youngster and Best New Artist nominee Chris Brown—and to a slightly lesser degree, John Mayer, Corinne Bailey Rae, and Ludacris, who had a great year and was the frontrunner in the hip-hop area, although closely pursued by Atlanta's T.I., whose nominations didn't really reflect his huge popularity.

Another strong possibility was the nomination given to U2 and Green Day for the track "The Saints Are Coming." This was a track both bands had recorded and performed at the urging of The Edge and his Music Rising project. After it was recorded, he asked us to produce the only-ever live and televised performance at the opening New Orleans Saints game at the Superdome, the sight of so much despair and death during Katrina. The live performance in New Orleans had all the makings of an incredible event, and as I thought about it, I went back to Edge and suggested expanding it to include pieces of "Wake Me When September Ends" (which was so on point to the tragedy in the Gulf region) and "Beautiful Day," which was already being used by the Saints as their unofficial official song for the season. So, on September 25, with 50,000 fans coming back to the Dome for the first time, the two bands took the field and kicked off the Saints' most successful season ever (getting to within one game of the Super Bowl) with an inspiring performance that I don't think anyone there will ever forget—oh, and by the way, the Saints beat their fiercest rival, the Falcons, 24–3. While I knew that this performance would be amazing, the most obvious factor working against booking it was that both U2 and Green Day had played significant parts in several Grammy shows over the past few years, and the question was raised, and legitimately so, "Is it too much already?"

I encouraged our group not to go too much further than our initial list, what with the holidays fast approaching. Before we broke up, though, I brought our group up to speed on a concept which involved Justin Timberlake that would have a major effect on this year's Grammy show, the promotion we were calling "My Grammy Moment."

"My Grammy Moment" actually had its beginnings two years earlier with a treatment that I had done for a show called *I Want to Be on The Grammys*, a series that would lend the Grammy brand to the currently raging *American Idol* talent competition idea. I had unsuccessfully pitched this series in various incarnations to our partners at CBS several times with no luck. I was convinced, and still am, that a Grammy-branded talent competition series, where the payoff was a performance on the Grammys itself, would not only be a major step forward in contemporizing the show itself, but also a real magnet to a younger audience which has become very used to discovering its music via this type of show. The series also had a strong Internet component, which gave it additional traction in the new world of participatory television.

But CBS was having none of it, so not content to let it die, I came up with yet one more twist: the idea of having the winner of the competition sing a duet on the show with a Grammy-nominated artist. We took that to CBS, and though they loved the idea of doing it on the show, they still wouldn't give us a limited series running up to the show.

I'm sure that the spate of failed copycat *Idol* shows was the reason the network didn't believe in this idea, but neither Neil nor I were willing to give up on the concept, and so we decided to move ahead with it strictly on the Internet, without the obvious boost a weekly network broadcast presence would have given us. Of course we realized that repetition and getting to know the participants was the real secret to the success of these types of shows, but we figured that even without a weekly network broadcast, we were still better off trying to make the competition work and hoping that the viral aspect of the Internet would be our friend.

Our first inquiry to an artist to join us as a partner in this proved to be the right one—an artist whose popularity has been closely aligned to the Internet generation, an artist who was a risk taker, and most of all, an artist whose accessible musical style and cross-generational appeal made him the absolute right partner for this project. Justin Timberlake was our man, and he and his manager, Johnny Wright, *got* it from square one.

Neil, Jack Sussman, and I met with Justin and Johnny and discussed the concept where we would open the competition through our partnership with Yahoo to all contestants willing to submit an a cappella video that would be judged by a blue-ribbon committee. Then through a series of eliminations, we'd wind up with three finalists who would actually rehearse a song with Justin during Grammy Week, come to the show and be seated together, and then wait as one name was called to the stage to duet with Justin as part of the Grammy show.

So it was that concept that Neil asked John Cossette and me to bring to the Academy Board of Trustees meeting in November to explain to the Board why this idea, which was very innovative and somewhat risky, should be embraced by the leadership of the Academy. After all, the Grammy has stood as a peer voted award for nearly 50 years, voted on by its membership with popularity perhaps factored in but not used as a criterion for a Grammy Award, and here we were, putting an amateur, a performer who had never had a released recording, on the biggest music show in the world. I'll say it needed a bit of clarification.

The meeting itself went well, and though a number of questions were asked and answered, as it turns out, it wasn't until after John and I left the room that the full impact of what I had said began to sink in to the leadership of the Academy, and with us safely out of the room, it went to Neil and Terry not only to defend our project, but to put themselves on the line that it was going to be a big win for everyone. And that's exactly what they did.

But even though we had the endorsement of the Board, Neil and Terry's support, and a great partner in Justin, the project took on a life of its own, becoming a pack of wild horses who kept on trying to break out of the pen. We did due diligence in coming up with the rules, worked closely with our partners at CBS and at Yahoo to make sure we had covered all the bases, and went online with our first announcement in mid December, with a cutoff of early January for submissions. And though it was slow in the beginning, all of a sudden the competition took off and before we knew it, we had close to 3000 videos entered in competition, and our small group of first-round judges found ourselves spending much of the holiday looking at version after version of "If I Ain't Got You" or "I Want to Dance with Somebody" or "Respect," three of the eight songs we had given as choices for our contestants.

~

For every segment that needed to be built from ground zero, sometimes with a logical song attached, there would often be one that just fell into our laps, and it was just up to us to recognize it. We were due one of those, and it happened shortly after the nominations came out when I got a call from Sting's longtime manager Kathy Shenker guardedly inquiring whether we'd be interested in opening the show with the reunion of the Police. Now, over the years, the show has developed a reputation for surprise openings, and nothing on the horizon even resembled the surprise we might get from Sting, Andy Summers, and Stewart Copeland getting together again, so I was all for it., but not without the ever-present nagging feeling I had when committing to an opening so early in the process. What if something were to come along to trump the Police, I thought to myself, and then realized that the Beatles weren't going to regroup, neither was Led Zeppelin, nor would Bob Marley walk onto our stage. So I told Kathy that of course we wanted the boys—having done a number of shows with Sting as a solo act, but never with the Police—but that I wanted to wait a bit to commit to the opening.

And so we approached the Christmas week break seemingly in pretty good shape. We had a potential dynamite opening act and had confirmed agreements with the Dixie Chicks, Justin Timberlake performing one song on his own and one with our "Grammy Moment" winner, Gnarls Barkley, Beyoncé, Mary J. Blige, and Chris Brown. We had offers out to the Chili Peppers and Carrie Underwood, and conditional offers out to Corinne Bailey Rae, John Mayer, and John Legend based upon their performing together in one segment.

Then James Brown died.

Our In Memoriam segment, which had become a staple of the show, and which I had come to accept despite the double-edged sword that it was, was "in work." Material was being gathered about those music people who had passed, and in my mind it would be key-stoned by a salute to Ahmet Ertegun, the longtime head of Atlantic Records who was one of my personal idols as well as being one of the real giants of the music industry. I was planning on building a segment that gave Ahmet the only soundbite and surrounding him with clips of Arif Mardin, Atlantic's longtime A&R head and pr oducer, Ruth Brown, one of the first-ever Atlantic Records stars of the '50s, and Gerald Levert, who was one of the great R&B voices of the past two decades and a personal favorite of Ahmet's—all of whom had passed away during the year. And it looked as though I had found a great clip of Gerald and his father Eddie Levert (of the O'Jays) singing "Wind Beneath My Wings" from an Essence Awards show, that I planned to use to pay off with Eddie onstage paying tribute to all of those who had passed.

But then . . . James Brown died. And then the promoter of the O'Jays show that was to be held on Grammy day wouldn't let Eddie out of his show . . . even to come to Los Angeles to be on the Grammys to pay tribute to his son. And we were then faced with the reality that both of these giants deserved to be paid proper homage on the Grammys, even though I had always been clear with all who listened that we needed to be very careful not to turn the show itself into a memorial service for artists who had passed away in the previous year. It was a trap that we couldn't allow ourselves to fall into, even though other award shows that didn't have the opportunities we had, still embraced the In Memoriam segment because it gave them some "business" to do other than giving out awards.

For me, there were no easy answers to this dilemma. I had known both Ahmet and James well. I had worked with both of them, having done the epic 12-hour Atlantic Records 40th Anniversary show at Madison Square Garden in 1988, a show that opened with Ruth Brown and Lavern Baker and ended nearly 12 hours later with the Led Zeppelin reunion (that featured Page and Plant's first appearance together in ten years, accompanied by Jason Bonham on drums and John Paul Jones). And as discussed elsewhere in this tome, we had done any number of shows with James, the most recent being his duet with young Usher on the Grammys two years earlier.

As I thought about James, a couple of ideas came to me. We had already committed to doing an extended segment that featured several generations of male R&B singers starring Smokey Robinson and Lionel Richie, both of whom were nominated for Grammys this year, and would pay off with Chris Brown, the hot young kid who very well might follow in the footsteps of popularity of the two legends who would precede him onstage that night. And then, in a meeting with Jesse Collins, a young producer who was working on other shows with John Cossette, we came upon an idea to do something totally different to this medley that paid tribute to the great male R&B stars—and that was to take a major left turn and ask Christina Aguilera to finish the piece with the James Brown classic, "It's a Man's World." I called Irving Azoff (who had been after me to put Christina on the show), and without hesitation, he got it and said he would talk to Christina, knowing that this could potentially be the biggest standing ovation of a show that was growing in standing ovations.

But there was a little more we could do for James, and while it might not have been an obvious thought, it turned out to be very special. When it was apparent that we couldn't get Eddie Levert out of his date, we switched back to James as the payoff, and with Jesse's help, found the perfect clip of James, from the *TAMI* show in the middle sixties, doing a classic dance routine. We then went to Chris Brown's manager, Tina Davis, and asked her if Chris would learn the steps exactly to mimic James's and that we would project them above Chris as he danced to Mr. Brown's steps. She loved it, Chris jumped at the chance of doing it, but we had one more thought, an idea that would not only honor Mr. Brown but put a button on the entire list of people who were to be remembered in this year's In Memoriam segment.

I asked Tisha to find Danny Ray, James's longtime "cape man," the man who always came out at the end of Mr. Brown's performance, put a cape on the Godfather and "attempted" to get him to leave the stage, providing one false exit after another for Mr. Brown to milk everything he could out of a usually already drained crowd. Only this time, on show night, Danny would come out, cape in hand, pause as he held the cape up to the audience, and then drape it gracefully over the microphone stand that Chris had used just as his mentor, James Brown, had. The spotlight would close into to a pinspot on the cape, the rest of the stage would be dark, and 12,000 people in Staples Center would rise to their feet to salute one of the fathers of modern music, James Brown.

So the show was half booked with what looked like at least a few Grammy moments, but there was still a long way to go, and the clock was ticking. And though we were back from the Christmas holiday two days after the New Year, the rest of the business was on its usual week-long slow trip back from any and everywhere, and we were once again scrambling, with five weeks to go to get the rest of the show together.

An important booking to me was to get Corinne Bailey Rae and the two Johns (Mayer and Legend) to come to the table and perform together a segment that had come out of a suggestion by Neil. It wasn't coming along. Corinne's nominations and my lack of a relationship either with her or her manager were making communication difficult, even with the help of Andy Slater, the president of Capitol Records, her label. And it was clear that with his nominations for two separate CDs, John Mayer felt that he deserved a solo spot on the show. John Legend, on the other hand, was very open to this trio, obviously contingent on the material and how it played out.

And then a good thing happened. I was speaking with a friend who works with Mayer and mentioned that I would really like to speak with John, who I knew from past experience was about the music first. This friend got a message to John and a day later John called and we began to talk about the segment. He explained to me that he wasn't at all against collaborating with John and Corinne, but he had been told that I wanted to do "Waiting for the World to Change" and that he was much more interested in doing "Gravity." As it turns out, I actually preferred "Gravity," with its slow build, to the bigger hit "Change," and I asked him to give me a day to lay out the segment musically using "Gravity." That night at home, I listened to all three artists' CDs again, changing my thoughts about Corinne's song from the hit "Put Your Records On" to the much moodier, almost butterfly wing-like "Like a Star," and then, after several listenings to Legend's CD, settled on the last cut, "Coming Home," a haunting anti-war song whose lyric and melody were so classic that it could have been written almost anytime over the past 50 years.

Inspired, and armed with what I thought was a killer medley for the three artists, I broke down each of the three songs, finding the places for each artist to drop in on the other artist's song, followed by a lovely piano fill for John Legend later in the song, and so on. These kind of things are what give me the greatest joy in the shows we do, and when I got to the office the following day, I couldn't wait to try all this out on John Mayer, who loved it. Later that same day, while I was on my way down to the Music Center to meet with Sting to talk about the Police's number on the show, I made a slight detour to the Capitol Tower unannounced to see Andy Slater, armed with three CDs and a scripted roadmap to what I wanted to do. He held a meeting off while the adrenaline rushed me through this nine-minute piece and at the end he said it was wonderful and not to even think twice about it, he'd make sure that his artist, Corinne, did it.

We were not having the same type of success in the country music world, where we knew we wanted both Carrie Underwood and Rascal Flatts, but with some strings attached. After all, Carrie had performed on both the Billboard Music Awards and the American Music Awards just two months prior to the Grammys (not to mention the Country Music Awards the month before) and her three hits had been seen by just about every type of music fan. And Rascal Flatts's sole nomination was a mid-tempo ballad that didn't in any way serve the band, known for being able to rock out country style. And so it was that we began to look for a way to book both of these acts but to present them in a way that would give our viewers not only something fresh to look at, but hopefully expand their core audience to include the broad spectrum of Grammy viewer.

It started out as a tribute to the Eagles, whose cofounder Don Henley was to be honored as the Musicares Person of the Year this year, and who at one point had expressed possible interest in being a part of the piece. But by the time it aired, it had become one of the more difficult special segments we had put on the show._

I thought Carrie did a great job on "Desperado" and was a game player to walk into Flatts's for a verse chorus of "Life in the Fast Lane." She also came up with an inspired idea to add a layer of authenticity to the piece by suggesting a Bob Wills song (he was being given a Trustees' Award this year) to kick the segment off, and allowing us to turn it into a Texas tribute, with both Wills and Henley coming from Texas. Rascal Flatts, who had sold more CDs than any other act, country or otherwise, agreed to do "Hotel California," and definitely scored in the house with that. As I've said earlier, it was not the easiest of combinations to pull off, but at the end of the day, I think it really worked for both acts.

On the other hand, the Chili Peppers were one of the easiest and smoothest bookings of the whole show, with the only request from the band being that we cover the arena in confetti at the mid-point in their performance, only appropriate since we had agreed that we wanted to do the song "Snow" from their multi-Grammy-nominated CD. There were numerous calls back and forth to insure that we had enough confetti, almost to an obsessive point from the band's management, but at the end of the day, there was enough confetti falling down on $50,000 diamond necklaces and designer dresses to float Staples, and the phone call from Gayle Fine, the band's co-manager two days after the show was that this was assuredly "the best television experience the band had ever had."

⌐

With the show still a few weeks away, we were in that very uncertain period of production where we were trying to finalize the acts who were already booked, let the few remaining acts in contention simmer a bit while we looked at the overall complexion of the show to determine what would help balance it a bit, and equally importantly, do the fine tuning we needed to do to create our trademarked Grammy moments, whether that involved pairing acts up or coming up with twists on the solo artists to find something truly unique to "plus up" their performances. Because of the sheer number of nominations she had received and the subsequent press interest because of them, Mary J. Blige needed very careful attention for her solo performance as well as her performance with Ludacris.

I had met with Mary just before the Christmas break and taken another copy of "Stay with Me," the Lorraine Ellison song that I had been trying to get her to sing for years, in another attempt to get her to consider it for her performance. Mary had already told me that she wanted to sing "Be Without You," the biggest hit from the nominated CD, her biggest ever, and though I was persistent, she wasn't having it. She told me that "Be Without You" exemplified her current life with husband and manager Kendu Isaacs, and that she couldn't sing a song like "Stay with Me," about needing a man so desperately that life was unbearable without one, while conceding to me that the song was pretty amazing. I left the meeting without any hope that she would sing the song that I knew could possibly take her to another level, just as our collaborative approach to "No More Drama" had done four years earlier on the same stage. That night was a career high point for her, and to this day people remind me that that was the moment when Mary J. Blige became a star in their eyes.

A couple of weeks later we had still not locked into the arrangement for "Be Without You" and I scheduled one more meeting on Saturday night with Mary, Kendu, and Ron Fair, who had produced much of Mary's record-breaking CD. I brought along a few other tracks for her, and Kendu and Mary had a couple of other thoughts as well, but I couldn't get "Stay with Me" out of my mind. And when we said goodbye that night, I was resigned to drop my quest for the song and accept the fact that whatever Mary did, it would be great.

So you can imagine my surprise when the following Saturday night as I was about to leave for dinner with friends, Ron Fair called to tell me that Mary had called him earlier that day with these words, "Ken is absolutely right about 'that' song. It would be amazing for me, and I'd like you to figure out a way to work it in so that I can do both songs for my performance."

And Ron had spent the rest of that day writing the chart for a full orchestra that would be the base for Mary's finest-ever performance on the Grammys, and one that would be talked about for a long time. Not to mention just how good she had made me feel by trusting me to know her musically once again.

But Mary's solo number would not be her only appearance on the show, since our discussions with Chris Bridges (Ludacris) and his manager Chaka Zulu kept coming back around to him performing "Runaway Love," an incredibly strong song about sexual abuse of young girls in the home. Initially, I had two reservations about this song, the first that it had been done elsewhere and secondly, that since Mary was performing elsewhere on the show, this could conceivably either take away from that performance or diminish the power of Luda's performance. Mary was on the track and provided the entire musical vocal bed of the song, so fans of the song would be expecting her to be a part of it.

Initially we talked about having two or three other artists take Mary's part with Mary making a cameo appearance at the end, and we even explored that with Mary and Kendu. But Mary wasn't having any of that. She said, and rightfully so, "That's my song and I want to do it," and she was right. What with her nominations and the performer that she is, there was simply no problem at all with Mary being seen in performance twice on the show—what was really happening was that as much as I'd like to discount it, part of my brain was still operating under the old regime, and one of Mike's rules that no artist could be seen more than once on the show. I had never agreed with that, and had won the argument a number of times saying that if the Grammy show as a whole was about the entire family of music, then it only made sense that since we had the world's greatest ensemble cast gathered together in one place for one night, we should be free to mix and match as fit. Over the past number of years, those moments have often proven to be magical.

On paper, the show was looking very rich, very balanced, and very full. But the truth of it was that I was still not feeling that we had everything we wanted yet, and we shouldn't give up looking for more magic.

For one thing, though we had earlier considered booking the New York cast of *Jersey Boys*, which was nominated for a Grammy in the Best Musical Score category, it began to lose enthusiasm once we learned that our plan to book Frankie Valli and a couple of the original Four Seasons wasn't going to work, and that, equally importantly, we wouldn't be able to get any of the Broadway cast and would only have the recently opened San Francisco cast to work with. Though Neil was reluctant to let this go, as happens with this show, when we looked at the overall landscape and what we had yet to do, it moved a couple of steps down on our priority list, just as booking Shakira and Wyclef to do the immensely popular (and nominated) "Hips Don't Lie" moved up.

This was not a difficult idea to grasp. Shakira, in addition to being beautiful and able to move her body in ways that only a salt water taffy machine can begin to emulate, is a great performer, understands the "moment" and was very much in sync with us in creating the standout musical dance tempo number of the show, something that was still not in the books. We worked with them very closely in developing a look, an approach, and a feel for a number that would be totally different than anything else on the show, and by the time it moved onto our stage for rehearsal, it had evolved into something quite special, made even better by the presence of Wyclef Jean, an old friend from the Fugee days.

We were now about three weeks away, most if not all of the production elements were moving along, and for the first time I was able to stand back for a moment, take a look at the overall, and let out the first sigh, a signal that this show felt good, good enough to put together a preliminary rundown and begin to lock in the categories. I can't really describe this process, since it's more of an evolution than an all-of-a-sudden realization, but there does come a time when it all seems to fit together, and that time had come. But in all honesty, it was colored by another event in my life, which while it had no direct impact on the show, had an enormous effect on me.

Sometime before the end of 2006, I got a call from Michael Levitt, a producer who had worked with us on a number of shows before going out on his own and becoming very successful. Michael was producing the Producers Guild of America awards dinner and the PGA had met and wanted to honor me with the "Visionary Award," whatever that was. I can't say that I wasn't excited to hear this news, particularly since for so many years the Grammy show has been ignored by the Television Academy Emmy voters, who seem to close their eyes and nominate the Oscars no matter what kind of show they do. I accepted his invitation and then pretty much forgot about the event until I looked at the calendar in mid January and saw that it was that Saturday night.

We had invited my mother and our kids, Matt and Dori, to come into Los Angeles for it, however, and the four of us showed up at the Century Plaza that evening with no idea of what to expect, other than the proverbial rubber chicken and a good-sized limo bill. I had invited Walter, Neil, Randy Phillips (my new partner with AEG), and their dates. Ron and Kim Basile were to join us at our table as well, and as I walked around a bit, I saw it was a pretty good room. Among others, also being honored were Jerry Bruckheimer, the über-producer of film and television and Ron Meyer, the head of Universal Studios. When I saw Tom Hanks, I knew that Ron Meyer was covered, and when I saw Marg Helgenberger I knew that Bruckheimer (CSI) was as well, but Michael took great pains to make sure that I was in the dark. I trusted him, but all I imagined was that someone would come up and talk, lead into a nice clip segment of some highlights of my career, and then I'd go up and give a short speech thanking everyone, but in particular my family.

After a couple of very nice honorary presentations, Melissa Etheridge was introduced and she came out, to my relief, to host my segment. Relieved, because in addition to knowing Melissa for 24 years, going back to when I auditioned her for a role in *Fame*, we had some pretty amazing moments together, the most recent of which was her triumphant performance on the Grammys following her treatment for breast cancer two years ago. We had seen each other since, but as I looked from my seat in the house, she looked more radiant and alive than ever, and I flashed back to that night two years ago when she launched into "Piece of My Heart" and made an entire audience as well as millions of viewers cheer and cry at the same time.

Melissa said all the requisite things about where I came from and how I got to where I was, and then she told the story of how I had called her when she was in chemo offering her a spot on the Grammys "if she was ready." She then introduced the clip segment, which I must say, was put together wonderfully by Gary Tellalian, who was co-producing the show with Michael and was also a Ken Ehrlich Productions alumnus. As it ended, I took a quick glance at my notes ready to come up to the stage to get this thing over with already.

But Melissa wasn't finished. There was someone who couldn't be there that night who wanted to wish me well, and then she introduced a tape of Katie Couric on the set of the CBS Evening News delivering a Motown song–filled couple of minutes about how much I had helped with her three colon cancer benefits, all of which were labors of love for me. And then Melissa quickly introduced three more clips, one from my friend Elvis Costello, another from Celine Dion, and a third from my great New Orleans buddy, Quint Davis. It was very sweet, and as it concluded, I thought, OK now, I go up.

But Melissa had more. And in quick succession, as I sat there in reasonable disbelief, out came Bonnie Raitt, who sang "Love Sneakin Up on You," followed by Paul Simon, who came out and sang "The Boxer," and then Stevie Wonder who did "Superstition" with his usual vamp sing-along this time with the added phrase, "Kenny Ehrlich Is the Way." It was pretty amazing, and I looked around a few times during all of it to glance at my mother, to whom this night would provide stories for months at the retirement home in Fort Lauderdale where she lived, stories that I suspect would be met with a certain amount of skepticism by her dinner mates, all of whom probably had children they could be even more boastful of.

Stevie finished, the four of them moved to the podium, and I snaked my way through the crowd to the stage and embraced each of them, all the while thinking about moments in our collective lives that we had shared in rooms like this, with people applauding. Over those years, I had done my best to create the moment where people were applauding those four, and the only difference tonight was that the audience was applauding for me, but really recognizing what I had done to help earn the love and affection for these and other artists.

Realizing that there were much more appropriate things to say, I put the notes away and spoke off the cuff. I recounted a few special moments with Melissa, Bonnie, Paul, and Stevie and thanked them on behalf of all of the artists I had been lucky enough to work with over the years. I then mentioned a few of the many people behind the scenes who have been so much a part of everything we do, singling out Walter for the past 26 years of the Grammys, and then saved my last thanks for Harriet, the kids, and my mom. I walked offstage with the four performers, and once we had crossed into the backstage all at once I felt remarkably more comfortable, because now I was where I belonged, backstage.

It had been a pretty wonderful experience, and I'm very grateful to Michael and Gary, and the PGA, for making it happen.

The effect it had on the upcoming Grammys was to give me one more shot of adrenaline, thinking about the pure music that each of those four great artists represented. It reminded me just how key it was this year, and every year, to imbue the Grammy show with a sense of that musicality in a world that was losing its taste for just that. The very next morning, a hazy winter Sunday in Los Angeles, I took a virtual walk through the show looking for little spots that could be touched up, or places where we could polish the little facets of our gemstone to take a great performance and just give it a couple of more highlights—and I made some notes, a number of which made sense and a few of which didn't.

The next week found us making real progress on pretty much each segment, and finalizing most of the looks for the acts, which could only be done once the songs had been selected, the arrangements were well along, and our team had the time to think fully about how we wanted to support the acts. With our stage being divided up into two main performance areas on the main stage, and a satellite stage in the house that could be used for small, acoustic performances, there were a variety of choices to be made, and this aspect of the show was one of the trickiest, but also one of the most enjoyable. A few years ago, when we went to the multiple-stage approach, we found ourselves committed to making an initial decision with each act whether to use video as the main scenic support, or to go with something other than video. We would usually stick with that decision, but every once in a while, because the structure of the show depended upon bouncing back and forth between the stages so that one could be set while the other was working, we would have to rethink and try and decide what was more important, the rundown of the show or the look for the act. In general, I would opt for trying to make the act work around the format, because in my mind, the most critical aspect of any event show like the Grammys is the overall structure, building a show whose pacing keeps viewers involved, and in fact, brings them even more into the show as it goes along.

So those are a few of the tradeoffs that go into making a Grammy show. One more thing that always affects the rundown is the complexity of the setup of each act—how many live musicians, how much of a set, and so on—would come into play to allow us to turn it around for the next act that would be on that same stage about 15 minutes later. And it was that fact that set the stage for the final booking of the show, which needed to once again be a choice between two worthy candidates.

Because of the difficult stage set-up on the stage-left side, it didn't look as though we would be able to make the turnaround to the next act on that side without some additional time, and since it was not a question of adding another award, my thought was to use the satellite stage out in the house for one additional, acoustic performance in addition to the start of Gnarls Barkley's number as well as the Lionel Richie performance in our R&B piece we had already placed there.

The choice came down to whether to book multi-Grammy nominee James Blunt, who was nominated in two major categories, Best New Artist and Record of the Year (for "Beautiful") or another Best New Artist nominee K.T. Tunstall, who had had nowhere near the success Blunt had but who I had seen do this incredible bit of using a foot pedal–operated hard drive to add one track at a time of a solo acoustic version of her song "Black Horse and the Cherry Tree," from a percussive "hit" to a full-blown multi-track version that rocked. Both performances would have fit the requirement for being intimate, acoustic, and in fact helping to create an environment where either one would feel absolutely right for the show. Blunt was the clear popular favorite although I had my doubts about booking him from the beginning because there wasn't anyone left on the planet who hadn't heard or seen him do the song, and that there wasn't much else to him but this one song. And there was a growing support for K.T., who has a great voice and probably a great future.

In the end, we opted for Blunt, and even though it turned out to be a good performance and he thanked Ahmet in his introduction, I believe that it would have served the show and the Academy better to have had a moment with a young artist who was relatively unknown and whose success would probably have been hastened by a virtuoso appearance on "music's biggest night."

Alas, we'll never know, but moments like that and our ability to try and work them into the show or not are some of the few regrets that we carry from show to show.

Now that the show was pretty much there, and we had begun to book a steady stream of presenters (since we were going without a host) to introduce the acts. Some were easy: Joan Baez said yes to the Dixie Chicks (how good a call that turned out to be); Samuel L. Jackson and Christina Ricci (who were in a film with Justin) accepted our invitation to introduce the R&B segment; Reba McEntire said yes to the Rascal Flatts/Carrie Underwood piece; Stevie Wonder came in to introduce our medley with Corinne Bailey Rae, John Legend, and John Mayer; Terrence Howard (who had been in Mary's video) was booked to introduce Mary's solo number; and Chris Rock (who had directed the Chili Peppers' new video) was confirmed to intro the Chili Peppers. What we didn't have until it hopped into our laps was anyone to introduce Beyoncé, and I was trolling when I got a call from my friends at AEG asking whether or not we'd be interested in Prince, who had just performed at the Super Bowl halftime show the week before. We offered him a simple, one word: "Beyoncé," (that's the way he likes it), and he accepted, and so on Grammy night, it was Prince, who with Beyoncé, had given us one of our all-time Grammy moments three years earlier, who walked up the stairs from our bunker and uttered that one word that introduced a great Beyoncé performance of "Listen" from *Dreamgirls*.

The week prior to the show is one of those really strange weeks where you alternately feel that the hours are passing so slowly that you think you're in a slow-motion movie, and then at other times you look around and ask yourself how you are ever going to get everything done in the time you have left before the show. It's kind of hard to explain but I suspect that everyone has similar situations in their lives. Every moment is filled, and the rare breaks in that week, while welcome, unfortunately give your brain time to create worries. One such worry for me was how the R&B number was shaping up and in particular how the number was working, so on Tuesday night, with Terry Lickona along for the ride, we went out to our rehearsal facility, Centerstaging, to take a look at the Chris Brown number. As it turned out, not only were my fears ungrounded, but it was obvious that this kid has a work ethic second to none and was committed to creating a moment on the show that people would not forget.

Rehearsals were reasonably smooth as we headed toward Saturday night and the last rehearsal, which would be a closed rehearsal for the Police, the first time they would walk on a stage together in years. Mary J. Blige came in on Thursday and started us up with an amazing version of the two-song medley. And then all of Friday morning was devoted to Justin, first to Justin's solo number, which was getting better with each performance even as Justin was getting physically sicker with each pass. He had picked up some kind of virus on the road, and this was going to be a tough day, with his rehearsals with each of the three finalists for the My Grammy Moment piece following up on his solo performance of "What Goes Around." And, as I've learned over the years, Justin is not the kind of performer who holds back, ever. He rocked out every time, and by the time we had the first number blocked and sounding great, it was time to move right into his second number with the girls.

What amazed me was that each time through—and each time it was a different girl—to give them each the experience of working onstage and with Justin in the arena environment, Justin gave it his all. What we had decided for "My Grammy Moment" was that we would have the winning girl (even when we narrowed it to the five semifinalists, they were all women) come to the stage, get warmed up by trading a couple of verses of the Bill Withers classic "Ain't No Sunshine" with Justin, and then they would launch into one of Justin's biggest hits from the current CD, "My Love," with T.I. joining the two of them as a surprise. Again, every rehearsal notched up a bit, and with each pass, you could see the three girls getting more and more into the excitement of the moment, and we knew it was nothing compared to what it would be like on show night.

Justin finished his five-hour rehearsal session and basically flopped onto a sofa in his dressing room where I thanked him for not just showing up and making this work, but also for being so considerate of each of the girls—not only putting them at ease, but also letting them know that they needed to notch up their performance to match his, something he said to them at a brief get-together before rehearsals began. My respect for him, which is considerable, grew even more in that couple of hours.

While we were rehearsing Justin, I was called into an on-site rehearsal room that we had set up several years ago to "tech in" some of the multiple-act performances where we knew we weren't going to get everyone involved until rehearsal day. The Corinne/John/John number was one of those, except that we had a slight leg up on it having rehearsed John Legend and Corinne with Ricky Minor's band the day before out at Centerstaging. They had done as much as they could do without John Mayer in the room, laying out the number musically to the point that they could just stay out of those parts where John would be, and then adding John, fresh off a plane from Japan, just minutes before we would bring them to the stage to rehearse. I know I've revealed this little secret to some of our collaborations here, but people still don't believe that we can put together a number this way—but we do.

I walked in just as they were getting ready to run it from top to bottom for the first time with John. Knowing that it wasn't really ready to be seen, I tried to melt into the woodwork so as not to intimidate—after all these years, I do have a sense of the moment the producer gets there—even though, in this case, the producer had heard this in his head long before the principals even knew they were going to be doing it. I laid out, walked to the back of the room, and listened—and when they finished I made my presence known and as I was thanking them for doing this, found myself on the verge of tears, so proud and so happy that this was going to get on the show in such great form and with such great musical integrity.

I returned to the house, just steps away, and to the last couple of passes with Justin and the My Grammy Moment finalists, and then we brought Corinne and the two Johns to the stage for camera blocking. Of course, after I left their rehearsal, it got even better, and from the response of the crew and other assorted people in the house for rehearsals, I knew this segment would be, as I had called it in USA Today, "a stunner." It didn't disappoint.

⌒

Saturday started with the Dixie Chicks, who were not only gracious, but also delivered much more than I ever expected at nine o'clock on a Saturday morning. "Not Ready to Make Nice" is a strong song and with the visuals, a series of nonlinear images that were nearly perfectly matched to the music, and Bob Dickinson's nearly perfect underlit look, the number had a powerful effect on everyone around for the rehearsal, even at an ungodly hour for most musicians.

We then moved through Carrie Underwood and Rascal Flatts smoothly, although until I saw Carrie come onstage and join Flatts for the last two minutes of "Life in the Fast Lane" I held my breath. It had taken the better part of a week to negotiate these couple of minutes, and though it seemed as natural as anything to those watching, to me it was one of the most arduous pieces of business to accomplish in the whole three-and-a-half-hour Grammy show.

Beyoncé was next, and as always, was ready to go and in perfect form. She looked radiant and after we had said hello, she walked to the circular, underlit platform that was at the head of another longer walkway, also lit, that led to three stairs that took her all the way over the mosh pit and as close to the audience as she could possibly get. We had laid out the number to match the build of the song, "Listen," and knew that she would get what we were going for and give us a great performance. But as I looked in her eyes, I saw that something wasn't right and asked her what was wrong. She told me that she was expecting the platform to rotate so that she could start upstage, turn toward the audience on the platform, and then begin singing as she was revealed and lit.

I told her the truth: that we had abandoned that idea early on when we decided to keep everything as simple as possible, even to not having any musicians on the floor with her, but only a string section that was kept in silhouette above her. There was obviously a missed communication somewhere and rather than disappoint her, I called for John Bradley, the man who really makes the show run backstage, and who has saved our lives countless times with his ability to solve a problem that seems insoluble, and asked him if there was anything he could do to make the circular platform turn. We don't call him "Silent John" for nothing, and though his brain was working, he shrugged his shoulders and said that he'd try and get it solved by the dress rehearsal on Sunday, if he could do it at all, but that we'd have to rehearse with the platform the way it was. Beyoncé, standing there, saw that we were going to try and make it happen, and we went on with the rehearsal, and she delivered, as she always does.

As we were rehearsing Beyoncé, out of the corner of my eye, standing at the foot of the stage, I caught my first glance of Sting, who was standing there with Andy and Stewart, and I breathed one more sigh of relief. They had made it this far, and there certainly wasn't any turning back now. I walked down the stairs designed for winners to walk up on show night and greeted them all. In this age of MP3s, Billy Francis, their longtime tour manager, had sent me a couple of downloads of rehearsals earlier in the week, including one that Sting had done for us to break the song down that began with that distinctive rasp going "OK, Ken, we're going to do 'Roxanne' for you now. Hope you like it." I guess I'll keep that one on the old iPod for awhile.

As I looked around the house, I saw the seats beginning to fill with even more people than had been around earlier, even though we had called for a "closed rehearsal." Despite that request, it seemed as if the entire camera-left side of the lower mezzanine was loaded with people, and I asked Garry Hood, our lead stage manager, to ask the ushers to move them at least in back of the center cross aisle, so they would be less prominent, and hoped that it would be done before we heard anything from the boys or Kathy Shenker, their manager.

And then the rehearsal started and the clock leapt back 20 years in an instant. For those of us of a certain age, "Roxanne," the song about a hooker, was a coming-of-age song. Since I had been introduced to it by my son Matt—who was much too young to be thinking about hookers when it first came out—I always associate it with family. Go figure! It was all good, all positive, and all the way home.

We ran the number a few times, Walter got his shots, and after the appropriate thanks, the boys left and we went on to the last rehearsal of the night, the tag to the In Memoriam piece that was to feature Chris Brown matching footage of James Brown dancing and then lead into Danny Ray placing an authentic J.B. cape on the microphone stand.

Earlier in the day and the day before, Walter had come to me a few times asking me to reconsider dropping this piece from the show. He said that we had done enough for James Brown, that this segment was overkill, and that it wasn't going to work. He said it enough times that, as happens occasionally, I began to doubt myself and my instincts. I knew this was a good idea, but the fact that a few other folks around us had heard this and hadn't taken a side one way or another led me to begin to question whether or not it was a good idea. As we rehearsed it, it looked like it was going to work, and when Danny Ray came out with the cape, though he never quite got it right in rehearsal, I still believed in the piece. But even after we broke rehearsal and went back to the office to clean up the few last remaining things we needed to talk about, Walter still felt that the piece wasn't necessary and might stiff.

Although I told him I would still continue to think about it and maybe drop it even on show day, my mind was really made up to keep it, risky or not, and go with it on the show. I couldn't imagine that the combination of this young kid paying tribute to Mr. Brown followed by Danny Ray placing the cape at the end of the In Memoriam segment wouldn't be a huge moment on the show, an emotional release that would allow the audience to give one last shout-out to the Godfather of Soul, and at the same time, recognize the entire group of artists and music industry people who were being saluted in the segment.

I drove home that night with some doubts, but for the most part, I was anxious for show day to come and for us to get this puppy on the air some 16 hours later.

And then, after a reasonably restless but not unexpected short sleep, show day was here and I was in a car on my way back to Staples Center for a full day of fun, commencing at around ten o'clock in the morning with the traditional dress rehearsal of the show, followed by a couple of hours of anxious pacing waiting for 5:00 p.m. (8:00 p.m. EST) when my friend Sting would shout out to the house, America, and the world, "We're the Police and we're back" before launching into "Roxanne" and beginning the fun and frivolity.

Following Academy Chairman Terry Lickona's very warm and personally affectionate speech before the show, I went out to do my traditional warm-up, a task that I generally enjoy.

The warm-up is a time to thank the people who make the show go, in particular my relatively unsung partner John, who does all of the below-the-line work and seldom if ever gets to do the fun stuff like I do; Tzvi Small and Ron Basile, who shoulder a lot more of that kind of stuff, making sure that Ts are crossed and Is are dotted, and in Ron's case, having amazing relationships with the talent support people; and finally the stage manager group, 12 remarkable people honcho'd by Garry Hood who somehow manage to get hundreds of pieces of talent to the right place at the right time and an incalculable amount of electrical equipment placed and working against near impossible odds. Being on headset with them during the show and listening to this army move, I can appreciate the gravity of the task, but to this day, after these many years and many shows, I still have no idea how they manage to do it. I ended my speech to tepid applause, which I am used to, and exited, arriving to a bit more tepid applause from my bunker mates, which had now grown to include Mr. Portnow, Ms. Little, Mr. Lickona, Mr. Sussman, Mr. Basile, and a couple of people I didn't recognize but looked like they belonged.

And off we were, courtesy of the Police, and into Jamie Foxx setting up the first award, which could have been anybody's, but went to Tony Bennett and Stevie Wonder's duet of "For Once in My Life." While the winners were older than the demographic we were looking for, the emotional acceptance speech of both, Tony about his son Danny and Stevie about his late mother, got the show off with a sense of respect and gravitas that was only heightened as Joan Baez introduced the Dixie Chicks by comparing her own activist life with that of the three girls. And the Chicks answered in their own way, earning the second standing ovation of the night (after the Police) before we had even gone to the first commercial.

And that's sort of the kind of night it was.

Prince warmed up the audience with one word, "Beyoncé," and then she drove it home with a great version of "Listen," and then Mary J. walked up to the microphone for the first of two visits to accept the Grammy for Best R&B Album. Justin came back from his sickbed with a vengeance and delivered a scorching version of "What Goes Around" in the first of his two appearances on the show, and then, in an act of perhaps not the best award structuring of my career, Pink read Mary's name a second time and she came up and accepted the Best Female R&B Grammy.

As we were setting Corinne, John, and John during the commercial, I went up to each of them, as I do to most of the acts during the show, and thanked them again for doing this and then winked and said, as I have done in the past, "This one counts." It was quite a performance, met with a huge standing ovation and carried over to John's win for Best Pop Vocal Album immediately after the performance.

We were now into the second hour of the show and Shakira and Wyclef proved once and for all that "Hips Don't Lie" and retired that song for the final time. Nobody ever has to see it again, and I don't mean that as a slight, rather that it'll never be done better or with more intensity and great production than it was that night—and Walter captured it with cameras that felt like they were attached to those legendary hips.

Burt Bacharach and Seal, both Song of the Year Grammy winners, presented that Grammy to the Dixie Chicks, and with the awards they had won earlier in the night, it was beginning to look like quite a night for these girls.

Gnarls Barkley performed, and with all the work we had done with Brian (Danger Mouse), it never felt like it reached the heights that it should have. Maybe it was because we had both agreed that we should change it up and do it at a slightly slower tempo. Maybe it was really that Brian and Cee Lo had made a great record, and that it was a better recorded experience than it could ever be live, but having seen it live at the Palace some months earlier and thinking it could be a great live number, I'm not sure. Sometimes you can do everything and it still doesn't quite get there. There were a lot of people, including a number of the critics, who loved the performance, but for me, it left something out, and to this day, I can't quite put my finger on it. All was redeemed however, as Ludacris came up to accept the Grammy for Best Rap Album and gave an emotional and caustic speech that in less than a minute thanked his extremely ill father (who would pass away two weeks after the show) and then thank Bill O'Reilly and Oprah, both of whom had taken shots (not literally) at the hip-hop community in general and at Luda in particular. Big ups, as we used to say.

And then, along came Mary—and she nailed it. In a performance worthy of an Oscar, an Emmy, a Golden Globe, and a Grammy, she set the table with "Be Without You," and cleared it with "Stay with Me." If there was anyone sitting at the end of that number, it was in the handicapped section, and even there, I believe "they had risen"—maybe not saved, but risen. It was spectacular and though I'll never forget "No More Drama" or "Piece of My Heart" that we had done with her in the past, they moved a bit back into the memory banks, crowded out by this incredible performance.

The Chicks made their second trip (on the show) to Grammyland as they accepted the award for Best Country Album, surprising no one but country radio, which had refused to play this album. This time, Natalie's acceptance was a bit edgier than the first time up, but one could see that if they made a return trip, confidence was building, and it might bubble over into some overly enthusiastic territory. Hey, it could happen.

As we moved into the third hour with the country Texas salute, the show was really sailing and I felt good enough to desert the bunker where Neil, Jack Sussman, Neil's assistant Claudine, Garry Hood, and I live for the better part of the show. I wandered out into the house to catch the eye of a couple of people whose reaction I was very interested in, namely Les Moonves (CBS), Ellen DeGeneres (my Grammy barometer), and my wife Harriet (is she smiling?). I sensed a very happy and involved house, seeming almost impatient for the next act and not at all fatigued with a show that still had over an hour to go. And I knew we had them once we headed into the R&B medley, which was up next.

Smokey got a huge and warm reception from the live audience, recognizing his 40 years of hits as much as this year's Grammy nomination, and he delivered a classic version of "Tracks of My Tears," as good a version as I've heard him do over the many times we've done that song on television. And then, from out in the middle of the house, came that familiar keyboard into the similarly classic "Hello," and the smoothest voice of the night, Lionel Richie, made us all remember where we were when we experienced his solo hits as well as those great Commodores' songs. And then, right back on the stage where Chris Brown slid down a Lucite slide following some pyro and launched into "Run It" complete with leaps, trampolines, and the requisite dance troupe that again had no bones to break. As the number finished, Chris took a moment and then came centerstage to join Smokey and Lionel for yet one more standing ovation from the crowd, who still didn't have a clue as to what they were in for next.

From under the stage rose Christina in a white tuxedo framed below a huge black-and-white profile of James Brown as the familiar intro riff to "It's a Man's World" kicked in. Three-and-a-half minutes later, the audience found itself as drained as Christina sank to her knees holding onto the mic stand for dear life just as Mr. Brown had done for so many years, and wrenching the final notes out of a song that had never before (to my knowledge) ever been sung by a blonde woman who wouldn't be born until 25 years after the song had been introduced by the Godfather. And like its father, the song could now rest in peace forever.

OK, so I'm given to a bit of overblown verbiage, I'll confess. But my enthusiasm is reasonably well rooted in truth. I can be very critical when things aren't right, and over the years, we've certainly had our share of moments that just didn't click. But then there are years where it all seems to go right, and if up to this point Gnarls Barkley was a "low point," then I was already feeling that we were going to be very happy in the morning both with the rating for the show and the public and media reaction—although I tempered my enthusiasm for the press because after all these years the Grammys were still a target, and the best I could usually hope for was a begrudging "Well, the Grammys finally got it right," a statement which I found somewhat redundant when from time to time I'd go back to the same writer or magazine and find that they had written that or a similar statement numerous times over the past several years. How many times could we be "finally getting it right" for the first time?

Anyway, it was now time for Neil Portnow to come out and tell the world what the Academy had been doing for the last 12 months. Now don't get me wrong, Neil is a lovely guy and as we tease each other on a yearly basis about some of my shortcomings, I love to tease him about just how much America is looking forward to seeing him, making him further agonize over his remarks and how he's going to come across. But it was his idea this year to surround himself with a couple of extremely talented kids to demonstrate just how important music education is and what the results can be, and with a musical underscore like he got, he did well, and as the minute-by-minute breakdown of the show proved days later, held the audience reasonably well—not Prince and Beyoncé well, mind you, but well. And then of course, following his speech we were into our In Memoriam segment, which as I had mentioned earlier, ended with a virtuoso dance performance by Chris Brown following (literally) in the footsteps of his namesake, James Brown. And we were about 50 minutes from closing credits.

This late in the show, I have this vision that our audience has lowered expectations for performances, but I wasn't having any of that. In addition to two of the biggest awards of the night, I knew we had a great Chili Peppers performance, a terrific duet between Justin and the My Grammy Moment winner, and, just ahead, the unexpected moment of the night, when Ludacris and Mary J. did "Runaway Love." And it didn't disappoint, delivered with a rhyming passion and urgency that was matched by Mary's vocal, and by the special guesting of Earth, Wind & Fire, whose Philip Bailey led off the number, and whose great sound augmented an already-memorable melody and made it even more distinctive. By the end of the number, as a group of candle-bearing young girls surrounded Chris and Mary, and the images of other young kids in peril were projected above along with an 800 number that urged people to get involved, we had created one more memorable event that more importantly would have an effect on people's lives.

And then, following the next commercial, Jennifer Hudson (who two weeks later would be rewarded with a Best Supporting Actress Oscar for *Dreamgirls*) walked onstage and called out Robyn Troup's name as the winner of the My Grammy Moment competition. Robyn took the stage as Justin began to sing "Ain't No Sunshine" and joined him right on cue to answer his verse with one of her own and then it was off to the races with "My Love." All of the work we had done to get to this moment seemed to be worth it, if for no other reason than to see the look on this 18-year-old's face as she came alive moving between Justin and T.I. and perhaps taking the first step on a road to stardom, and that first step being pretty high up on the ladder, an appearance on the Grammy Awards, for chrissake!!!

The standing ovation that greeted this performance was, I believe, not only for Robyn, but also for Justin in recognition of what had been an amazing year for this performer, only eight years older than Robyn herself. He won three Grammys that night, none of them on the air, but there is no question that he came out of the show as one of the big winners, with both performances landing on numerous highlights lists with critics in the next day's coverage of the show.

Record of the Year went to the Dixie Chicks for "Not Ready to Make Nice," setting the stage for Grammy guessers to figure that Album of the Year, still to be presented, would probably go that way too. I had mixed emotions about what was going on awards-wise: very happy at the Chicks' seeming sweep, but hopeful that things might get spread around a bit so that it would make more people happy at the end of the night. In my line of work, that is sometimes pretty important.

The last performance of the night, which would be followed by the presentation of Rock Album of the Year and then Album of the Year, belonged to the Chili Peppers, placed at the end of the night for a few reasons, the primary one being their coming confetti drop, enough to top Mount Hood. After being introduced by Chris Rock, the Peppers did what the Peppers do, they rocked—and when the confetti blizzard started to turn Staples into Cleveland in January, they still rocked, and were duly rewarded for bringing the Grammys home with a high when they walked onstage following their performance to accept the Grammy for Rock Album of the Year, the second of two Grammys they won that night.

And now we were almost home; the only one left was "the Big One," an appellation the Academy folks would not like me to use in reference to *any* one award, but, hey, Album of the Year is Album of the Year. And to use a well-turned phrase: "And the nominees are: The Dixie Chicks, Gnarls Barkley, John Mayer, the Red Hot Chili Peppers, and Justin Timberlake. And the Grammy goes to . . ."

Let's pause here for dramatic effect. Over the past three-and-a-half hours, all five of the nominees for Album of the Year had performed on the show, and each of them had delivered from really good to great performances. And while it seemed obvious from the earlier results that the Chicks would be making one more trip to the stage to collect their last Grammy of the year, for a moment—one of those moments that they say you have in the last moments of your life—everything went to slow motion and I relived moments of each of the previous performances: John Mayer's face scrunched up as he blistered through a guitar solo on "Gravity;" the Dixie Chicks bringing "Not Ready To Make Nice" alive to an arguably loving audience filled with respect for what they had accomplished that night; the Chili Peppers, reasonably oblivious to anything else that had happened on the show earlier and just there to rock out and have a good time much as they've always done; and even Gnarls Barkley's Cee Lo, earnestly singing those lines to "Crazy" that he had sung so many times, while making his way through the house to the stage. At that moment, before any name was said, I realized the worth in each of these offerings and that music, at its very root, still has the capacity to create change, to take us to a higher place, to remind us of who we are and who we might want to be—and if nothing else, to bring pleasure—and then:

"The Dixie Chicks!" exclaimed Don Henley and Scarlett Johansson in unison, and the audience rose en masse for the last time that night to say thank you to this group of southern women who had set the tone at the beginning of the evening both musically and philosophically and were now closing it out with some salient thoughts that might carry some of the 12,000 people still in the arena at least to the night of parties ahead. Scarlett said good night, credits rolled over one last reprise of "Not Ready to Make Nice" and in the truck technical director John Field pulled one last toggle switch down toward him and the 49th Annual Grammy Awards was off the air, two minutes over its allotted three-and-a-half hours.

Back in the office, Walter and I had our usual group hug, brought David Wild, Bob Dickinson, and Garry Hood into it and then shared it with Christine Bradley, Walter's longtime associate director and master of the sacred book (and by the way, the wife of the aforementioned John Bradley, who did succeed in taking a solid piece of scenery and miraculously parting it so that the circular part at the top was able to turn Beyoncé in a half turn, giving her the move she wanted).

The ritual "best show ever" speeches commenced, inevitably followed up by a vegetable garden's variety of reviews (from ripe, plump, and perfect to rotten). But the eternal quest for ratings proved to reverse the downward trend of the past two years, and we wound up with a 22 percent audience increase. What was equally important to me, the minute-by-minutes showed a remarkably low erosion rate, meaning that people really did get into the show and stay with it, even past the normal eleven o'clock drop-off time.

Were we to take from this that we had done a better show than usual? That our little *American Idol* "homage" (a kind word for you know what) paid off and we brought an Internet-savvy, audience participatory experience to the show in the nick of time? Or was it just that moving the show back to Sunday (where, granted, it had been beaten two years before by a newer and more press-friendly *Desperate Housewives*), plus the CBS Super Bowl boost the week before, that gave the show the lift it needed?

We could analyze, over-analyze, and over-think it to death. Rather, I felt, we should just accept the fact that we did good, that we put on consistently good music, and that while the record labels were struggling to stay alive, music that was interesting, involving and passionate was still more than a commodity. It was an art form, and that, goddamn it, compared to what else was out there, we're still the Grammy Awards, and we could celebrate the best and the brightest.

In a more perfect world, I'd proffer that it was the kind of show that we had been doing for years. But only more recently, thanks largely to CBS, were we able to market the idea that you *had* to watch the Grammys—to see things that you would never see elsewhere—and it was finally beginning to take hold with our audience. Not everywhere mind you, but enough to make a difference. This year we had our first major national break in a *USA Today* cover story. They finally got it. It is all about the *moments.*

Finally, it was beginning to register, and register in a good way.

Acknowledgments

This book would certainly not have been possible had Pierre Cossette not brought me into the Grammy fold in 1980 and, equally importantly, entrusted me with his most important asset, the faith of the Recording Academy, all these years. Similarly, to those Academy folks with whom I've worked most closely, the Television Committees over the years, staff people like Claudine Little, Doug Gore, Paul Madeira, and particularly Diane Theriot, a very special thank you. Going back to the beginning, I should also like to mention Christine Farnon, always a supporter and the backbone of the organization from its first days until the late '80s. Also, the honorary chairmen over the 26 years, including Jay Lowy, Jay Cooper, Joel Katz, Leslie Anne Jones, Ron Kramer, Mike Melvoin, Jimmy Jam, and—again to single out two individuals—Bill Ivey, the voice of reason for many years, and Garth Fundis, who oversaw the most critical period in the Academy's history five years ago. I would also like to acknowledge the only two paid presidents in the Academy history, Mike Greene, who, as you've read throughout this book, is painted in conflicting terms but who certainly did advance the goals and outreach of the Academy in a remarkable manner, and his successor, Neil Portnow, who has become a friend and confidante not to mention a marvelous collaborator. And finally, speaking of collaboration, Terry Lickona, the most recent chairman of the Academy and chairman of the Television Committee, with whom it has been my utmost pleasure to work closely.

On the production side, it's been a pleasure to work with so many talented and dedicated people over the years, and of course this show is a reflection of a tremendous funneling of ideas and execution. In particular, and in alphabetical order, I'd like to thank Steve Bass, Christine Clark Bradley, Ellen Brown, Bob Dickinson, Tisha Fein, John Field, Gungor, Bob Keene, Boey Kober, Rene Lagler, Terry McCoy, Paul Sandweiss, Tzvi Small, Brian Stonestreet, David Wild, and literally hundreds of others who band together for a couple of months at the beginning of each year to put this show on its feet. I am grateful to John Cossette, with whom I have shared a partnership in the show for the past several years, and his lovely wife Rita, who has stage-managed the show and stage-managed me for many years. To Ron Basile, there really aren't words to express what you and your family have meant to me and mine over the years. And finally, my partner Walter Miller, who signed on the same year I did and who will vouch for nearly every anecdote in this book for at least as many years as our respective memories hold . . . I would assume that in reading this book you've sensed my love and admiration for Walter.

There are too many artists, managers, record label people, and so on to mention, but over the years certain of them have become true partners and I'd like to acknowledge that, beginning with Rene and Celine Dion, Paul Simon, Stevie Wonder, Bonnie Raitt, Elton John, Bono, Edge, Larry and Adam, Gloria and Emilio Estefan, Bruce Springsteen, Herbie Hancock, Barry, Maurice, and Robin Gibb, Dr. John, Aretha Franklin, Ricky Martin, Luther Vandross, will.i.am, Melissa Etheridge, Billy Crystal, Tommy Mottola, John Hammond, Ron Fair, Tom Whalley, Clive Davis, Mo Ostin, Donnie Ienner, Paul Farberman, Jon Landau, Jeff Kramer, Irving Azoff, Paul McGuinness, Larry Jenkins, John Beug, Bob Merlis, and my agents over the years, Jay Venetianer, who introduced me to Pierre, Danny Schrier and Paul Heller, and Alix Hartley.

Although my company does shows for all the networks, the Grammys has been a CBS show nearly from the beginning, and I've been privileged to work with some very remarkable people there, including Leslie Moonves, Nancy Tellem, Nina Tassler, Fred Rappaport, Terry Botwick, Chris Ender, Susan Marks, Nancy Carr, and in particular, my friend and companion in crime, Jack Sussman. Ever since Jack's arrival at CBS, the show's course has been steadier, the journey more enjoyable, and our shorthand both reliable and appreciated. Plus, he hits the ball a ton, even farther when it's straight.

A special thanks to my New Orleans family and friends, most notably Quint Davis, who walked into my house and my life with Professor Longhair in 1975 and has been there ever since, through the great times and the tough times.

I must also mention a few people from Parts One and Two of my television life, first and foremost Marty Faye, whose talk/variety show I produced for six years in the same studio and a few hours later each Saturday night following Don Cornelius's *Soul Train* tapings. It was Marty who told a raw (and thereby very inexpensive) publicist that he could produce a two-hour live show and do it for $75 a week. And then to John

Rahmann, Bill McCarter, and Sherry Goodman at the Chicago Public Television station WTTW, who cut me the slack to handle publicity and fundraising activities at the same time I was developing programming like *Soundstage*, which was the show that brought me to the attention of the Hollywood community and launched my career out here.

To my family: my brother Steve, who took the white ceramic horse my grandfather offered so that I could have the palomino when we were kids; to my mother, who let the Continentals rehearse in the living room (she had to, it's where the piano was) and who faithfully watches endless hours of our shows to get to the credits; and to my dad, who passed away nearly 20 years ago and who I only wish had lived longer to enjoy a lot more Grammy moments, because I certainly had a great number of Daddy moments with him.

And finally, to the three people who have shared me with my work and the Grammy Awards all these years. My loving kids, Matt and Dori, of whom I am so proud as I've watched them grow up to be vital, involved, caring, and contributing members of this world, and to my wife, Harriet, who stayed the course through the good and bad times and saved my life two years ago when I wanted to go to the Bahamas to do the Patti LaBelle show rather than to the hospital and have bypass surgery—go figure.

Revisionist thinking can come pretty much at any time, and while I stick to my guns in repeating what I think I've said in numerous pages of this book, "They're not your friends," I guess in retrospect so many of them really are and it's only out of self-protection and self-preservation that I need to "protest too much." But to all of you whose names appear anywhere in this book, thank you. It's been a great ride, and here's to a bunch more great Grammy moments, Grammy shows, and most of all, great music to celebrate in the coming years.

Ken Ehrlich
Encino
June 2007

Index